Daily Strength
for Daily Needs

Daily Strength for Daily Needs

One Year of
Biblical Inspirations

Victor M. Parachin

Liguori

LIGUORI, MISSOURI

Published by Liguori Publications
Liguori, Missouri

Except where otherwise noted, Scripture quotations are taken from *Today's English Version Bible*. Copyright American Bible Society 1966, 1971, 1976, 1992. Used by permission.

Library of Congress Cataloging-in-Publication Data

Parachin, Victor M.
    Daily strength for daily needs : one year of biblical inspirations / Victor M. Parachin. — 1st ed.
        p. cm.
    ISBN 0-7648-0234-8 (alk. paper)
    1. Devotional calendars. I. Title.
    BV4811.P32 1998
    242'.2—dc21   98–6244

Copyright 1998 by Victor M. Parachin
Printed in the United States of America
02 01 00 99 98   5 4 3 2 1
First Edition

INTRODUCTION

A New Jersey couple, who love flowers, had a large greenhouse attached to their home so they could enjoy beautiful flowering plants during the harsh northeast winters. One snowy January evening the husband and wife went to a rehearsal of an amateur orchestra in a nearby town where they had previously lived. They decided to take a large bouquet of colorful flowers as a gift to the musicians, believing that the sunny colors—orange, yellow, red—would create a warm atmosphere that cold night.

As they got to the town, the husband turned onto a side street near the river. Because the snow was falling heavily, the area was deserted, except for an elderly woman who was walking alone. The couple recognized her as the mother of their former next-door neighbor. Stopping, they offered to give her a ride. Initially she seemed confused but finally told them where she was going, and they drove her there. As she was leaving the car, the couple spontaneously offered her the bouquet of colorful flowers.

Three days later they received a note from her, thanking them for the ride and the flowers. The woman explained that their gift had a profound impact upon her life. A nurse her entire working life, she realized that very day that she was too old and infirm to continue working. Not wanting to be a burden to her family, she made up her mind to throw herself in the river—*unless God gave her a sign* that he didn't want her to. She said the bouquet of colorful flowers was that sign, and it literally saved her life.

The woman who sought a sign from God about ending her life may not even have known that the origins of seeking a sign are traced to the Bible—in the Book of Judges, chapter 6, verses 36–40. In ways large and small, known and unknown, the Bible continues to shape our lives.

The purpose of *Daily Strength for Daily Needs* is to enable you, the reader, to experience the Bible on a daily basis. The meditations come from various books of the Bible. It is my hope that day by day you will receive uplifting information and fresh inspiration. I hope, too, that you will experience daily strength for daily needs by connecting to the diverse themes found in scripture.

—Victor M. Parachin, M. Div.

Daily Strength
for Daily Needs

Being Faithful Where We Are

Now if you obey me fully and keep my covenant,
then out of all the nations you will be my treasured possession.
Exodus 19:5

In the eleventh century, King Henry III of Bavaria grew tired of court life and the pressures of the monarchy. He experienced what today is termed a "midlife crisis." He went to Prior Richard at a local monastery, asking to be accepted as a contemplative, to spend the rest of his life in the monastery.

"Your majesty," said Prior Richard, "do you understand that the pledge here is one of obedience? That will be hard because you have been a king."

"I understand," said Henry. "The rest of my life I will be obedient to you, as Christ leads you."

"Then I will tell you what to do," said Prior Richard. "Go back to your throne and serve faithfully in the place where God has put you."

That story leads to these two thoughts:

First, faithfulness is intertwined with faith. We cannot honestly say we believe in God if we are not dependable and loyal to the highest of spiritual values.

Second, faithfulness is not simply a religious duty we employ on Sundays or when we are "supposed" to act like Christians. God expects us to be faithful where we are.

So, as a new year begins, let us resolve to be faithful. When we tire of our roles and responsibilities, let us remember that God has planted us in a certain place at a certain time and told us to be dependable and reliable in whatever responsibilities we have—as a parent, a spouse, an accountant, a welder, a dentist, a teacher—whatever.

~≈ *Prayer for the Day* ≈~

Loving God,
In all of my responsibilities and roles,
let me be faithful in the discharge
of my duties.
Day be day empower me to meet every
challenge with love and wisdom.
VMP

Stop to Pray and Listen for Guidance

Whether you turn to the right or to the left,
your ears will hear a voice behind you, saying,
"This is the way; walk in it."

Isaiah 30:21

A young couple recently moved to a rural part of New York state where each house had its own well. Soon after moving, the couple woke up one day to find they had no water. They checked their well and plumbing, but to no avail.

A neighbor suggested the lack of water could be due to a loss of pressure in their water tank. So they emptied the tank and refilled it. Still they had no water. Next they called in the contractor who had originally dug the well. After examining the pipes and water pressure, he, too, was baffled.

The next morning the woman woke up and started her day in her normal custom. She first read from scripture and then prayed. She prayed about the lack of water. Soon an idea came to her, and she telephoned the contractor. "Do you think there might be a connection between our loss of water and the fact we had a new telephone line installed the other day?" she asked. That led to a solution. The contractor returned and discovered the telephone worker, in grounding the line, had accidentally split a wire from the well pump.

That simple solution came as a direct result of the woman stopping to pray and then listening for guidance. The same is true for each of us. Whenever we face a dilemma, large or small, let us make time to pray about it, ask for God's guidance and help, and then prepare to be led toward a solution. Think about today's passage from the prophet Isaiah where God promises to guide us.

❧ Thought for the Day ❧
Simply wait upon him. So doing,
we shall be directed, supplied, protected,
corrected, and rewarded.
Vance Havner

Doing All the Good We Can

Trust in the Lord and do good.
Psalm 37:3

A woman named Marian Crawford was written up in a magazine as "one of the nation's most dedicated volunteers." The East Arlington, Vermont, resident is a seventy-three-year-old great-grandmother who gets up at five each morning and drives to the homes of several elderly neighbors. There she helps bathe and shower them, as well as prepare their breakfast. "Older people like to remain in their own homes," Crawford explains. "I saw a need to help some of them."

After doing her morning work, she returns home for lunch but leaves again immediately afterward to revisit the same seniors. This time she does their laundry, vacuums their homes, handles grocery shopping, or takes them to medical appointments.

Later, after spending part of the evening with her husband, Walter, Crawford begins baking bread. "I do about a hundred loaves at a time," she says. "The next day, I take them to the people I visit."

Not only does Crawford have a regular group of people she helps daily, but she manages to help when other needs emerge. She prepares casseroles for those who become housebound and mends clothing for those whose eyesight does not allow sewing. All this assistance keeps Crawford from getting much sleep. "I need only a couple of hours here or there," she explains. "I'd hate to think I was guilty of sleeping my life away."

The importance of helping others was instilled in Crawford by her mother. One of sixteen children, she remembers her mother often asking Crawford to check in with needy neighbors to see how she could help them. Today, at seventy-three, her philosophy is simple and sound: "We pass this way only once, and while we're here we should do all the good we can."

Today's passage from Psalm 37 reminds us to "do good." The importance of doing good and helping others is a command that appears many times in scripture. By doing good we not only help others by sharing their load but we infuse our own living with purpose, meaning, and vitality. Let us consciously seek to do good today.

⇒ *Thought for the Day* ⇐
No one has a right to sit down and feel hopeless.
There's too much work to do.
Dorothy Day

Serenity Suggestions

If only you had paid attention to my commands,
your peace would have been like a river.

Isaiah 48:18

Daily stress has been linked by researchers to headaches, backaches, high blood pressure, ulcers, as well as psychosocial difficulties with depression and eating and sleeping disorders. The impact of stress varies from person to person. The good news is that we can build up our resources to meet the challenges of stress. Here are some serenity suggestions:

1. *Eliminate the negative.* There are some life irritants that can be quickly removed, such as replacing a lumpy mattress, getting a new eyeglass prescription, searching out a new job.

2. *Get physical.* In one study, physically fit women showed heart-rate responses to stress that were thirty beats a minute lower than those of unfit women. Use exercise to reduce stress.

3. *Use the therapy of laughter.* The ability to laugh at life has positive effects on the physiological system. It reduces the level of three negative and harmful emotions: anger, fear, and depression.

4. *Shed tears.* Most people feel better after crying. God has given us the gift of tears to relieve our tensions.

5. *Schedule leisure.* Break the daily grind by doing something different and pleasant periodically. Go for a bike ride on a quiet country road. Play your favorite childhood game. Visit a local tourist site.

6. *Listen to music.* Think about the type of music that has a calming, soothing effect upon you. Then, when feeling stressed, find a quiet place and simply listen to that music.

7. *Don't be a perfectionist.* Don't be your own worst enemy. Ease up by reminding yourself that you don't have to be perfect.

8. *Build spiritual muscle.* Deepen your spiritual resources through prayer, scripture study, inspirational reading, and regular worship. God is the source of peace and serenity.

～ *Prayer for the Day* ～
Loving God,
Day by day guide my thoughts and actions
so that I can enjoy peace and serenity in my life
and thereby be a better and healthier person.
VMP

Controlling Life's Crises

Have faith in the Lord your God
and you will be upheld.

2 Chronicles 20:20

Monica, a young woman in her twenties, tells what happened in her life when her beloved father died in the summer of 1985.

She had recently graduated from university, moved to a new city, rented an apartment, and began working in an exciting career. After her father's death and funeral, she returned to work briefly.

Abruptly, she quit her job, left her apartment, moved home with her mother, and did nothing. "My excuse was, 'My mom needs me,'" she recalls. For several months all she did was eat, sleep, and watch television—a disastrous pattern for anyone. Soon her weight soared, and she became embarrassed by her physical appearance.

Finally, her mother urged Monica to return to school and seek out a career, saying, "You have to do something other than eat, watch TV, and sleep." That helped Monica came to terms with her father's death, and she corrected her unhealthy lifestyle.

Anyone who has had a loss to death can understand the despair and lethargy that took over Monica's life. However, the lesson from her experience is this: We must manage, shape, and control life's crises; they must not be allowed to manage, shape, and control us. Whenever we experience a stormy time let us use all of our creativity and energy to respond. And let us ask God to help us. The scripture reminds us that we will be "upheld" when we trust God.

⤳ Prayer for the Day ⤳
Loving and kind God,
As I face any crisis,
give me strength, insight, wisdom,
patience, faith, trust, and hope.
VMP

Sharing With God
the Pain of a Broken Relationship

Lead me, O Lord...make straight your way before me.
Psalm 5:8

Elisabeth and Barbara met in college where they became best friends. One of Barbara's great loves was the daisy; and so, when she was engaged, she and Elisabeth searched for a silverware pattern with daisies. As her bridesmaid, Elisabeth carried a yellow-and-white bouquet down the church aisle. And daisies graced each table at the reception.

After college and marriage the two women spoke daily. Then, unfortunately, their husbands had an argument. "That drove a wedge between us," Elisabeth explained. They stopped telephoning, quit celebrating birthdays, and suddenly were no longer friends. Elisabeth thought about calling Barbara to see if the wounds could be healed, but she kept putting it off. Then, through another friend, Elisabeth learned that Barbara died at the age of thirty-eight.

She was devastated and agonized over what had been left unspoken. "Oh, God, I'll never forgive myself for not telling Barbara how sorry I am and how much I loved her," she cried out in a prayer. Immediately she felt God directing her. So Elisabeth poured out her heart and spoke to Barbara the way they used to: "You were the best friend I ever had. I'm so sorry." That night Elisabeth went to bed with a lighter heart but still wishing she had reached out when Barbara could still respond.

Amazingly, the next morning in the corner of the yard, sprouting up from the freshly mowed lawn, was an unexpected bouquet. It was a foot-high clump of yellow-and-white daisies.

It is always good when an argument can be talked through, leaving the relationship clean and vibrant. However, there are times when a difference of opinion is not resolved. Rather than be haunted and hurt by that fact, let us, like Elisabeth, share the pain of a broken relationship with God. Then let us listen and be led by God's spirit to take the wise course of action.

❧ Thought for the Day ❧

If you expect perfection from people, your whole life is
a series of disappointments, grumblings and complaints.
If, on the contrary, you pitch your expectations low,
taking folks as the inefficient creatures which they are,
you are frequently surprised by having them perform
better than you had hoped.
Bruce Fairfield Barton

Head for the Light

The people walking in darkness have seen a great light;
on those living in the land of the shadow of death
a light has dawned.

Isaiah 9:2

Annually the giant female sea turtle leaves the safety of the ocean in order to complete her nesting pilgrimage. Laboriously, in the dark of the night, she heaves her two-hundred-pound bulk upon a beach, lays her eggs, and covers them with a mound of sand.

Later in the season, her tiny baby turtles will hatch and dig their way to the surface. Then, under the cover of darkness hiding them from their predators, they will begin their perilous journey to the ocean. Following an inborn instinct, they head toward the moonlight reflecting off the ocean surface. Years later they will return to the same beach to lay their own eggs for future generations.

God has created us human beings with a similar instinct to seek out the light, to seek a higher consciousness and a deeper spirituality. We are created by God to seek our highest good and develop our potential. Sadly, many fears keep us from hatching, from digging through the sand, from taking the first steps on an unknown journey. Some people live all their lives with their hopes and dreams unrealized. Others allow themselves to be devoured by feelings of inadequacy and insecurity, which keeps them from making important changes. They remain in jobs that inhibit their potential or stagnate in old patterns of living and unhealthy relationships.

Yet God calls us to "hatch" or break out, to change, take risks, journey in faith toward the future. If we do not respond we will be trapped and entombed all of our lives in drudgery and meaninglessness. Perhaps this is the day when you can express your potential and claim happiness. The first step is to stop making excuses and simply break out of the old shell. Today, ask God to help you dig through your suffocating environment and head for the light.

⇜ Affirmation for the Day ⇝
God is the source of my inner peace.
God is the source of my wisdom.
God is the source of my strength.
VMP

Remaking Ourselves

*I will remove from them their heart of stone
and give them a heart of flesh.*

Ezekiel 11:19

A man decided to entertain his boss, inviting him home for dinner. Earlier he explained how important it was that the evening meal go well. He asked his son to cooperate by behaving well and not speaking much. The man's employer was a tough, insensitive, self-centered individual. He was difficult to work for.

Throughout the evening the employer talked nonstop about himself, his work, his success. The young boy did not speak, but simply stared at the man. Finally, and somewhat annoyed, the employer asked the boy, "Why do you keep looking at me that way?"

Seeing his father was out of the room, the boy broke his silence, saying, "My dad says you are a self-made man." The employer beamed and proudly admitted he had made his own way in the world, carving out his niche through hard work and ability. With candor he told the boy he was quite wealthy. The young boy, with equal candor, asked, "But why did you make yourself that way?"

The truth is that we make ourselves what we are.

But the greater truth is that we can remake ourselves. We do not need to remain the way we are.

Today, examine your life. Ask yourself if you are happy with what you see in yourself. Are you pleased by the kind of individual you have become? If not, ask God to give you insight and the courage to act. Today's text is a reminder that, with God's help, we can remake ourselves!

⊷ Thought for the Day ⊶
The difficulty in life is the choice.

George Moore

Tears Are Not a Sign of Weakness

Then the man of God began to weep.
2 Kings 8:11

Norman Schwarzkopf, the general who headed the Gulf War, is a tender warrior. Not long after the Gulf War and the stunning victory over Iraqi forces, the commander of Desert Storm was interviewed on national television by Barbara Walters.

In the course of their conversation, something touched Schwarzkopf deeply. Millions of people watched on television as the eyes of this seasoned, career soldier with four stars on his shoulder, filled with tears.

Even the interviewer was surprised. Walters responded: "Why, General, aren't you afraid to cry?" Without hesitation the commander replied, "No, Barbara. I'm afraid of a man who won't cry!"

Tears are a gift from God. We cry with joy at the birth of a child. We cry with compassion for those who suffer. We cry when a loved one is ill or near death or has died. We cry when we have been wounded. We cry even when strangers are afflicted with great disaster. In today's text we read about the prophet Elisha who was moved to deep tears because he anticipated a declaration of war and the horrors it would bring. Because we are created by God with the capacity to weep, we should never be ashamed when tears flow freely.

∼ *Thought for the Day* ∼

I have always felt sorry for people afraid of feeling,
of sentimentality, who are unable to weep with
their whole heart. Because those who do not
know how to weep do not know how to laugh either.
Golda Meir

Fostering Hope in the World

In those days it was not safe to travel about, for all
the inhabitants of the lands were in great turmoil.
2 Chronicles 15:5

Many parts of the planet are in dire crisis. Today as I write, the headlines refer to conflict and killing in Rwanda and Burundi, Bosnia, Yemen, Israel and Palestine, North Korea, Haiti. Closer to home there are dreadful statistics: increasing incidents of gang violence, child abuse, AIDS, and so forth. As in biblical times, our world is "in great turmoil."

Yet people who believe in God are fundamentally people of faith and hope. In spite of overwhelming bad news, the people of God are called to foster hope on the planet. Here are seven ways to do that:

1. Spend ten minutes each day to pray for peace in troubled countries. These ten minutes can be used while you drive to work, during lunch hour, or even on a coffee break. If peace seems too unrealistic, then pray for stability. Stability is often the first step to full peace.

2. Pray for world leaders, that God will give them insight, as well as the courage to act wisely. Such world leaders include the president, the secretary-general of the United Nations, and heads of other countries, especially those where conflict is present.

3. Meditate each day in addition to praying. During meditation listen for God's calling and directing. Let silence be used by God to teach you.

4. Practice sending out "arrow" prayers. When you see or hear of someone in need, offer a prayer immediately.

5. Act as an agent of hope and faith in your daily surroundings. At work, in the community, and within your family, help resolve conflicts and maintain the attitudes of hope and love.

6. Acknowledge peace in your immediate community. If you are fortunate to live in a safe, pleasant environment, thank God for it. In prayer remember other families for whom daily existence is a struggle.

7. Acknowledge the peace in your personal and family life. Sincerely thank God for that as well.

⤞ Thought for the Day ⤝
The world has narrowed to a neighborhood before
it has broadened to brotherhood.
Lyndon B. Johnson

God's Help to Live in the Real World Versus the Ideal World

The Lord will fight for you; you need only to be still.
Exodus 14:14

For more than a decade, Christine and Michael were unable to have children of their own. Then, most surprisingly, Christine discovered she was pregnant. It was a conception that she and her husband and close friends considered a miracle. Like all new parents, they were excited at the prospect of a child.

At the time of labor and delivery, complications developed and the baby suffered a stroke. Although doctors said it would take awhile to determine the extent of brain damage, it appeared to be severe.

A close friend from church was anxiously waiting for information about the birth, but when she heard the problems she was reluctant to call the new parents. "What could I say," she explains. "Usually you phone and offer congratulations. Considering the circumstances, that seemed inappropriate." Gathering up her courage, she visited Christine and Michael. "I drove over to their home, wondering how they were dealing with this event," she said. "However, I soon realized I had underestimated the power of their faith."

When she arrived at Christine and Michael's home, they welcomed her. "We are not mourning a loss but celebrating a gift," Michael said. "We had to let go of the idea we had set for ourselves. Our role is not to live by our ideals and expectations, but to love the child in front of us now," Christine added. They went on to explain that their newborn son was already teaching them lessons. "He is providing us with a chance to love as Christ did. We are learning to love our son not for who he could be but for who he is."

People of faith are realists. God helps them to live in the real world rather than the ideal world. The ideal world is a fantasyland where there is no pain or suffering. Living in the real world means experiencing hurt. Yet God strengthens Christians and helps them live in the real world of pain and suffering. Christine and Michael are examples of people through whom the grace of God is active. Their suffering has become a medium of new growth, and they are becoming stronger people because of it.

❧ Thought for the Day ❧

When God is our strength, it is strength indeed;
when our strength is our own, it is only weakness.
Saint Augustine

Only God Can Meet Our Deepest Needs

I am God, and there is no other;
I am God, and there is none like me.
Isaiah 46:9

"It was a dark time in our marriage," recalled Maureen. "My husband was working more and more; I was feeling unloved and neglected." The brief times they had together were consumed by screaming fights, which often ended in pain and guilt but no resolution.

Maureen began to see a marriage counselor. After only a few sessions the counselor said something that transformed Maureen and her marriage: "You are asking from your husband what you can only ask from God."

Immediately lights went on for Maureen. "Here I had been demanding that he be always available, always understanding, always loving. I was asking him to meet my needs and blaming him when he couldn't," she realized. Her counselor's wise observation marked a major turning point in Marueen's thinking and acting. Their marriage crisis passed.

Many people live with an emotional "Black Hole," which they frantically seek to fill with human love. When parents, spouses, children, or friends fail, as humans inevitably will, they suffer deep, painful anguish. Too many people experience tear-soaked pillows, pain-wracked nights, broken relationships, and revolving divorces because they seek perfect love from another human being.

Only God can give us what we deeply and authentically need: unconditional acceptance, complete communion, unyielding honor, and eternal value. Human love, at its best, can only be a shadow of God's love.

Let us remember it is not fair to demand from human beings what they are incapable of giving. Rather, let us seek a closer relationship with God because it is in that relationship where we will have our deepest needs met.

∼ *Affirmation for the Day* ∼
God's love fills me with peace and serenity.
God's love fills me with wisdom.
God's love makes me feel secure and confident.
VMP

Large Lessons From a Little Girl

Blessed is the man who trusts in the Lord,
whose confidence is in him.

Jeremiah 17:7

The Associated Press carried a story filled with good news. The head-line read: "From Homeless to Harvard." It was the story of Lauralee Summer, who received a full scholarship to Harvard University. Most of Lauralee's life experience was that of being homeless with her mother. For years the two lived in Salvation Army shelters in various parts of the country.

Because of her mother's lifestyle, school and formal education were almost impossible. Consequently, Lauralee taught herself to read from a "See and Say" book that she bought with money from a fourth birthday. As she and her mother moved among shelters and welfare hotels in several states, little Lauralee took refuge in public libraries and turned to books for solace. She spent most of her rootless childhood feeling alienated from classmates.

In spite of a childhood of homelessness, constant moving, and lack of friends, Lauralee is not angry or bitter. In fact, she is quite at peace with herself and her life. On her college application she wrote:

I learned that wealth is not what I have; rather it is who I am. Being poor, being homeless, having my startled eyes opened to blinding lights and long rows of metal cots from which so many strangers were arising: These were not disadvantages, but blessings, because they taught me more about myself.

Lauralee credits her mother and her own faith in God for helping her with the demands of daily life.

There are several large lessons that come from the example of a little girl. Like Lauralee, we should live our lives becoming better not bitter, celebrating what we have rather than becoming cynical over what is missing. Like Lauralee, we must move forward step by step and day by day, with hope and faith.

✎ Thought for the Day ✎

Trust God where you cannot trace him.
Do not try to penetrate the cloud he brings
over you; rather look to the bow that is on it.
The mystery of God's promise is yours.

John R. MacDuff

Helping a Grieving Friend

I rescued the poor who cried for help,
and the fatherless who had none to assist him.
Job 29:12

Many people feel at a loss over what to say or do when a friend is in grief because of separation, divorce, or death. Here are some simple, but effective, ways to help:

1. *Go to him.* Don't delay. Your visit will tell him "I care," "I love you," "I want to be with you during this hard time."

2. *Go to her.* But don't say too much. Words get in the way of grief. Sit gently by her side knowing that comfort comes from your presence.

3. *Go to comfort.* Don't go to cheer him up or try to change his feelings. Be there to provide comfort and consolation. That means accepting your friend in whatever condition he is in. If he is sad and crying, accept the tears and sadness. They are part of his life just now. He will not be that way permanently.

4. *Go to listen.* Allow your friend to tell of her loss over and over again. The repetition defuses the intensity of her loss and makes it possible for healing to take place. Every grieving person needs people who will simply listen.

5. *Go to help.* Don't say, "Let me know if there is anything I can do." Rather, open your eyes and be sensitive to what is needed. Offer to wash dishes, make beds, vacuum, pick up people at the airport, answer the phone, do some shopping, mow the lawn. See what needs to be done, and do it with your friend's permission.

⚜ *Prayer for the Day* ⚜
Loving God,
Increase my awareness and sensitivity
to the hurts and sufferings of other people.
Like Job, let me be one who rescues the
poor and assists the fatherless.
VMP

Keeping Promises

Words from a wise man's mouth are gracious,
but a fool is consumed by his own lips.

Ecclesiastes 10:12

After nearly thirty-five years of marriage, George's wife, Martha, died from cancer. Shortly before her death she asked George to promise he would never allow grass to grow on her grave. He made the promise.

For several years after her death, George would faithfully weed out every blade, keeping his word. All around her cemetery plot green grass flourished, but her grave lay bare. It was an emotionally sad task, but George made a promise, so each week he devoted several hours attending to his wife's grave. Then he planted a pine tree at the side of Martha's grave. Over the next few years he watched the small tree grow as he made his weekly visits.

One day as George visited with his daughter, he told her about the promise and his weekly visits. He was now an old man and said to his daughter, "I don't think I could have been able to handle the weekly weeding without the pine tree because in time, its needles came to cover Martha's grave holding back the grass."

Since that conversation George has died; but the pine needles continue to cover his wife's grave, and so his promise is kept.

Today, his daughter remembers vividly what he shared with her during their visit: "Think before you make a promise," he cautioned. "If you can't keep it, don't make it."

The father's advice is important. Our promises become empty words if they are not backed up by our action. We display spiritual maturity and emotional health when we keep our word.

☙ Thought for the Day ❧
It is better to run the risk of being considered
indecisive, better to be uncertain and not promise,
than to promise and not fulfill.
Oswald Chambers

Using Time Wisely

Teach us to number our days aright.
Psalm 90:12

America's greatest inventor, Thomas Edison, provides us with an important lesson about using time wisely. Edison's formal education ended at age twelve when he began selling candy and newspapers on the railroad. When the train laid over in Detroit, the youth raced to the public library to read for a few hours.

While working on the train, Edison also used spare time to study business practices. He soon discovered that by wiring ahead to the next train station informing them of news about a Civil War battle, he could increase the sales and the price of his newspapers when he arrived.

In addition to selling newspapers, Edison started one of his own, a newspaper that featured information and gossip about the railroad and the towns along the line. He printed the newspaper in the baggage car. There he also set up a small chemistry laboratory spending his remaining free time conducting experiments described in a chemistry textbook.

The obvious lesson from Edison's life is this: There is always enough time and space to do what is important to us. Although God gives every human being twenty-four hours daily, those hours are used effectively by some and are squandered by others. Today's reading from the psalms is a mature prayer asking God to "teach us to number our days aright." It is a prayer that all of us should offer routinely, and it is a prayer that should prompt us to examine the way we spend our hours.

❧ Prayer for the Day ❧
Gracious and Good God,
thank you for the gift of life and
the gift of each hour.
Help me not to lose time,
abuse time, or misuse time.
Rather, empower me
to use each hour of each day wisely.
VMP

Having a Good Day Every Day

The day is sacred to our Lord.
Nehemiah 8:10

Here are "ten commandments" for having a good day every day:

1. Accept each day as a unique gift from God.

2. Each morning offer a brief prayer asking God to bless your day.

3. Ask also that God will use you to be a blessing to others during the day.

4. Do some spiritual exercises. Begin the day by counting your blessings.

5. Anticipate new blessings to flow over you throughout the day.

6. Believe you will have a good day. Outlook determines outcome.

7. Plan for a good day. Picture, in detail, how you will spend twenty-four satisfying hours.

8. Do all you can to enjoy the day. Don't let life's routine and small irritants ruin the day.

9. Let the doing of goodness be a vital part of your day.

10. End each day with a brief prayer of thanks for the day behind.

∽ *Affirmation for the Day* ∼

God gives me the gift of a new day.
God fills my day with blessings and opportunities.
God's love and vitality fill me
with creative energy for every task.
VMP

Being a True and Loyal Friend

Do not forsake your friend.
Proverbs 27:10

When Richard Nixon resigned the presidency in 1972 due to the Watergate scandal, he was at his lowest, both politically and personally. Many former colleagues, as well as friends, avoided him.

During that time of emotional turmoil and loneliness, Nixon received a letter from his friend Harold Macmillan, former prime minister of England. Macmillan wrote, "I feel impelled, in view of our long friendship, to send you a message of sympathy and good will. I trust that these clouds may soon roll away."

When Macmillan died a short time later, Nixon wrote a tribute to the prime minister in *The Times* of London. Foremost among the things he remembered about Macmillan was his letter of friendship and how he did not treat Nixon in an inferior manner because he was forced to resign from the presidency.

There is a good life lesson in the exchange between President Nixon and Prime Minister Macmillan, and it is this: Real friendship is permeated with loyalty. True friendship and a mature understanding of relationships is characterized by faithfulness through all times: the good and the bad; the joyful and the sorrowful; when the going is easy and when the going gets rough.

Often the times when we need our friends most are not when life is going smoothly but when we are facing major difficulties and great challenges. That is why the Bible offers this simple, straightforward command: "Do not forsake your friend."

Today ask yourself, "Am I being the kind of friend I would like to have?"

～ Thought for the Day ～
Friendship is one of the sweetest joys of life.
Many might have failed beneath the bitterness
of their trial had they not found a friend.
Charles H. Spurgeon

Maintaining a Healthy Outlook

Keep up your courage...have faith in God.
Acts of the Apostles 27:25

There are times when we are too harsh with ourselves, overestimating our problems and underestimating our resources. It is a trap any of us can easily fall into. Here are some ways to maintain a healthy outlook:

1. *Avoid exaggerating.* Be careful not to overestimate your problems and underestimate your abilities. Rather than saying to yourself *I'm always late for meetings,* say *I make it to most meetings on time.*

2. *Don't overgeneralize.* Do not take an isolated incident and make it your defining characteristic. If you make a mistake, don't say, "I'm stupid." Replace it with, "This time I made a mistake. It won't happen again."

3. *Avoid personalizing.* Be careful not to feel and think that everything you do is noticed by all sorts of people. For example, "Everyone noticed that I wore the same dress twice" can be replaced with the affirmation "I like this outfit, and I am properly dressed for the occasion."

4. *Don't use either/or thinking.* Be careful about seeing events as mutually exclusive: "Either I get the promotion or I am a failure." Replace that kind of thinking with the word "and": "My performance has been exceptional, *and* I have a good chance of getting promoted. If I don't get it this time around, there will be other opportunities."

5. *Avoid jumping to conclusions.* Make sure you have all the information and not just limited knowledge before you make conclusions. Replace the thought *I wasn't included as a member of the project because I am incompetent* with *I'll check with the manager and see if I can be helpful with the project.*

6. *Don't ignore the positive.* Beware of the tendency to focus on the negative while forgetting the positives. *I did not make my sales quota last month* can be replaced with the more positive, *I met my sales quotas eleven out of twelve months, and I will make it again.*

⤙ Thought for the Day ⤚
Do not feel that all is lost because of the revolt
you feel inside. It has rained hard. The thunder has crashed.
Is the weather any less beautiful because of that?
Be assured you are not, for all that, less dear to our Lord.
Saint Vincent de Paul

The Importance of Living One Day at a Time

So my heart began to despair over all my toilsome labor.

Ecclesiastes 2:20

Whether we are working inside the home raising children and managing household duties or working in a career, the daily responsibilities can wear us down. Today's biblical writer speaks of "despair" over "toilsome labor." Whenever we begin to feel discouraged and despairing over our daily activity, we should respond by intentionally living one day at a time. That practice is what restored television personality Deborah Norville.

In 1990 she was selected by television network officials to replace popular *Today* co-host, Jane Pauley. Although Norville had nothing to do with the decision, fans of Jane Pauley were outraged and directed their anger toward Norville. In addition, television critics skewered Norville. One even coined the word "Norvilled," meaning to be rudely pushed aside.

All of that criticism damaged Norville's self-esteem. Her confidence hit an all-time low. In less than a year she left the *Today* program—and television—and then did some radio work.

Finally, after several months, her confidence was renewed. She says what helped her overcome feelings of despair was learning to live one day at a time. "There are days—depression is part of it—when if all you do is get dressed, take a shower, and put on your makeup, then it's a good day. Your goals have to be much lower. But if you take one tiny little step, then you can take another and another. Then you have walked that city block."

❧ Thought for the Day ❧

Build a little fence of trust
Around today;
Fill the space with loving deeds,
And therein stay.
Look not through the sheltering bars
Upon tomorrow;
God will help thee bear what comes
Of joy or sorrow.

Mary Frances Butts

The Importance of Flexibility

A man who remains stiff-necked...
will suddenly be destroyed.

Proverbs 29:1

One night while performing a one-man show in New Zealand, actor Peter Ustinov was startled when a power failure knocked out all the lights. Fearing the audience might panic, Ustinov declared in the dark: "The performance goes on. From now on, I'm on radio. You're having a sleepless night, and you switch the bedside radio on. Ready? Here goes...."

For the next twenty minutes, Ustinov entertained his audience in the pitch blackness, using different voices to compensate for the fact he couldn't be seen. "I got more laughs than when they could see me," he recalls. "When the lights went on again, it wasn't at all the same thing. I regretted that the lights never went out again."

Ustinov's ability to adapt and change so quickly is admirable. However, many people have difficulty coping with change and transition. Yet, in today's world, change is inevitable. Everyone is subject to life's changes and chances. Not even an exceptional job performance is a defense against change. If a company decides to downsize, or is bought out, every employee runs the risk of a job loss or being forced into another position.

Today's scripture is a strong reminder that those who do not adapt to change will find their lives filled with frustration, fear, and even failure. Those who are "stiff-necked" will be suddenly destroyed. On the other hand, those who master the art of change develop a vital survival skill. In the process they will experience courage, confidence, and control over the various changes that life brings. Whenever changes come our way let us remember Ustinov's example. Let us seek God's help when changes invade our lives.

❧ *Prayer for the Day* ❧
Loving God,
Give me the insight to know when
I should stand firm and when
I should be flexible and adaptable.
VMP

Remembering God's Constant and Consistent Presence

I the Lord do not change. So you, O descendants of Jacob, are not destroyed.

Malachi 3:6

Yesterday we dealt with the fact of change. Today we want to think about the reality that God is constantly and consistently present. Even though there come events that may dramatically change and even traumatize your living, the Bible makes it clear that God remains the same. In addition to the scriptural verse for today, consider verses such as these:

Psalm 102:25–27: "In the beginning you laid the foundations of the earth and the heavens are the work of your hands. They will perish...but you remain the same."

James 1:17: "Every good and perfect gift is from above, coming down from the Father of the heavenly lights, who does not change like shifting shadows."

Hebrews 13:8: "Jesus Christ is the same yesterday and today and forever."

These and other biblical passages were written to instill deep faith and great confidence that God has not changed and can be trusted to provide love, support, strength, patience, wisdom, insight, and creativity when we have to face change.

As you face change, reflect on such Bible verses, affirming that God is present in all of your life changes and that God is filling you with divine love and wisdom.

❧ Thought for the Day ❧

Change and decay in all around I see:
O thou who changest not, abide with me.

Henry Francis Lyte

Identifying Resources

No one will be able to stand up against you
all the days of your life. As I was with Moses,
so I will be with you; I will never leave you
nor forsake you. Be strong and courageous.

Joshua 1:5-6

Some situations emerge in our lives that are highly traumatic, such as an abrupt job loss, learning of a serious illness, death of a loved one, or a divorce. Managing these challenging transitions often makes people feel helpless and hopeless.

Under such circumstances we must remember that God always provides us with a variety of resources. In the Bible, God promises: "As I was with Moses, so I will be with you; I will never leave you nor forsake you."

Thus it is vital that we take the time to identify God's resources for us. Although we may not have control over the situation, we can control the *strategies* we use by identifying resources available.

Consider the example of Rita, a factory worker who returned home after work and found a note from her husband. She had been abandoned and was left with no money and three children to support.

"My situation was unbelievable," she recalls. "My life and the lives of my children seemed to be out of my control. It was stressful, frightening, and horrible." After the initial shock receded, Rita wisely took stock of her resources. "By seeking advice from friends, I was able to find a lawyer who helped me for no money. In the yellow pages I found a therapist who saw clients on a sliding scale. She let me pay what I could when I could. I knew I would need a better job to support my children, so I took computer classes at the least expensive school in our area. I was able to keep my day job while attending night school. Those courses led me into a much better paying job."

When tough times and difficult days come our way, let us pause in the midst of the emotional chaos to identify sources of help that God provides for us. It may be the encouragement of a good friend, the wise counsel of a pastor, the comfort of a support group.

❧ *Affirmation for the Day* ❧
God knows all of my needs.
God provides me with ample resources.
God leads me in the right paths day by day.
VMP

Accepting the Challenge to Change

I am making everything new.
Revelation 21:5

Scripture often reminds us that God is always in the process of creating something new. Today's scripture reading is one expression of that truth: "I am making everything new." *I am making a way in the desert and streams in the wasteland.*

Those biblical verses should be read as an invitation to deliberately expand our comfort zones by accepting the challenge of change. Be willing to entertain a new idea or a different way of doing things. Take on the challenge of transforming yourself.

This is precisely what Jake Steinfeld did. Because of his television program, *Body by Jake,* he is a well-known bodybuilder and physical trainer. Recently he started the *Cable Health Club,* the first all-health cable network.

What many of his viewers do not know is that Steinfeld was not always the fine physical specimen he is today. "I started out as a fat kid with a terrible stutter," he says. The summer he turned fifteen his father bought him a set of weights and challenged him to begin exercising.

Those weights sat unused all summer. "One night, I picked up an easy curl bar to do bicep curls," Steinfeld recalls. "I liked it. I got into the habit of doing my bicep curls in front of this long, skinny mirror in my room. That was the beginning for me. The more I got into working out, the better I felt about myself, the taller I stood up, and the less I stuttered."

Today, take an honest look at yourself. Are there areas of your life that you would like to change and improve? Perhaps today is the day to accept the challenge to change.

❧ Thought for the Day ❧
Keep changing.
When you're through changing,
you're through.
Bruce Fairfield Barton

Learning From Role Models

Moses listened to his father-in-law
and did everything he said.

Exodus 18:24

God provides us with teachers and mentors. In today's reading, Moses responded to a suggestion made by Jethro, his father-in-law. When Jethro visited Moses and his family, he was surprised to note that Moses alone was serving as mediator and judge over every dispute that arose in the Israeli camp. The workload was too heavy for one person, so Jethro suggested Moses appoint other assistants to help him sort through the various disputes. Moses responded positively and could now devote his time to more important issues.

Along with helpful advice from friends, we can learn important lessons informally through role models. For example, there are many people who flow with change naturally and easily. Also, there are individuals who have been forced to make changes and have adapted successfully. Keep an eye out for such persons, and let them become your mentors.

Look for role models of people who have made a success of living. They can help us become comfortable with change and empower us to be victors and not victims over life's many transitions. Their example can help us stay on top, even when our world turns upside down.

⤳ *Prayer for the Day* ⤶
Loving and good God,
I thank you for the gift of good friends
and helpful people in my life.
I thank you for their experiences and insights.
Let me be a teachable person;
one who learns naturally
and responds to the positive
suggestions of others.
VMP

The Qualities of a Survivor

You need to persevere.
Hebrews 10:36

Sometimes the art of living is more like wrestling than a dance. Difficult times emerge in every life, times that call for courage. Getting through those times is to become a survivor. And surviving involves attitude. A survivor

- Refuses to give up
- Clings to a strong sense of hope
- Remains open to new possibilities
- Believes in life
- Sees fresh prospects for the future
- Continues involvement with people
- Looks forward to a better tomorrow
- Lives one day at a time
- Honors life
- Goes on loving and offering unconditional love
- Weathers discouragement, depression, and setbacks
- Knows the sun always rises
- Understands that sadness comes to every life

Remind yourself that you are a survivor! When facing tough times and difficult dilemmas, ask God for daily help.

~≪ Thought for the Day ≫~
Life is either a daring adventure or nothing.
Helen Keller

The Importance of Perspective

If this is how you are going to treat me,
put me to death right now.

Numbers 11:15

In today's reading, Moses has moved from discouragement to despair. Because he has lost his perspective, he asks God: "Put me to death right now." The loss of perspective often leads to emotional and spiritual despair. That issue plagued Moses, and it troubles people today.

A man, speaking with his pastor, sadly said: "I'm deep in debt from my failed business. I'm forty-three years of age and am ruined. I don't know how I'll pay off the debt or support my wife and three children. I've prayed, but God doesn't seem to hear or help me. Why doesn't God get me back on my feet, financially and emotionally?"

Like Moses, this man is indeed dealing with a major crisis. And, like Moses, he has made it worse through his loss of perspective. In fact, he would operate with more creativity and energy if he could:

1. Remember that God goes through a crisis with us. We are not abandoned.

2. Recall that God provides us with spiritual, emotional, intellectual, and physical resources to manage problems.

3. List the positive aspects of his situation. He could begin by thanking God for his wife and three children, then move on to thank God for his good health, as well as that of his family. Also, he could praise God for his education, experience, friends, and colleagues. By seeing the blessings in his life, and not only the burden, he would realize that while facing a crisis he does have many resources to draw on.

4. Remind himself there is no problem that does not have a solution.

5. Ask God to help him formulate a plan of recovery.

Hopefully, this man's situation changes, as does Moses'. Although deeply discouraged, Moses receives the grace and wisdom to regain his perspective. Whenever we face discouragement and despair let us remember to maintain balance and perspective.

⁓ *Affirmation for the Day* ⁓
Because of God's love I dissolve all negative beliefs.
Because of God's love I end all limiting behavior.
Because of God's love I eliminate all constricted thinking.
VMP

God Works With Our Circumstances

If at any time I announce that a nation or kingdom
is to be uprooted, torn down and destroyed, and if that
nation I warned repents of its evil, then I will relent and
not inflict on it the disaster I had planned.
Jeremiah 18:7-8

Today's scripture from Jeremiah is worth rereading, because too often God is viewed as a "bulldozer," who moves straight toward an objective. If God says something will happen, it will happen.

While that idea has some basis in the Bible, it can be taken to extremes and lead to a fatalistic view of life: "God is going to do what God is going to do, so it doesn't matter what I do."

That is why the eighteenth chapter of Jeremiah contains another picture of God. He is not so much a bulldozer, but more a potter. According to Jeremiah, God is capable and willing to change his mind. God works with circumstances as they emerge. God may intend to make a vase, but events may cause God to make a cereal bowl instead.

God is soft and pliable, not rigid and fixed. If we make a mistake, get ourselves into problems, feel despairing and believe that God will judge us harshly, we need to remember that God works with circumstances. If we show sincere regret, seek forgiveness, ask for guidance and help, God is committed to respond favorably.

❧ Thought for the Day ❧

To forgive ourselves we need to believe that
we are forgiven by God. We must meditate on
God's forgiveness of us. Even if you have to
struggle to believe it, even if there are voices of
guilt and shame screaming inside you,
believe in the depths of your soul
that you have been forgiven.
Begin to see yourself as a child of God.
Benedict J. Groeschel

A Lesson in Generosity

They brought as their gifts before the Lord
six covered carts and twelve oxen.

Numbers 7:3

The Associated Press carried a heartwarming story about a young woman who had just graduated from law school.

During the graduation ceremonies the president of the University of Virginia announced that graduating student Tracey Lenhard was establishing a scholarship for future students in the law school.

Lenhard pledged that, over the course of her legal career, she will donate at least $1,000 a year to support other black students. She named the scholarship in honor of her parents, Maj. Gen. Alfonso E. Lenhard and Jacqueling O. Lenhard. "As my parents stuck with me through law school, I want to stick with that person for three years," Lenhard explained.

The surprised parents said their reactions were a combination of "joy, shock, and disbelief." The young woman said the scholarship reflects the lessons stressed by her parents: study hard, and help the less fortunate.

Today's scripture reading cites the generosity of some ancient Israelites who "brought as their gifts before the Lord six covered carts and twelve oxen." That passage and the example of Tracey Lenhard should prompt us to ask what gifts we are bringing to God. For the biblical people, their gifts included covered carts and oxen; for Tracey Lenhard, her gift was a scholarship.

What is it that we are offering to God as an expression of our gratitude?

⚞ Thought for the Day ⚟
Sharing is something more demanding than giving.
Mary Catherine Bateson

Some Healthy Living Principles

*Some became fools through their rebellious
ways and suffered affliction because of their
inequities.*

Psalm 107:17

More and more studies reveal Americans live unhealthy lifestyles that lead to a variety of illnesses, such as heart disease, strokes, and cancers. "Some became fools through their rebellious ways and suffered affliction because of their inequities," writes the psalmist. However, there is this good news: Experts are saying that some small, simple changes in lifestyle can bring large benefits in terms of overall physical, emotional, and spiritual health. Here are some healthy living principles to adopt:

1. *Balanced nutrition.* Try increasing your consumption of whole grains, vegetables, and fresh fruit. At the same time, decrease consumption of fatty meats, whole dairy products, high cholesterol foods, and sugar.

2. *Proper exercise.* Begin by walking a mere fifteen minutes daily in the fresh outdoors. Also, increase your daily activity level by standing instead of sitting, walking instead of driving (whenever possible), parking several blocks from your destination, using stairs instead of elevators or escalators. When visiting with friends, suggest walking while talking, rather than sitting.

3. *Moderation.* Avoid overworking, overeating, and overresting. That means adhering to an eight-hour workday, not going back for seconds, and limiting sleep to seven or eight hours each night.

4. *Friendship.* Cultivate at least one or two deep and abiding relationships. This could be with your spouse, a child, or a colleague. Have someone you could turn to for support, encouragement, and guidance during a time of crisis. Also, be the kind of person your friend could confide in if he or she was struggling with an issue.

5. *Trust in God.* With the beginning of each day, seek God's guidance. Praise God for good and joyous times; trust God on difficult and tough days.

❧ Thought for the Day ❧
The first wealth is health.
Ralph Waldo Emerson

Transforming Ourselves

*Each of you must turn from your wicked ways
and reform your actions.*

Jeremiah 35:15

The prophet Jeremiah reminds us that we are responsible for our lives. According to the prophet, each of us must turn from our "wicked" ways and "reform" our actions.

One who turned from "wicked ways" and reformed his action is Carl Robins of Fort Worth, Texas. By the time Robins was forty, he had spent nearly half his life in prison on charges of burglary, alcohol and drug abuse. "Suddenly, in my early forties, I felt ashamed," he says. That personal epiphany led to a determination to make something positive emerge from his life. He began by joining a twelve-step program for drug and alcohol abusers. Robins also took courses to earn a high-school diploma and went on to do all but four credits of a bachelor's degree. He became a model prisoner.

Between 1977 and 1982 he was turned down for parole six times by a panel that included a former corrections officer known for his tough line on career criminals. "After the sixth time I was turned down, I just cried," Robins says. "Then I asked God for help." That prayer was answered in 1983 when he came up for parole again. His old nemesis was there once again for him, "You're my mercy case this year; but if you ever come back, your life is over," recalled Robins. After twenty-seven years behind bars, Robins has been clean, straight, and sober for more than a decade. He now works with project RIO (Re-Integration of Offenders) in his state. The governor of Texas issued him a pardon in recognition of his positive contributions. That pardon allows him the right to vote once again.

Although few of us are career criminals, the words of the prophet still apply to our living:

"Each of you must turn from your wicked ways and reform your actions." Let us think deeply about that sentence and scrutinize our thoughts and actions. What actions need reforming? What "wicked" ways must we turn from?

❧ *Thought for the Day* ❧

Strength, for a person who desires to acquire virtues,
consists in not losing heart when one happens to fall,
but in continuing once more on the way.
Not to fall is characteristic only of angels.

Saint Moses

Courageously Facing Loss

Be strong and courageous.
Joshua 10:25

Mary Wilson, a professional singer and formerly associated with The Supremes, was involved in an accident that claimed the life of her fourteen-year-old son, Rafael. While driving on January 29, 1994, Wilson nodded off at the wheel. The Jeep veered off the highway. Although she swerved back onto the highway, the vehicle flipped over at least once and landed upright. In spite of the fact that Rafael was wearing his seat belt, he suffered serious injuries and died before medics could get him to a hospital. Mary Wilson spent several weeks in the hospital, but her determination to deal with her grief in healthy, constructive ways has impressed many.

First of all, Wilson believes she is honoring her son by continuing her life, even though performing is difficult under the burden of grief. "People think that the only way to deal with pain is to cry out in public, and for a year you have to wear black and you can't go anywhere," says Wilson. "I am totally the opposite. I could say 'If only I'd stayed in Los Angeles, if only he'd never come along'—all those 'if onlys' are really foolish. My advice is to make your life a testimony to your child. Obviously, I'd like to have my son back, but I can't. So I need to do everything I can to bring myself to a higher level."

Second, Wilson has allowed others to bring her comfort and support. That has resulted in a surprising reconciliation with her one-time best friend and fellow Supreme, Diana Ross. The two had been estranged for several years. "My son's passing has brought a lot of love back into my life," says Wilson. "Diana called me, and I think our relationship is on the mend."

Finally, Wilson has chosen to experience and confront her pain, rather than avoid it. Some who don't know Wilson feel her zeal to recover is simply an attempt to block the tragedy out of her mind. "People say, 'She's just not dealing with it; she's in denial'—but she's not," says her friend Coolidge. "She talks about it all the time. She had her hospital room decorated with pictures of Rafi. That's not denial; that's walking into your worst nightmare."

Mary Wilson is proof that God gives us the courage we need to face our trials. Although we do not ask for suffering, we must ask for God's help in responding to it creatively, powerfully.

❧ *Thought for the Day* ❧
Have plenty of courage. God is stronger than the devil.
We are on the winning side.
John Jay Chapman

Breaking Free of Boredom

And I declared that the dead, who had already died,
are happier than the living who are still alive.

Ecclesiastes 4:2

Life should always be viewed as a thrilling adventure filled with challenging opportunities. However, for many people there is a tedious monotony connected to life. Some even share the experience of the writer of Ecclesiastes, who appears to be caught in feelings of futility and despair.

Here are some guidelines for breaking free of boredom and living life more abundantly:

- Daily make a list of reasonable tasks to accomplish. Compliment yourself at the end of the day when they are complete. Find simple but pleasant ways to reward yourself.
- Go out of your way to make a new friend.
- Plan a social event regularly, perhaps once or twice a month. Be sure to invite some new friends, as well as comfortable old friends.
- Change your scenery. Go on a one-day outing where you can be amused, informed, or just renewed.
- Change your habits. Once a week get up before the sun and watch it rise. Or, following dinner go for a walk and observe the sun set.
- Find someone who is hurting and help out. Provide encouragement; be a mentor; give financial assistance. Do whatever will be most helpful.
- Volunteer your time and talent to a worthwhile cause in your community or church.
- Finally, if you feel bored with life try to view it as God's "wake-up call." God may indeed be nudging you to move in another direction or to reevaluate your lifestyle.

❧ Thought for the Day ❧

Boredom has made more gamblers than greed,
more drunkards than thirst, and perhaps
as many suicides as despair.

Charles Caleb Colton

Dealing With Anger

In your anger do not sin.
Psalm 4:4

It should be noted immediately that this biblical passage does not condemn anger. It issues a warning against sin, while acknowledging the fact that all people will become angry at one time or another. Nevertheless, for most people anger is an uncomfortable and confusing emotion. Here are some ways to deal with anger constructively and creatively.

- *Acknowledge your anger.* It is unhealthy to pretend you are not angry or that angry feelings do not exist. When you experience anger simply say to yourself: "Yes, I'm upset." "I am irritated." "I am very angry."

- *Seek out the cause of your anger.* Try to find out what triggered it. Sometimes it is simple: The driver behind you blew his horn at you. Other times it is more subtle: Someone treated you in a demeaning way.

- *Explore how you feel about your angry feelings.* Take an honest look and ask yourself: "Am I ashamed of my anger?" "Am I afraid of my anger?" Or, can you come to the healthy place and say, "I feel okay about my angry feelings."

- *Decide how to respond and resolve your anger.* There are three ways to respond and resolve angry feelings.

1. *Pray about the issue, seeking God's guidance and strength.*

2. *Speak to the person who has made you angry.* By using first-person rather than second-person pronouns, you will be less threatening. For example, say: "I'm upset" or "I'm angry," rather than the more accusatory: "You deliberately…" or "You always…"

3. *Put your anger into positive energy.* If you are upset about a problem in your organization, community, or church, commit yourself to working on a solution. If the issue is a recurring family matter, make an appointment to see a family counselor to strengthen the family.

❦ *Thought for the Day* ❦
I was angry with my friend.
I told my wrath, my wrath did end.
I was angry with my foe.
I told it not, my wrath did grow.
William Blake

Choosing to Trust God

Though he slay me, yet will I hope in him.
Job 13:15

Last week in my community two families held funerals for their two teenage girls, tragically killed in a car accident. A large segment of the community shared their sorrow and sadness. Whenever such a tragedy takes place, profound questions about God emerge. For example:

- Did God know about this in advance?
- Doesn't God know all things?
- Does God have the power to prevent these situations?
- Isn't God sovereign?
- Isn't God in control of this world and our lives?

The answer to each of the above questions is "yes." An all-powerful God knows, sees, and anticipates all events. Because that is true, the question of God's love becomes difficult to comprehend. If God loves us, if God is in control, if God is not surprised by events, and if God could have prevented them, why did they occur?

Such questions tax both mind and spirit. There is no simple answer. The questions leave us with a choice about God. Even though we feel deep emotional pain and intellectual confusion, we can still choose to trust God. Like Job who suffered greatly, we can say, "Though he slay me, yet will I hope in him."

Behind that sentence is the choice to trust that God is loving and righteous; that the God who has spoken through the scripture continues to work for our good even though the path is currently painful and mysterious. Let us choose to trust God.

❧ *Thought for the Day* ❧
Courage, brother! Do not stumble,
Though thy path be dark as night;
There's a star to guide the humble,
Trust in God and do the right.
Norman Macleod

Extending Kindness to the Stranger

The alien living with you must be treated as one of your native-born.
Love him as yourself, for you were aliens in Egypt.
I am the LORD your God.

Leviticus 19:34

A young woman wrote a well-known advice columnist asking help to thank a stranger who treated her with profound kindness. "I will remember him for the rest of my life," the woman declared. This is what happened:

In the spring term of her final college year, she flew from California to Washington state to be interviewed for admission to a veterinary school. She made reservations for a rental car and motel room so that she could go directly from the airport to her motel room to prepare for the interview. She had two hours from her arrival at the airport to the time of the interview.

Upon landing, she went directly to the rental car agency's desk where she planned to pay for the car with her credit card. She had carefully mailed her monthly payment five days earlier so that her new charges would clear. To her shock the credit-card transaction was rejected. She had no other form of payment. Furthermore, she was planning to pay for her motel room with the credit card. The young woman was stranded at the airport with no money and her credit card rejected.

Crying hysterically she raced to a phone booth and called her roommate back in California. While she was on the phone, a gentleman came up to her, tapped her on the shoulder, and handed her a hundred-dollar bill. Then he disappeared.

This young woman is extremely grateful and wrote the advice columnist because she wants him to know how appreciative she is. The anonymous benefactor not only made it possible for her to arrive on time for the interview, but he made it possible for her to enter veterinary school.

Today's reading from Leviticus is a direct command from God, reminding each of us about our duty toward the stranger in our midst. We are to treat him or her as we would treat a member of our family, with love and kindness. The man in the airport who helped the young woman in distress is an excellent example of what God requires. Let us reflect on that incident and open ourselves to assisting a stranger in need.

❧ Thought for the Day ❧

We cannot possibly let ourselves get frozen into regarding
everyone we do not know as an absolute stranger.

Albert Schweitzer

Be Nonconductors of Evil

If you come across your enemy's ox or donkey
wandering off, be sure to take it back to him.

Exodus 23:4

Today's reading from Exodus is a morally demanding one. It declares that we are to treat even our "enemies" with fairness and respect. In the ancient context, the Bible says if an enemy's valuable, domestic animal is seen wandering away it must be captured and returned to the owner.

The Bible reminds us that moral and social responsibility must transcend personal animosity and antagonism. We are to be nonconductors of evil. The chain of retaliation must stop with us. Doing so opens the possibility that greater understanding and healing may be achieved.

One person who understood this was President John F. Kennedy.

In October 1962, after more than two weeks of tense confrontation and negotiation, the Cuban missile crisis was resolved when Nikita Krushchev, the Soviet leader, agreed to remove all missiles from Cuba. In exchange, Kennedy promised that the United States would not invade the island.

According to Kennedy adviser and biographer, Theodore Sorensen, the president then "laid down the line for all of us." Kennedy told his aides there was to be no boasting, no gloating, not even a hint of victory. "We had won by enabling Krushchev to avoid complete humiliation— we should not humiliate him now," the president explained.

After reflecting on the ancient text, as well as the example of President Kennedy, let us consider how we can be more effective as nonconductors of evil. Let us ask ourselves:

- Will I honestly try to respond to evil with good?

- Will I honestly try to treat all people, including "enemies," with respect?

- Will I honestly try to be kind to those who are unkind to me?

- Will I honestly try to be fair with my "enemy"?

❧ *Thought for the Day* ❧

Never cease loving a person and never give up hope for him,
for even the Prodigal Son who had fallen most low could
still be saved. The bitterest enemy and also he who was
your friend could again be your friend;
love that has grown cold can kindle again.

Søren Kierkegaard

Creating New Possibilities

I will restore their fortunes.
Jeremiah 33:26

Jacqueline was fourteen when doctors informed her she had scoliosis, a curvature of the spine. In her case it could lead to paralysis and even death if not corrected. She underwent a major operation that reduced three curves in her spine and fused together most of her vertebrae. As part of the surgery, bone fragments were removed from her hip and used to strengthen the spine. In addition, two rods running the length of her back were inserted to hold her repositioned spine in place.

That procedure meant the teenager had to wear a body cast for four months and a brace for another three months. Jacqueline was forced to experience the trials of being a teen while her body was developing inside a cast. During the recovery, she spent most of her time alone at home. The confinement and lack of activity resulted in a deep depression, which lasted long after the cast's removal.

One source of her depression was the medical view that Jacqueline had to curtail physical activity. She could no longer participate in diving, gymnastics, skateboarding, and dance—some of her favorite activities. She questioned medical wisdom and cautiously began to exercise. Joining a health club with her mother, Jacqueline took aerobics and lifted weights. That gave her a sense of freedom, control, and power over her life. "I realized that I should be thankful for what I could do, rather than dwell on what I couldn't do."

Her thinking was completely transformed. For example, Jacqueline used to think the scar on her body was the sign of a handicap. She went to great lengths and suffered many discomforts to hide it. Today she views her scar as a symbol of her survival. Jacqueline has created new possibilities for her life that no one could ever have imagined for her. She went to a university where she studied fitness and exercise. Today she holds three fitness certifications, teaches step aerobics, does personal training, and lectures before fitness instructors. She is so physically oriented and has adapted so naturally to the rods in her spine that students are not aware that there was or is anything different about her.

Jacqueline is an excellent example of today's reading from Jeremiah.

⚕ *Prayer for the Day* ⚕
Glorious God,
Give me the courage to be creative.
Help me see and create new possibilities from my life.
VMP

The Healing Power of Silence

Miserable comforters are you all!
Will your long-winded speeches never end?
                    Job 16:2–3

Robert, a North Carolina pastor, tells about a time when his brother suffered a massive heart attack. Robert rushed to the hospital to be with his brother and wife. The brother lay in a coma in the hospital's coronary intensive-care unit. Tubes and wires hooked up to machines kept the man alive. A scope showed the weak lines of a faltering heartbeat. As a pastor, Robert had often been with other families in similar circumstances. But this time was different.

During those difficult hospital days, his sister-in-law and he were torn between hope and resignation. They appreciated every visitor. They were grateful for stories of people who had snapped out of comas and returned to normal. Robert and his sister-in-law knew that people meant well. However, "many visitors came through the door talking and kept talking," he recalls. *Was that how I had dealt with my nervousness when I didn't know what to say,* he wondered to himself.

Then, a casual friend came to visit. He stood with Robert and his sister-in-law by the bed looking at the comatose patient. There was a long silence. Suddenly overcome with emotion, he said simply, "I'm sorry." There was another long, silent pause. Finally, he hugged Robert's sister-in-law and shook Robert's hand, holding it a second longer than necessary. As he looked at Robert, tears came to his eyes. Then the man left. Robert's brother died a week later.

"Years have passed and I still remember that visitor," Robert says. "I do not recall his name, but I'll never forget how he shared our grief, quietly and sincerely and without awkwardness. His few words spoke volumes."

Job, like Robert, experienced the discomfort of friends who talked too much about his crisis. "Miserable comforters," he called them. That is a good lesson for all of us. When a friend is experiencing hard times, we do not need to say much or anything at all. Our caring presence conveys the message of love and support. Our silence can heal.

❧ Prayer for the Day ❧
Loving God,
As I seek to comfort those who hurt,
guide my thinking, my speaking, my acting,
so that I truly bring gifts of support and love.
VMP

Take the Time to Hurt and Heal

He will bind up our wounds.
Hosea 6:1

Life is less like a prairie, flat and level, but more like a mountain re-
gion. There are heights and depths, joys and sorrows. The next time you
experience life's harsh side, such as a prolonged illness, job loss, separation or divorce, the death of a loved one, take the time to hurt and heal.

- *Take the time to hurt.* The pain is real and honest. Avoid the temptation to ignore it or flee from it. Taking the time to experience the pain
  is the only way of recovering from it. Covering it up means it will only
  resurface later in a potentially more destructive way.

- *Take the time to feel sorry for yourself.* Cry when you need to. You have
  every reason to weep when you are hurt.

- *Take the time to "fall apart."* A crisis has come into your life. If you
  broke an arm, you would not expect to function at full capacity. If
  your heart is broken and your spirit is hurting, there will be confusion,
  depression, lethargy, feelings of despair. These are all a normal part of
  adjusting to life's blow.

Having done the above, then move on to the next level, that of healing.

- *Take the time to identify resources.* Seek out individuals who can help
  and guide you. A counselor, a financial planner, a clergyperson, compassionate friends.

- *Take the time to care for your health.* During a stressful time be sure to
  look after body and soul. Eat properly, exercise, pray and worship.

- *Take the time to be patient.* God has created us to heal, but the healing
  and recovery can take longer than you expect. Be patient. The ebb
  and flow of life will return to a more normal pace.

⇾ *Prayer for the Day* ⇽
Loving and gracious God,
Day by day guide me through the storm
and into safer, calmer waters.
Day by day empower me to trust you
and follow your guidance.
VMP

Wonderfully Created by God

I praise you because I am fearfully and wonderfully made...
Psalm 139:14

God has created us with powerful bodies that are adaptable to various circumstances. For example, the human body's remarkable resilience to aging is demonstrated by the following people:

Jack LaLanne. On his seventieth birthday he completed a one-and-a-half-mile swim in Long Beach Harbor, handcuffed, shackled, towing seventy boats full of friends and reporters.

Mavis Lindgren. This "senior" citizen took up running at the age of sixty-two and ran her first marathon at seventy. She has run forty-eight more since then. At age eighty, she was still running marathons.

Hulda Crooks. After turning sixty-five she began mountain climbing and has climbed ninety-eight mountains, including Japan's Mount Fuji.

Lucille Thompson. When she began to experience the crippling effects of arthritis at eighty-eight years of age, she took up karate to overcome her arthritis. Since then she has earned a black belt and the nickname "Killer."

These exemplary people are a reminder that we should take care of the bodies that God has given us. We can make our bodies work for us or against us. If we exercise, eat moderate and healthy meals, our bodies will serve us well until we die. However, if we abuse our bodies through drugs, alcohol, or overeating, they will become a burden and end our lives prematurely.

Let us join with the psalmist who thanks God saying, "I praise you because I am fearfully and wonderfully made." Then let us treat our bodies—and ourselves—with respect.

⤛ Prayer for the Day ⤜

Loving and Eternal God,
I thank you for eyes that see,
for legs that walk,
for arms that serve me,
for a mind that thinks and reasons.
Let me treat the body you have given me with respect,
so that I may continue to serve you and others
until you call me home.
VMP

An Example of Healthy Humility

What does the Lord require of you?...
to walk humbly with your God.
Micah 6:8

Inventor Thomas Edison held more patents than any other individual in history. He had 1,093, covering inventions, such as the phonograph, electric light bulb, and motion-picture camera. His life and work remain the standard by which all other inventors compete.

Although Edison was extremely successful, wealthy, and famous, he did not live by the illusion that he was a self-made individual. All his life he exercised a healthy humility through which he acknowledged his debt to others.

Of great importance to Edison was the influence of his mother. He attributed much of his success to the fact his mother nurtured and encouraged him to read. Although his formal education ended with grade school, his mother instilled in Edison a love of books. Later in life he paid this tribute to his mother: "My mother taught me how to read good books quickly and correctly, and as this opened up a great world in literature, I have always been very thankful for this early training."

True humility resides in the hearts of people who know that behind their successes are many individuals sent by God to provide encouragement, instruction, guidance, and teaching. The truth is that no one is self-made. We have had many guides and instructors along the way. A mature spirituality acknowledges that reality and expresses gratitude.

❧ Thought for the Day ❧
Humility is nothing but truth, while pride
is nothing but lying.
Saint Vincent de Paul

Keeping an Open Mind

Moses saw that though the bush was on fire
it did not burn up. So Moses thought,
"I will go over and see this strange sight—
why the bush does not burn up."

Exodus 3:2-3

Today's scripture stresses the importance of keeping an open mind to events, comments, and even criticisms. Had Moses ignored the sight of the burning bush, which was not consumed by the flames, he might never have received the call of God to lead the people of Israel out of slavery and into freedom.

There is an important lesson in that experience for each one of us. People whose personalities are rigid and inflexible deprive themselves of opportunities to grow and learn. On the other hand, those who keep an open mind pave the way to unlimited growth and learning. For them, even criticism can become a positive force.

An example of keeping an open mind is Sir James Barrie, author of *Peter Pan*. When the play first premiered in London in 1904, Barrie began to hear from parents who were upset with the play. They asked him to make a change.

In the original version, Peter told the Darling children that if they believed strongly enough they could fly, they *would* fly. Parents who took their children to see the play contacted Barrie saying their children had taken Peter's word literally and hurt themselves attempting to fly. Immediately, Barrie altered the script to include in the play a cautionary statement that the children could fly, but only if they had first been sprinkled with "fairy dust." From then on, because fairy dust was in short supply, children were no longer injuring themselves.

⤳ Prayer for the Day ⤶
Loving and gracious God,
Teach me to be an open person.
Remind me that I can have convictions,
principles, standards, beliefs, and still
be open to new thoughts, suggestions,
ideas. Like Moses, keep me soft and pliable,
so that when your spirit calls I respond
quickly and obediently.
VMP

Evaluate Your Change Ability

I am sending you to Pharaoh to bring
my people the Israelites out of Egypt.
Exodus 3:10

Take an honest look at how you feel about change and transition. Ask yourself if you are so loyal to the past that you are preventing growth and joy for the future. Remember that when God calls us to do a task it often interrupts our normal routine. This was true of Moses when God spoke to him and called Moses to leave behind his comfortable life as a rancher. If Moses was an inflexible person he would have missed God's calling. The same is true for us. Here are some characteristics of people who are overly rigid and fearful of change:

• Taking the safe way

• Reacting, instead of taking risks

• Avoiding decisions

• Daydreaming and talking, rather than acting

If, after evaluating your change ability, you discover that your style is to resist or avoid change, then begin consciously cultivating flexibility. This means making a mental decision to become more comfortable with change. Here is an "ABC" approach for cultivating flexibility and making changes more comfortably:

• Accept the fact that change is inevitable and impossible to avoid.

• Believe that new opportunities for your growth exist within the change.

• Be confident that you will adapt and adjust, becoming healthier and happier as a result of the change.

⊱ *Thought for the Day* ⊰
Your mind can be your best friend and a tremendous asset.
If your mind is working for you, it can produce a happy, creative,
worthwhile existence or it can also be your most vicious enemy,
destroying your creativity, making you unhappy and depressed.
So to handle your life successfully, you must bring your mind
under control and train it to be obedient to your will.
Norman Vincent Peale

God Knows Our Needs

But God remembered Noah.
Genesis 8:1

Last year on St. Valentine's Day, Alex, a recently widowed man, attended 9 a.m. Mass at his parish church. There were the usual number of faithful in attendance, along with the fourth-, fifth-, and sixth-grade pupils from the parochial school.

As the service concluded, and just before the final prayers, the pastor asked all adult parishioners to remain a few moments after Mass.

"It was a very sad Valentine's Day for me, having lost my wife a few months earlier," Alex recalled. "For the first time in many years, I did not buy chocolates and a valentine card." Nor did he expect to receive a card from anyone that year.

His sadness turned to gladness when the children from school approached the adults, many of whom were elderly, and handed each one a handmade valentine. "My surprise quickly turned to joy. It was a beautiful gesture by the school and the children, which reminded me that God knows our needs."

Today's biblical text is from Genesis and concerns Noah and the catastrophic flood that took place. The text is a very simply theological statement: "God remembered Noah."

That verse should encourage all of us because it says that in spite of great disaster and personal crisis God is never the God of the end of things. Our God is positive. Our God is the God of fresh mercies and new beginnings. Our God knows our needs and can provide for them.

❧ *Affirmation for the Day* ❧
I keep faith with the God who is always faithful to me.
The strength of God holds me above the floods of life.
I know that God remembers me.
VMP

Behaving Differently

Rid yourself of all offenses you have committed,
and get a new heart and a new spirit.
Ezekiel 18:31

From time to time, all of us identify patterns of behavior in ourselves that we want to change. Yet it is not easy to change these old patterns. They have become very much a part of us. Here are seven helpful ways to push forward the process of behaving differently:

1. *Develop a rationale.* Establish intellectually what you want to change and why you want to change. Develop arguments why the change will be better for you.

2. *Create a mental image of success.* See yourself as already different and having completed the change. What the mind perceives, the will achieves.

3. *Make a public commitment.* When you tell other people that you are going to change your behavior, you will probably work harder just to keep from embarrassing yourself.

4. *Seek guidance.* Get expert advice. Consult a psychologist, a spiritual leader, or a sensitive friend skilled in the issue you are seeking to change and resolve. These guides will help you build bridges to new ways of thinking and living.

5. *Join a support group.* If possible, join a group of people who are trying to make the same change. There you will gain insight, confidence, and strength from others moving toward the same goal.

6. *Pray over the issue.* Pour your feelings into prayer. Explain to God what you want to do and ask for God's guidance and strength.

7. *Trust God to help you.* Day by day live in the truth that God is guiding and strengthening you to make the necessary changes.

❧ *Prayer for the Day* ❧
Gracious and loving God,
I freely admit my errors, my shortcomings,
my patterns of life which I want to change.
I want to begin behaving differently and ask you
to guide, strengthen, and support me
moment by moment and day by day.
VMP

There Is Life After Loss

How blessed you will be,
sowing your seed by every stream.
Isaiah 32:20

Losses and tragedies of all sorts come to every person. Yet those losses and tragedies should not make life less worth living. Consider the inspiring example of widower Jesse McElveen.

As a youth growing up on a farm in southern Georgia, he was determined to attend college in spite of poverty. He attended the University of Georgia and later the Atlanta College of Pharmacy. Upon graduation he worked with an Atlanta pharmacy for forty-seven years.

Viewing his retirement as a golden opportunity to help others, Mr. McElveen donates his time as a volunteer at a large medical center. In 1992, he was honored for a record of 1,086 hours of volunteer work at the medical center.

Today, at ninety-two, he continues to volunteer four days a week in the mailroom and the personnel department. There he has learned to use the computer and helps with patient discharge records. In addition, he helps serve food and wash dishes at a needy men's club that meets in a downtown Atlanta church.

Mr. McElveen's philosophy is simple: "My mate Louise is gone. My daughter has her own life. As long as God gives me the strength of mind and body, I'll try to keep on keeping on."

His life is a wonderful testimonial that there is life after loss. In spite of trauma and tragedy, each of us can continue to grow, develop, learn, and help others. God's blessings flow on us when we sow our seeds.

❧ *Thought for the Day* ❧
You cannot make yourself feel something
you do not feel,
but you can make yourself do right
in spite of your feelings.
Pearl Buck

Acknowledging Your Strength and Endurance

Act with courage.
2 Chronicles 19:11

Dr. Julius Segal, a psychologist and author, was a member of the special health team assigned to the fifty-two American men and women held hostage in Iran from late 1979 to January 1981.

In addition, Dr. Segal has spent more than three decades studying victims of overwhelming trauma, including concentration camps survivors, POWs liberated from years of captivity, terrorized hostages, and bewildered refugees.

His study leads him to conclude that there is a remarkable human capacity for endurance and strength under "crushing stress." Dr. Segal affirms "the magnificent ability of human beings to rebuild shattered lives, careers, families, even as they wrestle with the bitterest of memories. Buried in the human breast are undreamed-of powers of healing—and even growth—in the face of stress. We are rarely as fragile as we imagine ourselves to be."

In fact, Dr. Segal quotes former Iranian hostage Bruce Laingen: "We're like tea bags. We don't know our strength until we get into hot water."

Those thoughts ought to inspire each of us, especially when we face difficult, harsh times. Let us remember that God has created us with inherent strengths, natural wisdom, and powerful coping abilities. And when we feel deficient, God provides additional energy for living. So let us face problems with courage, dignity, and great hope. Today's Bible passage reminds us that we have good reason to "act with courage."

❧ Affirmation for the Day ❧
I open my eyes to see my God-given strengths.
I exercise my will to use my God-given strengths.
I make the choice to overcome and triumph.
VMP

Hope for the Imperfect

Let us hold unswervingly to the hope we profess,
for he who promised is faithful.

Hebrews 10:23

A professor stood before his class one morning deeply upset. Earlier in the day, he neglected to look in his sideview mirror before pulling into traffic. In a matter of seconds, his beautiful new sports car had been mangled.

The man had not even made his first payment; but now his small convertible, something he had desired for years, was completely smashed on one side. Sharing his experience with the class, he posed the question, "Why do you think this accident has affected me so deeply?"

Several suggestions were made: the cost of the repair; the time he would spend waiting for his car to be fixed; the embarrassment of the accident.

However, the answer that seemed to best explain his sorrow came from a young woman who suggested, "I think it is because your sense of loss and your recognition that, no matter how good the repair workers do their job, you car will never completely be the way it was before."

Later that day when he was alone, the professor cried as he thought about that comment. He knew what his student said was true. He was grieving because what once had been perfect was now marred. His special vehicle would never be the same again.

That incident parallels our lives. As we move through life, we have high expectations: We will be successful in careers; have strong, satisfying marriages; raise good, responsible children; enjoy deep, abiding friendships. Instead, though, our careers may falter, marriage can be disappointing, children frustrating, and friends unable to live up to our expectations. The dream of living the good life can easily slip away.

When life's hurts emerge, let us remember we have a God who can take our losses, our failures, our disappointments, our imperfections, our sins, and can give us a new beginning.

There is hope for the imperfect because God does not give up on us. God did not give up on Adam and Eve, and God will not give up on you and me.

❧ Thought for the Day ❧

It is right that our hearts should be on God,
when the heart of God is so much on us.

Richard Baxter

Turning Relapse Into Renewal

"I will cure you of backsliding."

Jeremiah 3:22

Lapses and relapses happen to all people. The biblical term for a relapse is "backsliding." Despite our best efforts to change, we can slip into old patterns and fail to achieve goals, such as taking on an exercise program, losing weight, stopping smoking or drinking. Sometimes the relapse can make us feel ashamed and guilty, so we resolve to try again. Several such setbacks can make us feel that our lives are moving in circles, rather than achieving goals and moving forward.

The good news is that the circles can spiral upward. Here are some ways to turn relapse into renewal and thereby assure us that we are ascending the spiral staircase of change:

- *Be aware you are not the first person to slip.* Research reveals that only about 20 percent of the population conquers long-standing problems on the first try. That means you should not be too hard on yourself.
- *Think less about the past and more about the future.* Self-blame is not a good motivator. Rather than focus on past failure, remind yourself that you can move ahead to a second, third, and fourth chance.
- *Learn from a relapse.* Experience is an effective teacher. Look at your situation and learn the lessons. For example, if your goal was to lose weight, perhaps you did not allow enough time. Most weight-control programs recognize that it takes from ten to twelve weeks for a diet to begin working. Or perhaps you did not take advantage of other resources, such as group support, exercise, rewards, etc.
- *Regroup and renew.* Never give up. Think of a relapse as an opportunity to redouble your efforts. Surround yourself with people who will be support and not those who will distract and dissuade you from your goals. Remember that the most common way of change is taking two steps forward and one step back.
- *Seek God's strengthening.* We are not soloists in life. We are created by God whose love and concern for us extends all of our years. When seeking to change, ask God for daily strength and support.

Affirmation for the Day

I carefully establish priorities for my life.
I carefully move forward toward my goals.
I trust God to strengthen and guide me, day by day.

VMP

The Mother Teresa Effect

The Lord's servant must be kind to everyone.
2 Timothy 2:24

David McClelland, Ph.D., of Harvard Medical School, has demonstrated the power of love to make the body healthier through what he calls the "Mother Teresa Effect." He showed a group of Harvard students a documentary of Mother Teresa ministering lovingly to the sick, the dying, the "poorest of the poor" in Calcutta, India.

Next, Dr. McClelland measured the levels of immunoglobulin A (IgA) in their saliva before and after seeing the film. (IgA is an antibody active against viral infections, such as colds.) IgA levels rose significantly in the students, even in many of those who considered Mother Teresa as "too religious" or even insincere. The conclusion is obvious: "Tender loving care" is a valuable element in healing.

Dr. McClelland was also able to achieve similar effects in another way. He asked his graduate students simply to think about two things: past moments when they felt deeply loved and cared for by someone else, and a time when they loved another person. That information should nudge us to respond in two ways.

First, we should look back over our lives and mentally identify all those who deeply loved and cared for us. Then we ought to praise God for sending such fine, caring people into our lives. Because of their love we are stronger, emotionally *and* physically.

Second, the information about the "Mother Teresa Effect" should heighten our desire to touch others with our love and caring. We must remember that in the giving of love not only does the recipient benefit but so do we.

God is so good!

✎ *Thought for the Day* ✎
Love cures people—
both the ones who give it
and the ones who receive it.
Karl Menninger

February 21

Examining Our Ethics

Let the wicked forsake his way and the
evil man his thoughts.

Isaiah 55:7

A survey of one thousand adults in *Money* magazine reveals that young people are more dishonest than older people, men more dishonest than women, and the rich more dishonest than the poor. And worse, the survey shows that our country's ethical standards are falling. Here are some facts uncovered by the survey:

- 24 percent of people today would not correct a waiter who undercharged them, versus 15 percent in a 1987 poll.
- 9 percent of people would keep the $1,000 found in a wallet, versus 4 percent in 1987. Those aged eighteen to thirty-four are ten times more likely to keep the money than those sixty-five and older.
- 23 percent would steal $10 million if they knew they wouldn't get caught—more men (31 percent) than women (16 percent).
- One-third would cheat on taxes, especially the wealthy; 45 percent of those earning $50,000 or more a year would not report $2,000 in cash income on returns—versus 24 percent of those earning $15,000 or less.

A poll like that should stir our conscience. Combining that survey with today's scripture to forsake wicked ways and evil thoughts, let us conduct this examination of conscience about our personal ethics:

- *How would I respond to a waiter or store clerk who undercharged me?*
- *What would I do if I found a wallet containing $1,000?*
- *Would I steal money if I knew there was no chance of being caught?*
- *Am I honest in my tax declarations?*

Let us remember that as the people of God we are called to live lives of personal integrity and social responsibility.

◆ Thought for the Day ◆
A person of honor would prefer to lose his honor
rather than lose his conscience.
Michel Eyquem De Montaigne

The Art of Negotiation

He who humbles himself will be exalted.
Luke 18:24

A magazine described the first date of a young man and young woman. They were both students at Yale University in the 1970s. Their first date took place while they stood in line to register for classes. When they were finished filling in various forms, he invited her out for a Coke.

She agreed, and the two walked and talked for a long time. Finally, they ended up in front of the Yale University Art Gallery. It was closed, but the young man had been there earlier in the week. He wanted to show his date the exhibition inside, as well as a Henry Moore sculpture.

Looking around, the man found a worker who confirmed the gallery was closed because of a labor dispute. Thinking quickly and creatively, the young man made this offer: "If we pick up the garbage, will you let us in?"

Bill Clinton and his date, Hillary Rodham, picked up a pile of accumulated trash and then had a leisurely private viewing of the Yale University Art Gallery.

The ability to negotiate is an important life skill that can be utilized for personal and professional purposes. People who know how to negotiate are optimists and people of faith. They do not give up easily, hang back, or fear defeat. Rather than think something is "impossible," those who understand the power of negotiation reach for what may be possible in a situation. The next time you find yourself in an awkward, difficult, or even painful situation try to see what can be negotiated for everyone's satisfaction.

⊸ *Thought for the Day* ⊱
Let us never negotiate out of fear.
But let us never fear to negotiate.
John F. Kennedy

God Hears Ineloquent Prayers, Too!

Fear not...When you pass through the
waters, I will be with you.

Isaiah 43:1,2

Dr. James Dobson, a psychologist, author, and founder of Focus on the Family, received a letter in which the writer asked, "I've often heard that God will not abandon us when we go through fiery trials. What can we expect from him in the stressful moments?"

Rather than respond academically and theologically, Dr. Dobson shared a personal experience of God's wonderful care for him during a crisis. On August 15, 1990, Dr. Dobson was playing an early morning round of basketball. At fifty-four he believed he was in excellent physical condition and had recently undergone a medical examination that verified his perception. "I could play basketball all day with men twenty-five years my junior," he says.

Suddenly, stricken by moderate pain in the center of his chest, he excused himself, telling friends he did not feel well. Quickly he drove to a nearby emergency room, knowing that he had experienced a heart attack. When the medical report came back, it confirmed he had suffered some damage to the heart muscle. "I knew I was in serious trouble," he recalls.

He was taken back to his hospital room and left alone—overtaken by anxiety. "That's when I uttered a brief and ineloquent prayer from the depths of my soul," he says. Dr. Dobson simply prayed, "Lord, you know where I am right now. And you know that I am upset and very lonely. Would you send someone who can help me?"

A short time later, a good friend and pastor of a nearby church unexpectedly walked through the door. They greeted each other warmly and then Dr. Dobson asked, "Your church is on the other side of town. Why did you take the time to come see me today?" Dr. Dobson did not tell the minister about his prayer. The pastor replied simply: "I came because the Lord told me you were lonely."

This story is a powerful demonstration of God's constant care over us. We are not forgotten by God. Of course, God does not always resolve our difficulties so quickly. There are times when we walk through the dark valley; but even then, we do not travel alone. God is with us.

⫷ *Prayer for the Day* ⫸

Loving God,
I thank you that you know me, understand me,
watch over me, and love me unconditionally.

VMP

Why Is It Hard to Pray?

Look to the Lord and his strength;
seek his face always.
1 Chronicles 16:11

One man, confiding in his pastor, declared, "Praying comes hard for me. I believe in it, but it's hard work. Prayer has seldom been easy. Why?"

His honest dilemma is one shared by many people. Today let us briefly examine reasons why it may be hard to pray.

1. *Self-reliance.* Perhaps we would rather *do* something than pray. While taking action to correct a problem is good, there may be wisdom in delaying our response in order to pray over the matter first. God's guidance and direction may prove to be better and more efficient.

2. *My life is free from crisis.* When there is no pressing trauma, prayer does seem to be a less urgent force. Yet freedom from crisis should prompt a prayer of deep gratitude from us.

3. *I don't really know anyone who needs my prayers.* Because my family and friends are doing well, I don't pray much for them. However, if we open our spiritual eyes we will quickly see all sorts of people in all kinds of dilemmas who need our prayers of intercession on their behalf.

4. *I just don't have the time.* No one has enough time to do everything they want. The issue is one of priorities. What about rising a mere ten minutes earlier? or staying up ten minutes later? or offering prayers for ten minutes during the lunch hour? or using commuting time for prayers? The truth is, if we try hard enough we can usually find time for prayer.

5. *What's the point of prayer?* God knows what is best and will work his will without my advice and my pleading. So what's the point of praying? That view is a serious misunderstanding of prayer. The purpose of prayer is for us to be in a relationship with God. Just as human relationships are formed and deepened by talking and sharing thoughts, so is our relationship to God formed and deepened by talking and sharing our concerns, anxieties, joys, and hopes. Besides that, God himself invites us to pray.

⚬ Thought for the Day ⚬
Prayer is weakness leaning on omnipotence.
W. S. Bowden

The Prayer of Desperation

They turned to attack him, but Jehoshaphat cried out,
and the Lord helped him. God drew them away from him.

2 Chronicles 18:31

Everett Alvarez, Jr., has the distinction of being the second-longest-held American prisoner of war. He spent eight-and-one-half years in North Vietnam's prisons. The former navy pilot says his active war consisted of only two missions. The Navy Skyhawk he flew was shot down during the second one, on August 5, 1964. "My longer, real war was an inner one, against pain and fear in the face of torture, against hopelessness and loneliness during months of solitary confinement," Alvarez says. He won that war, returned to the United States, and put his life back together, serving as deputy director of the Peace Corps, deputy administrator of the Veterans Administration, and later founding a successful business.

During the first days of his confinement, Alvarez created a worship space for himself. He found a rusty nail, and on the wall in the courtyard behind his cell he scratched and nicked at it until he carved the outline of a cross, a foot high and eight inches wide. Beneath the cross he also scratched his name and the date he was shot down. From then on he held daily services before his makeshift cross.

Because he had been an altar boy at the Church of St. Mary of the Nativity in Salinas, California, he was able to recall from memory the rituals. So, in North Vietnam he became again an altar boy performing each ritual of the Mass. He held up an imaginary hand bell and remembered the priest's words: *Sanctus, Sanctus, Sanctus*. Alvarez recited the Lord's Prayer, the Hail Mary, and the Apostles' Creed. "Prayer helped sustain me through those long days and nights and through the brutal interrogations in the room next door," he says.

Fortunately, very few of us will be forced to experience such a severe test of life and faith. Yet Alvarez's words are a powerful reminder about the sustaining power of prayer. Prayer does link us to a power greater than ourselves and greater than any circumstances that threaten us. Let us continue to pray, to pour out our concerns—large and small—to the God who loves and cares for us.

ᘓ *Thought for the Day* ᘓ

The main lesson about prayer is just this: Do it! Do it! Do it!
You want to be taught to pray. My answer is: Pray and never
faint and then you shall never fail....
A sense of real want is at the very root of prayer.

John Laidlaw

God's Answers to Prayers We Haven't Offered

Before they call I will answer.
Isaiah 65:24

Yesterday we considered the plight of POW Everett Alvarez, Jr. There is more to his story. Recently a film producer invited him to return to Hanoi with a small group of former POWs to make a documentary. Alvarez agreed, but his friends were worried. "You'll need a psychiatrist along to give you support," said one. "You have pent up rage in you," declared another. "Don't deny it."

Although Alvarez did not feel he would have a problem returning to North Vietnam, his friends' comments created some worry for him. Perhaps the trip would be harmful by reopening old wounds. After further thought, Alvarez made the trip. Actually, he was eager to visit his old cell and view the courtyard wall where he had created his worship space.

Back in his cell, he looked up through the bars above the door at the sliver of sky beyond and tried to explain to the people with him how, month after month, he lifted his eyes to that same piece of sky and prayed through another day. Alvarez had to blink back tears and swallow hard. There *was* something buried inside of him. But it was not regret or remorse or hate.

"It was gratitude that God had answered not only those prayers so long ago but others that I had not thought to ask," Alvarez recalls. "He had delivered me back to freedom and my family, and he had allowed me to leave behind all the anger, resentment, and fear. God had allowed me to forgive and forget."

Let us consider the truth that God is wise enough to answer prayers we may not have thought to offer. People who are able to leave behind such negative emotions as anger, resentment, fear, hostility, desire for revenge, are emotionally and spiritually healthy. It is a gift from God that we are not burdened with carrying such excess emotional baggage.

⚜ Thought for the Day ⚜
More things are wrought by prayer
Than this world dreams of.
Alfred Lord Tennyson

Things You Will Never Regret

For I know my transgressions,
and my sin is always before me.
Psalm 51:3

All of us can identify with the psalmist's lament, "I know my transgressions." All of us have regrets over words spoken and actions taken. Although we do know our faults and failures, today let us consider ten things that we will never regret:

1. Showing respect to the elderly.
2. Acting kindly toward a stranger in need of help.
3. Destroying a letter written in anger.
4. Offering an apology and restoring a relationship.
5. Extending forgiveness to an "enemy," someone who has hurt you.
6. Listening to a hurting person.
7. Refraining from gossip.
8. Living according to your conviction.
9. Maintaining personal ethics and integrity when everyone else is "doing it."
10. Treating all those around you with dignity, diplomacy, and kindness.

⤳ *Thought for the Day* ⤳
The idea that you do unto others as you would
have them do unto you, that will make a better world.
I've seen that. I've been the receiver of it. And I was
always taught that if you had a piece of bread and
somebody was sitting there who didn't, then you
made your one piece of bread two.
Whoopi Goldberg

Our Example Teaches Others

Then you will lift up your face without shame.
Job 11:15

When the people around us—family, friends, neighbors, colleagues—see us in our daily tasks, what do they learn from us? Does our living inspire or injure? heal or hurt? Does our living teach people to live larger and more noble lives?

We should always remember that what we say, how we act, what we do and not do, makes an impact upon those around us. Our example teaches others.

Consider a man who responded to this question posed by a newspaper columnist: "If there is a simple way to instill in children the qualities that will keep them happy and help them contribute to the world while doing no harm to others, what is it?" The man's answer to that question was "by imitating my father. He taught me by example."

The man went on to say his father grew up in the Depression. His education ended before the eighth grade because he went to work to help support the family. Even though his father was very poor, he turned in a five-dollar bill he found on the floor when he was visiting his grandmother in a nursing home.

"My father had a strong faith in God. If he could help someone in need, he did. He was always considerate of his parents and treated my mother with respect." The admiring son also said his father taught him honesty, courage, faith, responsibility, courtesy, and kindness—all through his personal example. There were no formal lectures on those virtues. "I thank God every day for giving me such a fine role model. I have four children, and hope I can instill the virtues in them that my father taught me." Clearly, this was a man whose life could be described by the words of today's text: "Then you will lift up your face without shame."

Let us ask ourselves:

- *What are people learning from my example?*
- *Would anyone thank God for me as a role model?*

⤚ *Thought for the Day* ⤙
The entire ocean is affected by a pebble.
Blaise Pascal

A Spiritual Lesson From a Sparrow

My soul thirsts for...the living God.
Psalm 42:2

One hot summer afternoon a man noticed a sparrow trying to quench his thirst at a dripping faucet by the house. The little bird would wait for a drop of water to drip, take a sip, and then fly away. Again and again he would come back for a sip of the cool water.

To help the small creature the man placed a container of water on the ground near the faucet and watched to see what would happen. Soon the sparrow returned to drink from the faucet, but when he spied the container of water, he drank to his fill and flew away. Before long other sparrows came to drink from the container. "I like to think that the first sparrow told his friends about the source of water," says the man.

We all have something in common with the sparrow. Created in the image of God, we must turn and return many times to God for living water to sustain the spiritual life. Often the circumstances of daily living create pressures upon us and soon our spirits thirst. Then we turn to God for a refreshing of the soul. It is always good to feel God's care, comfort, strength, and support.

And, like the sparrow, we should be encouraged to tell others about God's love and warmth.

⚘ *Thought for the Day* ⚘
Our task is to live our personal communion with Christ
with such intensity as to make it contagious.
Paul Tournier

There Is Life After Loss

So do not fear, for I am with you;
do not be dismayed, for I am your God.
I will strengthen you and help you.

Isaiah 41:10

Be encouraged! There *is* life after loss, crisis, and tragedy.

Here is one shining example of that reality:

Mary Finnegan, a retired high-school French and Latin teacher, found herself widowed at sixty-seven years of age. After a couple of lonely years, she decided to go back to school. At seventy-two, she earned her master's degree in classics.

Energized by academics, Mary Finnegan continued to pursue doctoral studies. After writing a dissertation, defending it, and passing comprehensive examinations, she was awarded a Ph.D. (Doctor of Philosophy).

And by 1992, at age eighty-four, she was in residence at Dartmouth College as a visiting scholar in classics.

"She is a brilliant teacher," says the department chair.

Here are some lessons from Mary Finnegan's life:

- Grief does not permanently dampen the eagerness for new experiences.
- Grief does not permanently empty life of meaning and joy.
- Grief last for a "season" and then life opens up fresh possibilities.

No matter what our loss—due to death, separation, divorce, disability—God has instructed us not to fear because God will heal, strengthen, and help us through.

❧ *Thought for the Day* ❧
Where there is an open mind,
there will always be a frontier.
Charles F. Kettering

God Needs Well Diggers

He would give you...wells you did not dig.
Deuteronomy 6:11 (*Jerusalem Bible* translation)

In today's biblical passage, God promised the nomadic Israelites they would come to wells they had not dug. What a refreshment it must have been for the weary desert travelers to come upon supplies of water that their own efforts had not created!

We, too, are challenged to become "well diggers": women and men who dig wells for others, so that they will be refreshed, nurtured, comforted, and helped during difficult times.

Consider the example of Anne. As a young woman she married a student in medical school. The intensity of his program meant he studied day and night and was on call every third night for many months. It was difficult for the couple to find much time together to nourish their marriage. Yet their relationship weathered the pressures. One reason for that was due to a "well digger," Anne says.

"During those busy and hard years, a dear, praying woman in our church would occasionally come to me or my husband to quietly say, 'I'm praying for you,'" Anne recalls. "Here was the secret of our strength," she says. "She and others were digging wells for us. Those were days when we probably would have neglected to dig our own if others had not interceded for us."

So be a "well digger." Be the one who intercedes for others and prays regularly for those who may be too tired, burdened, preoccupied, to pray for themselves. A quick glance at people who come into my sphere of influence leads me to pray for

- A divorced mother struggling to work and raise two smallboys

- A woman married to a physically abusive husband

- A retired man whose beloved wife of forty years died recently

- An unemployed father who is extremely anxious about his circumstances

- A teenage girl exercising her independence in unhealthy, destructive ways

- A mother and father whose twelve-year-old was killed while riding his bicycle

⋰ *Thought for the Day* ⋱
A Christian fellowship lives and exists by the intercession
of its members for one another, or it collapses.
Dietrich Bonhoeffer

Combining a Vacation With a Pilgrimage

Send forth your light and your truth, let them guide me;
let them bring me to your holy mountain.

Psalm 43:3

When planning a vacation consider combining it with a pilgrimage, so that the time away from daily work is both emotionally and spiritually renewing. The ancients often made a pilgrimage to a "holy" mountain or a "holy" city. Recently, one family managed to squeeze the following vacation/pilgrimage out of a fourteen-hour day-trip from their home:

- The first stop was a visit to the Norman Rockwell Museum in Stockbridge, Massachusetts, approximately 160 miles from their house.
- Next was a visit to the nearby Marian Helpers Center in Stockbridge.
- Third, they drove south into Connecticut where they visited the Lourdes of Litchfield. It was built forty years ago by Monfort Missionaries and is modeled after the grotto where the Blessed Virgin Mary appeared in 1858 to the French peasant girl Bernadette Soubirous.
- At the end of the day and just in time for vespers, the family visited Regina Laudis, a Benedictine abbey, which has a spectacular eighteenth-century Neapolitan crèche, an art shop, and a chapel where the entire family heard nuns sing Gregorian chant.

Of course, it is not necessary to squeeze that much into a fourteen-hour trip, but it is certainly more memorable and formative than simply wandering from amusement parks to museums to resorts to gift shops. Some other ways to combine a vacation with a pilgrimage:

- Consider a special trip to the Holy Land or Rome.
- Visit local shrines, churches, and other holy sites close to home.
- Make a family heritage pilgrimage to ancestral homes and churches where relatives were baptized, married, and buried.
- Plan a pilgrimage to personal spiritual sites where you were baptized, where you received your first communion, where you were married.

⤙ Thought for the Day ⤚
Pilgrims and tourists aren't the same. Tourists focus on enjoying the sights, sounds, and bargains of far-off places. A pilgrim is on a journey to rekindle the fire of faith.

John J. Boucher

Do Not Underestimate Your Strength

But as for me, I am filled with power,
with the Spirit of the Lord.

Micah 3:8

You are stronger and more resilient than you think!

In October 1996, Chicago police officer Jim Mullen was shot in the face during a scuffle. The bullet ripped into his spine, permanently paralyzing him from the neck down. As a quadriplegic on medical disability, Mullen was entitled to his $42,000 salary for one year, followed by ten years at a 25 percent reduction, and half salary after that.

Instead, Mullen took stock of what he had left and felt he could still offer the Chicago Police Department a service. As a result, he asked to remain on the job and to keep his uniform. Today Mullen is outreach coordinator for the department's community policing program, a position that pays $60,000 per year and combines desk work with speaking engagements at schools, churches, and community centers.

So even though you may struggle with a life crisis, remember God has given you the inner strength to face it with dignity, courage, strength, and creativity.

Repeat to yourself the words of the prophet Micah: *But as for me, I am filled with power, with the spirit of the Lord.*

You will triumph!

⋘ *Prayer for the Day* ⋙

Creative and loving God,
Thank you for filling me with
determination and desire to overcome.
Thank you for filling me with power
and with your spirit.
I can cope and I can overcome.

VMP

Neutralizing Despair

So I hated life.
Ecclesiastes 2:17

The stresses and strains of life can conspire to rob us of hope and leave us feeling discouraged and despairing. "So I hated life," declares the writer of Ecclesiastes. One way to neutralize despair is by intentionally cultivating hope: by recalling that others have experienced hard times and yet gone on with the task of living productive, creative, fulfilling lives.

Consider these courageous women and men:

Barbara Jordan, a Texas congresswoman, who served the public well despite being in a wheelchair because of a neuromuscular disease.

Bobbi Clarke, a fifteen-season veteran of the Philadelphia Flyers hockey team, who at the age of thirteen was diagnosed with diabetes. Nevertheless, he pursued his dream of being a professional hockey player. In his entire career Clarke never missed a game because of diabetes-related problems.

Elizabeth Browning, bedridden with a back injury, wrote enduring romantic poetry from her sickroom.

Marcel Proust, who wrote his brilliant works under the stress of a disabling respiratory disease.

Franklin D. Roosevelt, who led the nation and vigorously pursued wartime victory while confined to a wheelchair following the paralysis of polio.

Florence Nightingale, whose disabling lung disease didn't stop her from giving advice to the military authorities on how to set up wartime medical services.

Robert Louis Stevenson, who continued to give us the pleasure of his adventure novels written from the confines of his sickbed where he suffered from tuberculosis.

Martha Graham, who, in spite of severe arthritis, brought soaring joy to millions with her innovative dance choreography.

Ludwig Beethoven, who continued to write music as his hearing faded and ultimately deserted him.

❦ Thought for the Day ❦
In the kingdom of hope there is no winter.
Russian proverb

Living Wisely

Where is the wise man?
1 Corinthians 1:20

Each new day is a glorious gift from God. Upon awakening we should rejoice in that fact, plan to live wisely and start the new day with confidence. Here are some thoughts to help us live wisely each day:

1. I refuse to be shackled by yesterday's failures.

2. I will not be intimidated by people or issues, but will view those as my growth opportunities.

3. I choose not to allow others to define my mood, method, message, or mission.

4. I will not tolerate self-pity, no matter what happens.

5. I will abstain from gossip and negative talk or thinking.

6. I will live not only for myself and my family, but will work to make at least one person happier because of me.

7. I will treat each person I encounter with dignity and courtesy.

8. I will be kind.

9. I will help whoever is in need of assistance.

10. I will remember my mission in life is to serve God and do his will.

⫷ *Prayer for the Day* ⫸
Eternal and loving God,
I have but one life to live;
help me to live wisely
and to make a difference.
With each new day, empower me
to serve you with purity of heart
and with the courage of my convictions.
VMP

Making Healthy Choices

Go and enjoy choice food and sweet drinks...
Nehemiah 8:10a

Some people are like Doctor Manette in the Charles Dickens novel *A Tale of Two Cities*.

The doctor had been in prison for twenty years prior to the French Revolution, which freed him. While in prison he learned the trade of being a cobbler. In the gloom of his small cell, Dr. Manette spent his days tapping shoes.

Finally, the day came when he was given liberty and let out into the brilliance of the sunlight. But the freedom intimidated and even terrorized him. He had spent too much time in the darkness of a cell and had grown comfortable with it. Sadly, a servant was given the duty of locking Dr. Manette each night in an attic room the size of his old cell. From there he could be seen, in the twilight, tapping out shoes.

Like Dr. Manette, some people have grown accustomed to living constricted and confined lives. Because the fear of freedom and liberty is so great, they allow themselves to be imprisoned and continue old patterns.

Yet our happiness, fulfillment, and joy in life is up to us. It all comes down to a choice: Remain bound by the past or break free to embrace the opportunities of the present and future.

Happiness, fulfillment, and joy are dependent upon our attitude toward what has happened. It is not dependent on what happen to us.

The truth is that problems, crises, trauma, and tragedies do not have to make us permanently unhappy.

The large reality in life is that happiness is a choice we make. Scripture challenges us to "enjoy choice food and sweet drinks."

Today, choose to move in the direction of happiness, fulfillment, and joy.

⊰ *Affirmation for the Day* ⊱
I choose to celebrate the life that God gives me.
I relax and let go of irritation, fear, anxiety, turmoil, and worry.
I let the sweet harmony of God fill me.
VMP

God Makes a Way When There Is No Way

Not a hair of your head will perish.
Luke 21:18

Although the near disaster took place many years ago, what transpired remains fresh in the memory of the pilot. Flying his Piper Cub light plane over the mountains of North Carolina, the sky was clear and blue and the air was clean and crisp. It was an ideal day for a leisurely flight. A few moments later, the pilot pushed the throttle of the Cub all the way forward and the plane nosed up into the sky.

Checking his navigation maps, all checkpoints revealed the pilot was on course. After several hours and fuel running low, the pilot decided to land the plane. As he neared the airport, he saw a sight that filled him with dread. Straight ahead was the boiling, swirling, black fury of a sudden summer storm. Beneath him were the mountains. Landing was impossible, and he did not have enough fuel to fly to another airport. His small Piper Cub was not equipped to fly and land through such a storm.

When pilots don't know what to do, they fly in a circle. So he circled while desperately trying to develop a plan of action. Soon, a larger plane with better navigational equipment flew by and signaled for the pilot to follow him. The pilot of the Piper Cub pulled up close behind him, and they plunged into the storm together.

However, the rain came down in torrents, and black clouds completely enclosed the small plane. Within seconds he could no longer see the larger plane. His small craft was tossed about like a canoe on an angry sea. He had no way of knowing if the Piper Cub was flying upside down, on its side, or right side up. He couldn't see the ground or the sky—only a swirling blackness. His instruments were spinning and provided no guidance. With only a few minutes of fuel left, he was completely helpless. In that moment of deep desperation, the pilot called on God to help him.

Suddenly, there was a break in the clouds. Through the hole in the sky, he could see the ground. With a tremendous shout of joy, he dived the little Cub through the small hole. Directly below he could see the airport. Because he came in from the wrong side, he overshot the runway, ignored a wave-off, but landed anyway. The tiny plane rolled off the end of the runway and narrowly missed some trees. Later he heard the airport manager say that the small break in the clouds lasted only a few moments. It was the only break in the ceiling all afternoon.

⚜ *Thought for the Day* ⚜

God is above, presiding; beneath, sustaining; within, filling.
Hildebert of Lavardin

Bright Ideas for Easter

The Spirit of the Sovereign Lord is one me.
Isaiah 61:1

The text cited today was quoted by Jesus (Luke 4:18) to announce and define his mission. Easter is the Christian season when we are challenged to deepen our spiritual lives. Here are seven ways to make Easter more meaningful:

1. *Research the Jewish roots of the Christian celebration.* Visit a library and select some books on Easter. Find out about Passover—how it is observed, how it relates to Easter.

2. *Reflect on the fourteen Stations of the Cross.* This practice is common for Catholic, Orthodox, and Episcopal Christians. Protestant Christians should make themselves familiar with this spiritual exercise as well.

3. *Begin a prayer journal.* Write out your personal prayers. Use the journal to track your spiritual journey to see God's faithfulness in answering prayers.

4. *Listen to Easter music.* Most of us have tapes and recordings of Christmas music. Purchase some interesting classical and contemporary music celebrating Easter.

5. *Conduct an examination of conscience.* Reflect on your strengths and weaknesses. Thank God for your gifts and consecrate them to God's use. Ask God's help in better managing and triumphing over shortcomings.

6. *Visit a cemetery.* Consider death. Praise God for resurrection.

7. *Participate in as many Easter services as possible.* In addition to main worship services on Easter Sunday morning, attend an Easter cantata, Maundy Thursday, Good Friday, Holy Saturday, and an Easter sunrise service. They will provide you with more opportunity to concentrate on the deep meaning of Jesus' ministry.

～ Thought for the Day ～
Tomb, thou shalt not hold him longer;
Death is strong, but life is stronger;
Stronger than the dark, the light;
Stronger than the wrong, the right;
Faith and hope triumphant say,
Christ will rise on Easter Day.
Phillips Brooks

Optimism Should Not Be a Choice

God saw all he had made, and it was very good.
Genesis 1:31

Today's text presents the theological fact that there is no such thing as a pessimistic creation. For us, it means that if we have to choose between positive expectations or gloom and doom, we must take positive expectations each and every time. As a rationale for that statement, consider this insight.

A pessimistic creation is almost impossible to imagine. No animal species comes into this world saying, "It's not going to work." "It's too hard to make it." "I can't do it." "We're all doomed." The newborn calf would never stand up. A bird would never build a nest. And why would an egg hatch?

When the Bible says, "God saw all he had made, and it was very good," it means that optimism is the foundation of life. Thus optimism is not merely a choice but a necessary and spiritual response to God's goodness. The optimistic view is the only way to fulfill God's destiny in us. Optimism drives creation. It is what brings every new birth enthusiastically bouncing out of their nests, burrows, and wombs.

Optimism means being into life for the long haul. It is what flowers the desert after a rainfall. It walks in the shoes of the unemployed. It energizes those who have an illness. The young are vitalized to take risks, while the elderly can peer expectantly over the rim of eternity.

Of course, optimism does not mean going through life never questioning anything, never doubting a course of action, never feeling regret or grief. At its best, optimism helps us transcend immediate plans, goals, and events. When there is an impasse, optimism reminds us there is the reality of a yet unseen solution. Where there is a failure, optimism is more interested in learning from it than assigning blame. Optimism helps us move through life's unfairness, injustice, contradictions, fears, and unhappiness, because it knows that underneath is the love of God which directs us to goodness.

No, optimism should not be a choice. It must be a way of life!

❦ *Affirmation for the Day* ❦
I am confident I will be led through despair.
I am confident that confusion will give way to clarity.
I am confident in my ability to challenge and transform problems.
VMP

God Will Meet Your Needs

You prepare a table before me in
the presence of my enemies.

Psalm 23:5

The meaning in today's verse is powerfully illustrated through the life of a woman named Darlene Rose. During World War II she served as a missionary in Asia. When the Japanese invaded the island country where she worked, Rose was imprisoned.

As a result of harsh treatment by her captors, Rose's weight dropped to a dangerous low of eighty pounds. Making matters worse was the malaria that invaded her system. She knew she was starving to death and was now very, very ill.

One day she watched the courtyard from her small cell. Prisoners were allowed to walk in the courtyard. As she observed the people, Rose noticed one woman sneak over to the fence partially covered by creeping vines. Someone was handing bananas to her. The women then hid them carefully under her sarong.

Extremely hungry and near the breaking point, Rose could actually smell those bananas. Desperately she fell to her knees and cried out to God, "Lord, I am not asking for many; I want just one banana." Then, Rose began to negate her desperate but sincere prayer. She began to rationalize and realized there was no way that God could get her a banana.

Amazingly, a short time later the Japanese camp commander from her former prison came to visit her. Rose had befriended the man and shared her faith with him. The official had not forgotten her and visited her while at the camp. After he left Rose, the guards returned to her cell. Opening the door they tossed inside a gift from the Japanese official—bananas. God sent Darlene Rose ninety-two bananas. *You prepare a table before me in the presence of my enemies*, declares the psalm writer.

When life becomes difficult and even a desperate struggle for survival, it is worth noting that God can come through in unexpected and unusual ways.

⤐ *Affirmation for the Day* ⤐
I am totally open to God's abundance.
I am completely receptive to God's prosperity.
I am divinely guided and protected.
VMP

An Example of Deep Commitment

Let us acknowledge the Lord; let us press on to acknowledge him.

Hosea 6:3

Duke University was honored with a visit by Bishop Emilio de Carvalho, the Methodist bishop of Angola. The godly man was asked, "What is it like to be the Church in a Marxist country?" Specifically, he was asked, "Is the new Marxist government supportive of the Church?"

"No," the bishop responded, "but we don't ask it to be supportive."

"Have there been tensions?" he was further asked.

"Yes," he responded. Recently the government decreed that the church must disband all women's organizations in the Church. "But the women kept meeting," Bishop de Carvalho explained. "The government is not yet strong enough to do much about it."

When asked what the Church would do when the government became stronger and more oppressive, the bishop said, "We shall keep meeting. The government does what it needs to do. The Church does what it needs to do."

Aware that continued practice of the Christian faith could lead to imprisonment, the bishop said simply: "Jail is a wonderful place for Christian evangelism. Our Church made some of its most dramatic gains during the revolution when so many of us were in jail." He went on to say that in jail, "you have everyone there, in one place. You have time to preach and teach. Sure, twenty of our Methodist pastors were killed during the revolution, but we came out of jail a much larger and stronger Church."

Sensing that his hearers were troubled and concerned for Christians in Angola, Bishop de Carvalho sought to reassure them by saying, "Don't worry about the Church in Angola; God is doing fine by us. Frankly, I would find it much more difficult to be a pastor in Evanston, Illinois. Here, there is so much. So many things. It must be hard to be the Church there."

Whenever we read or hear of Christians who remain faithful in spite of persecution, we should pause to engage in two actions. First, we should remember to pray for all believers who suffer at the hands of hostile governments. Second, we should ask ourselves if we could be faithful to God under such circumstances. Of course, it is impossible to know how we actually would respond; but it is a healthy discipline to examine the depth of our commitment. In times of trial and peril could we truly "acknowledge the Lord"?

❧ Thought for the Day ❧
Salvation is free, but discipleship costs everything we have.
Billy Graham

Be a Sideliner

Encourage the timid.
1 Thessalonians 5:14

The young woman stared intently. Concentration creased her forehead. Suddenly she thrust her body forward and leaped. On the sidelines was a woman who watched intensely and held her breath as the judges measured the jump length. Two feet! The woman on the sideline ran to hug her chubby, wide-eyed, delighted friend.

That was an event at the Special Olympics, the athletic competition for people with mental and physical challenges. Each athlete has one special person on the sidelines who showers him or her with praise and encouragement.

All of us need to have a "sideliner," someone who loves us no matter what happens. Knowing that there is one person who believes in us increases creativity and diminishes feelings of inadequacy.

Perhaps today you can accept the challenge to be a sideliner, that one person who believes in another and urges them on in life. Here is what sideliners are like:

- *Sideliners bring comfort.* They see hurts that others do not notice. They offer realistic, practical help without taking over your life. They are good listeners, extremely patient, and never talk down to you.

- *Sideliners don't criticize when you're down.* When you fail, others may pass harsh judgments and make critical comments, but sideliners hold back. They factor in your humanity and accept you as you are.

- *Sideliners believe the best about you.* Even if they have seen you at your worst, sideliners will give you a break. They know anyone can say and do rash things. However, they continue to believe the best about you.

- *Sideliners don't keep score.* They support and encourage you without expecting anything in return. They don't keep track of who paid for lunch the last time you ate together.

❧ Thought for the Day ❧

Apt words have power to assuage
The tumors of a troubled mind
And are as balm to fester'd wounds.

John Milton

A Prayer of Confession

Now make confession to the Lord,
the God of your fathers, and do his will.
Ezra 10:11

In scripture we are commanded to "make confession to the Lord." The practice of identifying our sins and shortcomings should be a regular spiritual discipline. Here is one prayer of confession that can be used:

Forgive us, O God, for each and every transgression we commit:
    for squandering money and abusing time;
    for speaking about love but acting indifferently;
    for avowing mercy and responding unkindly;
    for stressing equality but practicing discrimination;
    for keeping the law and distorting its spirit;
    for desiring peace but promoting strife;
    for raising questions and ignoring answers;
    for worshiping failures and forgetting forgiveness;
    for limiting alternatives and denying results;
    for making a promise and breaking our word;
    for advancing generosity but hoarding money;
    for elevating faith but living with despair.

From these devious sins we sincerely repent,
asking for your grace and strength not to repeat
the same errors over and over. Amen.

❧ *Thought for the Day* ❧
A fault confessed is a new virtue added to a man.
James S. Knowles

Exercising the Gift of Laughter

A cheerful heart is good medicine.
Proverbs 17:22

When William Howard Taft ran for reelection in 1912, he suffered the worst defeat of his political career. "I have one consolation," he commented. "No candidate was ever elected an ex-president by such a large majority!"

In today's scriptural verse the writer assumes the role of physician—"A cheerful heart is good medicine." Though the writer does not say how laughter makes us healthier, the assertion does have scientific verification. Many researchers believe that laughter may be a protection against disease and that without it we might be sick more often than we are.

Perhaps the biblical writer had in mind the emotional and spiritual benefits of laughter, which include:

- lifting feelings of depression
- generating more positive and hopeful thoughts
- maintaining emotional balance in the face of problems
- returning a sense of proportion when dealing with difficulty

God has created each of us with the ability to laugh because everyone, children and adults, experiences pressures, hurts, and disappointments. A little laughter can have a large impact on the spirit. Laughter can keep us sane and flood us briefly with healing happiness and make us more effective in solving a problem and rising to the challenge.

So today consider viewing events from the perspective of humor. If frustrating matters emerge this day, try to lighten the feelings through a humorous perspective.

～ *Thought for the Day* ～
The power of laughter
lies in its ability to lift the spirit.
Bob Hope

The Therapy of Serving

Bring water for the thirsty...
food for the fugitives.
Isaiah 21:14

Let the following story help us think about the truth that there is *therapy in serving* and *healing through helping*...

Oscar-winning screenwriter Robert Towne tells how his career and personal life crashed simultaneously in 1982.

Unable to find work in his field, he was also involved in a bitter custody battle with his ex-wife and became depressed by the death of a dog to which he had been "shamelessly attached."

"I walked out on a desolate beach filled with garbage from Santa Monica Bay and felt I had nothing left," Towne says.

There on the beach a man and his wife approached the screenwriter saying: "Excuse me, but we made a mistake. We came out here, but because of the bus strike our transfer tickets don't work and we can't get back downtown. Can you help us?"

Towne reached into his pocket and gave the couple all the money he had.

"I realized this was the best thing anybody could have done for me. I was feeling completely impotent, and here on this beach was the one guy I could do something for. It made me feel that I was not completely useless, that somehow things would be okay."

❧ *Thought for the Day* ❧
I often try to put depressed patients in contact
with someone they can help,
for there is something therapeutic
about doing another person a favor.
Dr. Alan Loy McGinnis

Remembering to Pray
for Those Who Abuse You

Do not gloat when your enemy falls;
when he stumbles, do not let your heart rejoice.
Proverbs 24:17

As Karen was stepping onto her driveway while retrieving the morning newspaper, a flash of red caught her eye. Curious, she walked to the edge of the driveway for a closer look. Her heart wrenched at the sight of her favorite geranium plant lying uprooted on the ground. Wilted and broken, its brilliant red petals bled profusely onto the sidewalk.

Oddly, Karen did not experience anger but sadness as she tried to envision what kind of person would take pleasure in willfully destroying an object of beauty. Assuming the offender was someone who passed by her home routinely, Karen wondered what message she would convey by her response to the inconsiderate act.

Should she replant the tangled mass, demonstrating the plant was valued by her? Or should she simply abandon it, as though the geranium didn't matter?

Unwilling to leave it lying there, she carefully returned the plant to its original spot. As she worked, the words of Jesus ran through her mind: "But I tell you: Love your enemies and pray for those who persecute you" (Matthew 5:44).

As she gently replanted the geranium, Karen found herself praying for the person who had committed this senseless act of destruction. She asked herself, *Was it possible this person's own roots had been damaged and were in need of being restored? Did this person need someone to heal the brokenness so that he or she could grow into a healthy human being?*

Karen prayed that God would speak directly to the individual and bring him or her healing and wholeness.

Several hours later she noticed, with pleasure, that the soft, heart-shaped leaves of the geranium plant had already begun reaching toward the sky. *I could only hope my prayer had done the same*, she thought to herself.

❧ Affirmation for the Day ❧

Today is a wonderful day because I choose to make it so.
I freely extend goodwill and peace to all I meet today.
God guides all my thoughts and actions today.
VMP

Cultivating the Best in Ourselves

I will build you up again and you will be rebuilt.
Jeremiah 31:4

Commit yourself to daily growth. Day by day consider ways to cultivate the best in yourself. Here are some simple suggestions for enriching your life:

1. *Pray and meditate.* Make time to heighten spiritual awareness. This can be done quietly in the privacy of your home or during a lunch-hour walk. Ask God for the desire and strength to do what is right.

2. *Be gentle with yourself.* Avoid the twin demons of self-pity and inappropriate shame or guilt.

3. *Concentrate on the present.* Learn from the past, but don't dwell on it. Do not allow yourself to become imprisoned by past events and actions.

4. *Focus on the future.* Remember that God can help you take charge of your life. No matter what has happened to us, God's intention is to "build you up again."

5. *Reflect on virtues.* Cultivate daily virtues such as compassion, honesty, respect. Read about people in whose lives such virtues were preeminent. Some good individuals to start with could include Albert Schweitzer and Mother Teresa of Calcutta.

6. *Act on virtues.* Seek ways, both simple and demanding, to spread kindness, compassion, honesty, and love.

7. *Solve problems.* Consider using your talent, insight, wisdom, and energy to solve problems, not to run from difficult situations.

8. *Learn from others.* Observe good people. Praise and imitate their virtues.

9. *Have fun.* Read a book for pure pleasure. Play a sport. Enjoy a hobby. Take a walk.

❧ *Affirmation for the Day* ❧
I am guided by a higher wisdom each day.
I make choices that are beneficial for me.
I learn and benefit from every experience.
VMP

Discovering and Deploying Our Gifts

The God of heaven will give us success.
Nehemiah 2:20

If you are feeling unfulfilled with life, hold to this powerful thought… *your best years may still lie ahead of you!* God has created all of us with many and diverse talents. Sometimes we discover and deploy those gifts later in life. "The God of heaven will give us success," declares Nehemiah. Consider these notable individuals:

- At age 64, Francis Chichester sailed alone around the world in a fifty-three-foot yacht.
- At age 75, Ed Delano of California bicycled 3,100 miles in thirty-three days to attend his fiftieth college reunion in Worcester, Massachusetts.
- At age 81, Benjamin Franklin skillfully mediated between disagreeing factions at the U.S. Constitutional Convention.
- At age 80, Winston Churchill returned to the House of Commons as a member of parliament and also exhibited sixty-two of his paintings.
- At age 96, George C. Selbach scored a 110-yard hole-in-one at Indian River, Michigan.
- At age 100, ragtime pianist Eubie Blake exclaimed, "If I'd known I was going to live this long, I'd have taken better care of myself."

❧ *Thought for the Day* ❧
The world stand aside to let anyone pass
who knows where he is going.
David Jordan

The Safest Place You Can Be

The Lord is my rock, my fortress, and my deliverer.
2 Samuel 22:2

The Golden Gate Bridge in San Francisco is one of the world's most famous sights. Although it is built directly over the San Andreas fault, the Golden Gate Bridge is probably the safest place a person could be during an earthquake.

The reason for that is careful engineering. Builders know that two principles are key for a structure to withstand an earthquake. First, the structure must be anchored securely to a foundation. Second, it must be flexible. The Golden Gate is supported by two towers sunk deep into the rock beneath the water of the bay. Yet the network of cables make it so flexible that the bridge can sway twenty-two feet horizontally and twelve feet vertically. Thus the towering, masterful structure is both securely anchored and designed to adapt to external changes—wind, storms, and earthquakes.

There is this lesson for living from that information.

Just like the weather, changes can come into our lives creating great turbulence. Emotionally, we can feel as though we are being blown away by the winds of crisis and trauma.

Before such events come our way we should ask ourselves two questions: "Am I anchored securely?" and "Do I have the flexibility necessary to go with the flow?"

As for an anchor, each one of us should be deeply imbedded in the rock of faith. Day by day we should be deepening our spiritual lives in ways large and small so that when a crisis emerges, we can tap into spiritual resources already cultivated.

As for flexibility, each one of us should strive to have spiritual and emotional adaptability.

That means understanding that life is a process of ebb and flow; that things change. When unpleasant events can come our way over which we have no control we must work to adjust and adapt knowing that God will help us and take care of us.

❧ Affirmation for the Day ❧
I am always safe, divinely guided, and protected.
I am one with the God who created me.
I am willing to change when necessary.
VMP

Act on Your Highest Hopes

Do not be afraid of them or their words.
Ezekiel 2:6

In May 1969, Jan Scruggs was in South Vietnam when his infantry unit was attacked. Seriously wounded, Scruggs was sent home to recuperate. During his brief time in Vietnam, over half of the men in his company were killed or wounded. Recovering from his injuries, Scruggs left the Army and returned to college, earning a degree in counseling. During that time he dreamed of establishing a memorial for soldiers killed in Vietnam. But he let his dream drop because all he could see were limitations—no organization and no money.

Then, in 1979, Scruggs saw *The Deer Hunter,* a movie about the impact of Vietnam upon a group of small-town friends. Scruggs was deeply affected by the film and couldn't sleep after seeing it. Memories of dead comrades flooded his mind. His dream of a memorial reemerged and with it, great determination. Using his own money he registered the Vietnam Veterans Memorial Fund as a nonprofit organization. On May 28, 1979, ten years after his injury, he held a press conference to announce his plans.

Quickly he assembled a large volunteer force of fund-raisers. In July of 1980, the government set aside a site near the Lincoln Memorial giving Scruggs five years to raise money for construction. Thirty-six months ahead of schedule, on November 13, 1982, Scruggs saw his dream become reality as he attended the dedication services for the Vietnam Veterans Memorial. Today, the Vietnam Veterans Memorial is Washington, D.C.'s most popular visitor site.

All people entertain high hopes and have great dreams. Yet many never act on them because of fear: the fear of failure, the fear of rejection, the fear of ridicule, the fear of disappointment.

Today ask yourself what are some of your highest hopes and dreams. Do you deeply want to engage in creative work—music, art, writing? Do you desire a graduate degree or to pursue professional studies such as law or medicine? Perhaps you would like to engage in a mission of service to the needy? Do not let fear hold you back. Act on your highest hopes and dreams. Remember the biblical promise: *Do not be afraid, for I am with you.*

❧ Affirmation for the Day ☙
I choose to live with faith, not fear.
I am capable of acting on my dreams.
I know God will guide and provide for me.
VMP

Letting Failure Be Our Most Important Teacher

Let the wise listen and add to their learning.
Proverbs 1:5

One fact of life is that all of us fail at something, sometime. No one is immune to failure. Failure can result from a lack of experience, immaturity, or carelessness.

However, failure can become a powerful ally when we take the time to glean the lessons in the failure. By doing that, we transform something bad and unpleasant into something good and useful for further growth.

Laura, a twenty-nine-year-old public relations executive, is a good example of one who learned important lessons from failure. "I was asked to give a speech before a group of our East Coast sales persons. To my utter embarrassment, the speech bombed. I vowed I would never speak in public again."

Yet Laura was asked to make a similar presentation to another company group. "Although tempted to say 'no,' I decided to accept the challenge. By then I'd had time to think about my first disastrous presentation. I realized I could learn from my failure. So I reviewed what went wrong the first time: There was lack of organization in my speech, not enough material to fill the time, and far too few human interest anecdotes. I made the corrections and delivered the speech. That time I was very well received. Later in the day I was delighted to be faxed a memo of thanks from our corporation president, who also praised my speaking ability."

Like Laura, let us remember that failure can be our most important teacher. *Let the wise listen and add to their learning* declares the writer of Proverbs. Let us "listen" to failure and thereby add to our learning.

~ Thought for the Day ~
I would never have amounted to anything were it not for adversity. I was forced to come up the hard way.
J. C. Penney

There's Always Enough to Share

She opens her arms to the poor and
extends her hands to the needy.

Proverbs 31:20

For fourteen years, a single mother of two schoolaged boys volunteered to arrange flowers for the altars of her church. Every Friday, after a long day on her feet at a local cannery where she worked to support her boys, the woman would drive directly to her church and begin preparations for weekend services. Depending on the number of weddings, she sometimes had as many as ten flower vases to prepare.

After school, her boys would often walk over to the church so they could all be together. Soon it became a family routine for the mother to create arrangements while her boys spritzed flowers, swept floors, and squabbled good-naturedly.

On one such Friday evening, the mother declared it was time for dinner. She took the boys across the street to a restaurant. It was a great treat for the family because her income was minimum wage, and there were months she could barely meet her financial obligations. Because it was a warm evening, the three sat outside enjoying their meal out.

The boys noticed a homeless man nearby looking for food in the garbage bin. They were uncomfortable and quickly looked away. But not their mother.

As they finished eating and stood to leave, the boys were surprised when their mother placed another order, paid for it, and instructed the cashier to give the food to the homeless man. "Mother never spoke to the man or drew attention to him in any way; she just made sure he had something hot to eat that night," recall her sons.

This is the lesson from that story: No matter how tight our finances, no matter how poor we may be, we always have enough to share. So let us train our eyes to see the needs of others and find ways to respond. In so doing we not only lighten their load but brighten their day.

⚜ Prayer for the Day ⚜
God of all life,
Expand the boundaries of my heart.
Give me a willingness to share freely,
generously, and lovingly with those
who are in need.

VMP

A Blueprint for a Satisfying Life

Oh, that you would bless me and enlarge my territory.
1 Chronicles 4:10

Too many individuals are engaged day after day in work that is unsatisfying, unchallenging, and without meaning. Yet it does not have to be that way. Our emotional and spiritual "territory" can be enlarged. Here is a simple blueprint for a more satisfying life:

- Decide while others delay.
- Plan while others play.
- Prepare while others daydream.
- Learn while others ignore.
- Persist while others quit.
- Begin while others stall.
- Listen while others are talking.
- Advance while others retreat.
- Work while others pause.
- Act while others hesitate.
- Believe while others doubt.
- Trust while others vacillate.
- Affirm while others deny.
- Venture while others falter.

❧ *Thought for the Day* ❧
We must dare, and dare again, and go on daring.
George Jacques Danton

Choosing Our Attitude

How long will you waver between two opinions?
1 Kings 18:21

Consider these realities: *It is possible to let go of regret and to redefine life events so that they don't seem so oppressive….It is possible to choose our attitude when life deals us a low blow.*

And, here is an exceptional example:

Steve Skallerud, a Minnesota teenager, was pinned between his parent's car and another automobile as he was filling up the gas tank. His right leg had to be amputated.

When the anesthetic subsided, he had to stare at the cold truth of life in which he would no longer be able to do what most other teenagers could do. No running, skiing, bicycling, or kicking a football.

Nevertheless, a mere ten months after the accident, Steve Skallerud was again skiing a mile-long mountain run at sixty-eight miles per hour. In so doing, he won the second National Handicap Ski Championship at Winter Park, Colorado.

A reporter for the *Minneapolis Star and Tribune* chronicled the amazing young man's journey and concluded: "It is comforting to be bitter about bad luck, but it is more practical to create." That reporter was further inspired by other achievements made by the youth:

"He can squat on a water ski one-legged. And not long after, he can be skiing barefooted on the slalom course. And a little later, he can swing a driver on one good leg and the artificial one, and shoot within five strokes of his old score the first time down the course."

This young man offers an important lesson for those who struggle with the loss of a loved one: While we cannot always control what transpires in our lives, we can control how we will respond. We can choose to become angry, bitter, self-absorbed; or we can choose to adapt, adjust, and advance in spite of the loss.

❧ Thought for the Day ❧
He who has a firm will molds the world to himself.
Johann Wolfgang Von Goethe

Using Your Mind As a Lifesaving Tool

But you said, "It's no use!"
Jeremiah 2:25

Consider this reality: You can use your mind as a lifesaving tool or a self-destructive weapon. No matter what has happened in your life, you can move forward with faith and confidence or give up hope and live with despair—*"It's no use!"*

The way we think is often an indicator and predictor of what may actually occur. That is the conclusion of Dr. Daniel Mark, a researcher at Duke University whose study revealed the power of optimism and faith.

After asking 1,719 male and female patients whether or not they thought they would make it, he discovered that 14 percent said they doubted they would ever recover enough to resume their daily routines.

Checking on these patients a year later, he found 12 percent of the pessimists had died, compared to only 5 percent of those who were optimistic about their outcome.

"When people give up and feel they are not going to make it, it's usually a self-fulfilling prophecy," says Dr. Mark.

Although his study showed that optimism plays an important role in the survival of heart-disease patients, some of the principles apply toward those suffering from any of life's hurts.

So the lesson and challenge for everyone is to think of reasons and strategies to help you manage and overcome life's hurts rather than being overcome by them. Therefore, *think the best, hope for the best, work for the best,* possible in your life.

In so doing, you will use your mind as a lifesaving tool, instead of a self-destructive weapon.

～ *Affirmation for the Day* ～

Dark, depressing thoughts have no hold over me.
Despair has no power in my life.
I exude confidence, hope, and great faith in myself and in my God.
VMP

Knowing When to Unload

If the Lord had not been on our side...
the raging waters would have swept us away.
Psalm 124:1,5

A woman tells of her childhood in England during World War II. Once when her father was home on leave from the army, he took her to the Liverpool dockyards near their home. He explained that many of the ships coming into the port were merchant ships that resupplied the British people with food, medicine, and munitions. "Courageous people risk their lives to bring us those supplies," he said.

The little girl noticed each ship had a line painted around the center of the hull. "What's that for?" she asked.

"To show the people loading up the ship how much it's made to carry," he said. "If they put too much on, the line disappears. That could cause the boat to sink. But if they put too little inside, it won't be full enough to do what it was made to do. Each boat is made by its builder to carry just the right amount," he carefully explained.

That simple story has this deeper implication:

God is the master boatbuilder. God has created us and therefore knows who we are, how big our holds are, what he wants us to carry. If the load of life we carry is heavy and we feel as though we are sinking, it is God who can lighten the load and give us the strength to carry on.

However, we must be careful not to overload ourselves with too much responsibility, too many cares, too much work, too many activities. If we say "yes" to everyone and everything, we may thwart God's design and find ourselves frustrated, overwhelmed, and feeling submerged.

～≈ *Thought for the Day* ≈～

It is impossible to get exhausted in work for God.
We get exhausted because we try to do God's
work in our own way.
Oswald Chambers

You Can Be Fearless

Do not be afraid, but let your hands be strong.
Zechariah 8:13

There are large groups of people who live constantly with fear. They are afraid of people, issues, and events that can come along. Repeatedly, the scripture of Jesus reminds us that we can be fearless—*Do not be afraid, but let your hands be strong,* declares the prophet Zechariah. But, to overcome our fears we must understand them. To minimize and overcome your fears try asking:

- What do I fear?

- Why am I afraid?

- What previous experiences cause my fear?

- What do I believe about this situation?

- Am I jumping to conclusions?

- How many "uns" contribute to my fear: *Un*substantiated stories, *un*familiar ideas, *un*kind accusations and judgments about me, *under*mined unity and support, *un*due influence to respond in an expected way, *un*balanced treatment of a topic or person?

- Am I willing to talk with someone who can help me see more clearly, or do I only talk with those who reinforce the fear?

- What are my motives behind this fear?

- Why do I allow it?

- How would a strong, spiritual leader embrace this aspect of life—Moses, Jeremiah, Isaiah, Jesus, or a spiritual person still living whom I admire?

Such questioning is an effective way of attacking your fears. As you begin to question and examine your fear it will begin to unfold. Observe it as its size diminishes. Look for opportunities to triumph over it.

❧ Thought for the Day ❧

We are so outnumbered
there's only one thing to do.
We must attack.
Sir Andrew Cunningham

Consider Developing
a Personal Philosophy of Life

Wisdom is supreme; therefore get wisdom.
Proverbs 4:7

The first disabled Miss America in the pageant's seventy-five-year history is the bright, talented, beautiful, and articulate Heather Whitestone, who also happens to be deaf. Originally from Birmingham, Alabama, Heather was born the youngest of three daughters in 1973. At eighteen months of age, she contracted a dangerously high fever. The antibiotic given to save her life also deprived her of hearing.

In spite of that major handicap, Heather excelled in school, is an accomplished ballet dancer (hearing the music in her heart rather than in her ears) and was crowned Miss America. Along with that crown came a $35,000 scholarship and the opportunity to inspire others. Heather attributes her success to her number one role model, her mother, Daphne. "She believed that I could have a normal life," Heather explains.

Along with her mother's encouragement and her own determination, Heather has lived her life by this personal philosophy which she calls STARS (Success Through Action and Realization of Your Dreams). Its five principles

1. Have a positive attitude

2. Believe in your dreams, especially education

3. Face your obstacles

4. Work hard

5. Build a support team

Today entertain this idea: Heather Whitestone's success and accomplishment is not only due to her mother's guidance and her own fierce determination, but to the fact that she developed and embraced a personal philosophy of life. Have you?

Like Whitestone, keep yours basic, simple, and easy to explain. Perhaps if more people took the time to develop a personal life philosophy they would be better able to overcome obstacles, beat discouragement, and emerge feeling more fulfilled and satisfied with life.

❧ *Thought for the Day* ❧
Philosophy is a longing after heavenly wisdom.
Plato

Arm Yourself With Prayer

Is any one of you in trouble?
He should pray.

Hebrews 5:13

Here is a fascinating modern story that highlights today's text: "Is any one of you in trouble? He should pray."

A newspaper reported this unusual encounter between a woman and two thieves. When the twenty-six-year-old woman discovered two men robbing her Arkansas home, she immediately dropped to her knees and prayed for them. Included in her prayer were statements of God's love for them and for God to direct their lives into more noble pursuits.

As soon as she completed her prayer, one of the robbers exclaimed to the other, "We can't do this! This is a Christian home!" Then, the two men returned all their stolen goods, left their gun with the woman, and walked out of her home.

Today, because so many people are frightened by high crime rates, they are arming themselves with weapons of all sorts. This newspaper story is a refreshing reminder that those who believe in God can arm themselves with prayer.

Prayer is a form of power. Sometimes prayer delivers us from evil, as it did the woman who was being robbed. At other times prayer may not lead to an instant resolution, but it will empower us to face and master the difficult situation that threatens us. And, on other occasions, prayer becomes a power that lifts us up, so that we can get a higher look, an objective view, of our lives. From the vantage point of prayer, things can look markedly different. The perspective of prayer can lead us to take wiser and more courageous actions.

❧ Thought for the Day ❧

Prayer is the easiest and hardest of all things;
the simplest and the sublimest;
the weakest and the most powerful;
its results lie outside the range of
human possibilities;
they are limited only by the omnipotence
of God.

Edward McKendree Bounds

Do You Have What It Takes?

Unless your righteousness surpasses that of
the Pharisees and the teachers of the law,
you will never enter the kingdom of heaven.
Matthew 5:20

It takes courage—
  to stand up for truth, justice,
    and what is good.
It takes patience—
  to support another person
    who is trying to rehabilitate himself.
It takes concern—
  to donate your time and money
    with people less fortunate.
It takes love—
  to consume less
    so that more can be shared with others.
It takes commitment—
  to follow through on promises made.
It takes compassion—
  to see "Christ" in every other human being.
It takes dedication—
  to continue loving those
    who act in "unloving" ways.
It takes perseverance—
  to work through a personal crisis.
It takes faith—
  to keep believing God's light
    will shine in the darkness.

❧ *Affirmation for the Day* ❧
I celebrate God's gift of life.
I gladly work for harmony, peace, and wholeness in my world.
I let the presence of God fill me and flow through me to others.
VMP

Healing Through Helping

Give to the one who asks you, and do not turn away.
Matthew 5:42

Today's scripture is a reminder that every Christian is called to engage in acts of love, kindness, and compassion. That call is, in itself, a great gift from God. Acts of love, kindness, and compassion not only bring joy to the recipient, but produce happiness and serenity in the life of the giver. One who is convinced that acts of compassion help the giver more than the receiver is Everett Alvarez, Jr. On August 5, 1964, Alvarez was shot down over North Vietnam while flying his Navy Skyhawk. He would spend eight-and-one-half years as a war prisoner, making him the second-longest-held American POW. Alvarez maintains that his own acts of caring were critical in helping him survive the desolation and brutality of captivity throughout his long confinement.

During one period, Alvarez was held apart from other POWs in a section of the prison containing only Vietnamese prisoners. Periodically he would be let out of his small jail into a courtyard in front of his cell where he could wash his few clothes and bathe. The door of his cell contained a tiny pinhole, and if he looked through it he could see a person standing ten feet away. Apparently one of the Vietnamese prisoners knew about the pinhole because he would come and stand in front of it waving and gesturing at Alvarez. Using hand signals, he would point at Alvarez's clothing left behind to dry overnight and then point to his own rags.

"Now maybe he was putting me on. Maybe he was just a professional prison beggar, but I truly felt sorry for him," Alvarez says. "I had two pairs of trousers and two undershirts, and all he had was holes. So I arranged to leave him my extra clothing. When I saw how elated he became, it lifted my own spirits and helped me to go on."

An important spiritual lesson that comes through the experience of Everett Alvarez is this: We gain strength by giving strength. Inherent in God's call to act with love, kindness, and compassion is our own experience of healing through helping. It is a grace of God that when we ease the pain of others, our own burdens become lighter. The truth is that when we are busy serving others, life is no longer meaningless.

❧ Thought for the Day ❧
If I cannot do great things,
I can do small things
in a great way.
James Freeman Clarke

The Victory of Faith

I will put my trust in him.
Hebrews 2:13

Rev. Norman Vincent Peale, best-selling author, tells of a faith insight that took place in his New York City home in 1940. At the time, German military had just bombed the port of Rotterdam and invaded Holland. The steamship cruiser *Statendam* was burned and destroyed at the dock. During the bombing, the ship's captain, George Barendse, was on his way to the United States on another vessel.

When he arrived in New York, Captain Barendse tried to communicate with his wife and son in Holland. He had read of the Rotterdam bombing, which reported that a third of the city was reduced to rubble and many people were killed. All his efforts to reach his family were unsuccessful. With his ship destroyed, his wife and son possibly injured or even dead, his city in ruins, his country overrun, Captain Barendse attended church that tragic Sunday morning in May of 1940. "I saw him sitting in the pew, seemingly crushed by this weight of sorrow," Dr. Peale recalls.

After the service, Rev. Peale invited the captain to join him and his family for lunch. Asked to offer a prayer before the meal, Captain Barendse prayed, "God, help me not to hate; give your guidance in thought, in speech, and in action to those who rule over the countries in war." Each word came one by one, slowly, as if hewn out of his soul, Dr. Peale remembers. "God, watch over my wife and boy. Before my wife was mine, she belonged to you, Lord; before my little boy came to me, he was yours, Father. They are in your hands. I trust you. May your will be done." There at a simple family dinner, the Peale family sat awestruck before a profound expression of faith. In that Dutch captain, undaunted amid ruins, they saw the superb grandeur of the Christian faith; the magnificence of soul and spirit it creates in a human being. "Something caught at our throats and stirred our hearts as we watched the triumph, the ineffable victory, of faith in the soul of a man," Dr. Peale says.

An incident like that challenges us to look at our own faith. Is our faith strong enough to sustain us during a time of great peril and crisis? Do we trust God completely enough that we can place our loved ones in God's hands and then live in confidence and peace?

⤙ *Affirmation for the Day* ⤚
God strengthens me for every demand of life.
God makes me flexible for meeting and dealing with change.
God fills me again and again with refreshing energy and vitality.
VMP

The Gift of Friendship

*Have we not all one Father? Did not one God
create us? Why do we profane the covenant
of our fathers by breaking faith with one another?*
Malachi 2:10

The lament of Malachi rings with amazing truth today as individuals, families, and nations are disconnected from one another. "Have we not all one Father? Did not one God create us?" asks the prophet. Those questions are raised to nudge us to respond with greater understanding, kindness, compassion, and love to the people around us. Consider this heartwarming encounter between a ten-year-old girl and a man in his seventies.

Quinn Petry doesn't have a grandfather, but she has made a special friend—a man named Ellie Crossman. Quinn used to see the older man walking his dog through her neighborhood in Westborough, Massachusetts. Although she didn't know his name, she looked forward to talking with him and playing with his greyhound, Iris.

Then one day the man disappeared. He was no longer seen walking his dog anywhere in the neighborhood. "I was worried that he died," says the ten-year-old. After asking friends and neighbors about the man, she eventually tracked him down in a nursing home, where he was recovering from foot surgery.

Quinn then began visiting Mr. Crossman in the nursing home, and the friendship continued after he recovered. Quinn bought Mr. Crossman a Father's Day card and asked him to be her honorary grandfather.

In December she filled Christmas stockings for both him and Iris (who devoured the candy-cane bone Quinn gave him). At Easter Mr. Crossman sent Quinn flowers with a card which read: "To my best friend."

Clearly the friendship means a great deal to Mr. Crossman, and Quinn is also benefiting from the relationship. "I feel good that I've helped someone," she says. "Mr. Crossman will always be part of me."

~ Prayer for the Day ~
Loving God,
Day by day remind me of the
truth that friendship doubles joy while
dividing grief. Let me be intentional
in reaching out to all others with
courtesy, respect, sympathy, understanding
compassion, kindness, and love.
VMP

The Power of Expressing Appreciation

A wise man has great power, and a man of
knowledge increases strength.

Proverbs 24:5

It was the movie *Silverado* that launched Kevin Costner's acting career. But first he had to weather a huge personal disappointment and a major professional setback. After completing his role in *The Big Chill*, Costner was called to a meeting with Lawrence Kasdan, the film's director. Kasdan gently told Costner he had to cut out the ending and his part was eliminated completely. Kasdan explained he felt terrible about the decision, but it had to be done.

"To my amazement, Costner was totally cheerful, sanguine, delightful," Kasdan recalls. "Larry," he said to me, "this has been the experience of my life. It has shown me what kind of actor I want to be, and I wouldn't trade it for anything. You have nothing to apologize for—you have given me a great gift."

It was at that moment that a strong friendship began between actor Kevin Costner and director Lawrence Kasdan. "I was already planning *Silverado*; and suddenly I thought, *I'm going to write a part for Kevin Costner in that*," Kasdan says.

Through Costner's classy response, he communicated this important three-word message: *I appreciate you*. As a result Costner and Kasdan became good friends. Appreciation, when spoken or conveyed has the power to forge new friendships, deepen old ones, and restore those which have cooled.

Why not consider reviewing your style of interaction with others. Monitor yourself to determine how you respond to disappointments.

Even though disappointed, can you, like Kevin Costner, find reasons to express gratitude? Ask if your appreciation level is high enough. Most of us can always increase our levels of gratitude and appreciation.

People with wisdom and maturity know the importance of maintaining the attitude of gratitude.

❧ *Affirmation for the Day* ❧

I choose to see and acknowledge the beauty all around me.

I choose to see and acknowledge the good that flows to me.

I choose to see and acknowledge the opportunities that shower me.

VMP

Remembering That Grief Is So Limited

Gladness and joy will overtake them, and sorrow
and sighing will flee away.

Isaiah 35:10

Although you have suffered a loss—death, separation, divorce, un-employment, relocation—try to remember what grief cannot do.

Grief is so limited…

It cannot kill friendship,
It cannot destroy memories,
It cannot silence courage,
It cannot abolish compassion,
It cannot cripple love,
It cannot destroy enthusiasm,
It cannot eliminate hope,
It cannot crush faith,
It cannot steal dignity,
It cannot silence music,
It cannot rob life of beauty,
It cannot exterminate integrity,
It cannot block the sunshine,
It cannot prevent personal growth,
It cannot conquer the will to live.

Grief is so limited!

❦ Thought for the Day ❧

At any moment in life we have the option to choose
an attitude of gratitude,
a posture of grace,
a commitment to joy.

Tim Hansel

In Love With Life

They will still bear fruit in old age,
they will stay fresh and green.

Psalm 92:14

Life is a precious gift generously given by our creator. Yet so many people squander their hours and eventually their lives. Today's passage reminds us to be "fruitful," that is, productive people, contributing members of society and learning new things even into old age. Here is a truly inspiring eighty-five-year-old woman who is in love with life. Although she has had her share of losses, her living is remarkable.

She is in excellent health and takes no medications. The woman exercises daily. Her state Department of Motor Vehicles has just renewed her driver's license for another four years. She wrote a play which is being produced by students at a nearby college. The woman belongs to a book-study group, to an art group, and a music group that requires members to present papers. Last year her Mother's Day gift was a computer, which she has mastered. "I find it invaluable," she declares.

What is truly important is the quality of your life, not necessarily the quantity. Your most precious resource for living well is time. Take the time to

- *Read:* It rejuvenates the mind, motivates the will and energizes the personality.
- *Think:* It is a source of self-renewal and self-discovery.
- *Volunteer:* It will return more than you give.
- *Laugh:* It restores your emotional balance.
- *Play:* It will make you feel briefly like a child again.
- *Worship:* It connects you to a higher, benevolent power.
- *Love:* It produces satisfying relationships.
- *Forgive:* It is the path to peace of mind.
- *Dream:* It provides a mental road map for your future.
- *Plan:* It determines whether you will have the time for everything you want to do.

∼ *Thought for the Day* ∼
Do not walk through time without leaving
worthy evidence of your passage.
Pope John XXIII

Cultivating an Eye to See the Good

All who have an eye for evil will be cut down.
Isaiah 29:20

Today the prophet Isaiah reminds all who believe in God that they must cultivate an eye to see the good around them. He issues a dire warning to those who "have an eye for evil." Here are two lists for expanding our vision to see the good and the beautiful in life and in people:

"Do Not" List

I will not speak words that belittle others—they show a lack of respect.

I will not make harsh comments—they show a profound lack of love.

I will not express doubts easily—they show a lack of trust.

I will not reveal the secrets of another—that shows a lack of honor.

I will not boast—it shows a lack of humility.

"Do" List

I will express encouragement—it will uplift the sad.

I will accept a challenge—it is important to try again.

I will speak good words—it will refresh burdened hearts.

I will notice beauty—it will triumph over life's ugliness.

I will listen to troubled people—it will lighten their load.

❧ *Thought for the Day* ❧

The proud who trust in themselves may fear to undertake anything, but the humble are bold in proportion to their sense of insufficiency. As they acknowledge their weakness, they acquire strength, because they rely on God.

Saint Francis de Sales

Be Like God—Choose to Forget

I will forgive their wickedness and
will remember their sins no more.
Jeremiah 31:34

Consider the scrapbook that usually contains no tokens of bad memories. We usually include only mementos that warm and nourish the spirit. They contain a childhood or even a lifetime of pleasant keepsakes. Then, when we're in a nostalgic mood, we drag out the old scrapbook and delightfully relive good times gone by.

Yet consider how different our mental and spiritual "scrapbooks" can be. When we review and relive our life we tend to dwell on regret and self-reproach. We have managed to fill our mind's "scrapbook" with volumes and volumes of past shortcomings and sins.

As clearly as yellowing photos and newspaper clippings in a tattered album, our mind recalls each ugly grievance: impatience with children or a spouse; our lack of gratitude; our failure to be kind and thoughtful; harsh words carelessly uttered; actions which hurt another. Sometimes the list can be endless and terribly oppressive. Such a review does nothing to nourish our spiritual development and much to sabotage that growth.

The way to end that spiritual suicide is to be like God who chooses to forget: "I will forgive their wickedness and will remember their sins no more."

Those words clearly tell us that God forgives and forgets—period! Therefore, after expressing regret and remorse to God for our sins and shortcomings, we must not continue to create our own guilt but let go. We must treat ourselves the way God treats us. We must release our forgiven sins and forget them.

So today let us resolve to build scrapbooks like God treats our sin— recalling good memories.

Let us think about times when we acted with courage, dignity, justice, love, kindness, and compassion. Let us thank God for loving mercy and acceptance. Let us thank God for forgiving and forgetting. And let us do likewise.

◝ *Thought for the Day* ◜

If God forgives us, we must forgive ourselves.
Otherwise it is almost like setting up ourselves
as a higher tribunal than him.
C. S. Lewis

Commitment to God Has Practical Consequences

The Lord will be your everlasting light,
and your days of sorrow will end.

Isaiah 60:20

Commitment to God makes a practical difference in how we live. Isaiah tells us that God will be our "everlasting light," dispelling the shadows and darkness in our lives. Our "days of sorrow will end." Consider actor Mickey Rooney.

Although his fame and wealth were established as a child actor, Rooney's life has been difficult. Today he is on his ninth marriage. His first two wives died, one with cancer, the other as a victim of a tragic homicide. That was followed by five unhappy marriages for Rooney.

He has been married to his current wife for twenty years. A television interviewer asked Rooney, "What changed?" Rooney's response is memorable and important:

"What changed?" he responded. "I gave my life to Christ. That changed everything. I had lived my life in chaos. I was a millionaire when I was a child. Participated in every form of lust and human degradation. Then, twenty years ago, I gave my life to Christ—warts and all. That has made all the difference."

Obviously, Rooney's commitment to God has had practical consequences in his life. That is as it should be.

As we come closer to God, virtues should grow stronger as vices grow weaker and are even eliminated. Virtues, such as peace, love, serenity, kindness, patience, joy, should replace chaos, hate, anger, cruelty, impatience, despondency.

Let us take a close look at our faith and see if that is indeed taking place. If so, let us thank God for continued growth. If not, let us ask God for aid to make necessary changes.

⤐ Affirmation for the Day ⤏
God calls me to change, and I am willing to change.
I choose to change the way I see, think, speak, and act.
I move from the old to the new with joy and ease.

VMP

Affirmation for Forgiveness

Do not hate your brother in your heart.
Leviticus 19:17

Much unhappiness in life could be eliminated if we extended forgiveness generously, spontaneously, and freely. Some of the most unhappy people in the world are those with emotional photographic memories. They never forget a hurt. Every slight ever received is permanently etched in their mind. A wound inflicted decades ago remains fresh in the memory. Some continue to be angry people who have died years earlier.

The way out of such emotional turmoil is forgiveness. The next time an angry memory emerges over someone who has hurt you, try to forgive and then forget.

Today's text does not instruct us to tell the individual you forgive him or her. Nor does it tell us to love them as we would love a dear friend or beloved spouse. It simply says, "Do no hate your brother in your heart." It calls for an action of the heart that is private and personal.

So, in your heart, extend forgiveness to others, wish them well, and let go of all negative energy connected with the painful event.

It may help to recite affirmations such as these:

- *Beginning now, I freely and willingly forgive those who have hurt me.*
- *Beginning now, I release all grudges and hatred.*
- *Beginning now, I extend goodwill toward those who have cause me pain.*

- *I allow God's love to flow over me and heal my memories.*
- *I allow God's love to flow through me, empowering me to forgive.*
- *I allow God's love to flow over me and purify my thoughts, feelings and actions.*

◈ *Thought for the Day* ◈
Every human soul has a right to be free from hate,
and we claim our rightful inheritance when we
forgive people who hurt us.
Lewis Smedes

What We Should Save for Senior Years

Moses was a hundred and twenty years old when he died,
yet his eyes were not weak nor his strength gone.

Deuteronomy 34:7

When I was in my early twenties and at college, I was approached by an insurance agent, who stressed the importance of buying an insurance policy that would grow financially. That way I could be independent upon retirement at age sixty-five.

Skillfully, he presented impressive statistics of several hundred thousand dollars I would receive at retirement if I began early. He also painted a glowing picture of a life of loafing: fishing, golfing, eating out, owning a home in a warm climate.

While the idea of financial planning for senior years is valid, saving money is not enough. In order to truly enjoy serenity and peace, there are many other things which we should save.

We should save *friendships* and make new ones so we will have others with whom to share our lives—the good moments and the bad.

We should save *books*. Over the course of our years, we should become acquainted with great thinkers and inspirational writings, so that we can turn to them for comfort and strength.

We should save *music*. Every home and apartment should have a library of music to lift hearts and spirits.

We should save our *physical health*. Unlike Moses cited in today's text, too many senior people lose their independence because of physical problems, many of which could be prevented through regular exercise.

We should save our *emotional health*. Maintaining friendships and being socially active leads to a longer, healthier, more satisfying life.

We should save our *outlook*. Rather than become bitter, angry, and disillusioned with the world, always see and work for a better future.

We should save *memories*. Store in the mind beautiful people you have experienced and places you have seen. Keep pictures of children, grandchildren, friends, and neighbors.

We should save a sense of *contribution*. Work to improve community, city, state, and nation. Those actions will live on after we are gone.

Here is the reality about a meaningful life: *It takes more than a check each month for a life to feel contented and happy.*

⇜ Thought for the Day ⇝

What most counts is not to live, but to live aright.

Socrates

Ideas for Redeeming the Time Alone

Our days on earth are like a shadow, without hope.
1 Chronicles 29:15

Many people experience the frustration of time that feels wasted and lost. That is the lament of the biblical writer who says, "Our days on earth are like a shadow, without hope." Consider these contemporary expressions about time:

"I can't bear to spend one more evening alone," says the wife of a busy physician. "My husband is at the hospital seeing his patients at least three nights a week while I am stuck sitting at home, watching TV with the kids until after nine each evening."

"Ever since my wife of thirty-eight years died, I can't bear the long, quiet, lonely hours of the evening alone. Weekends are equally difficult to bear," says a recent widower.

Yet life and time are gifts from God to be used wisely and properly. Here are some ideas for redeeming the time that we have:

- Deepen your spirituality by reading and memorizing scripture passages.

- Get closer to God through increased time spent in prayer.

- Take a home Bible-study course and get to know the Bible better.

- Learn a new skill—sewing, painting, playing a musical instrument.

- Read inspirational books or poetry.

- Write letters to friends with whom you have not communicated for some time.

- Call someone who may be very lonely.

- Volunteer to be the phone chairperson for your child's class or sports team.

- Once a week volunteer to visit a hospital, nursing home, or rehabilitation center.

↠ Affirmation for the Day ↞
I am divinely guided to use my time wisely.
I make choices that are good for me and for others.
The wise use of my time makes me feel good.
VMP

April 14

Some Reasons to Be Confident

*But I the Lord will speak what I will,
and it shall be fulfilled without delay.*
Ezekiel 12:25

A woman recalls when her teenage daughter was an infant. At that time she was diagnosed with an incurable illness. Although devastated emotionally by the physician's report, the woman and her husband balanced their fear with their faith. "For several months we clung to the promises of God's faithful care with every fiber of our being because our daughter's very life depended on it," she says.

Eventually her symptoms completely disappeared to the amazement of her doctors. Today she is a healthy college student. Based on that frightening but ultimately faith-building experience the woman shares these reasons why Christians can always be confident:

God has everything under control. As the Creator of the universe and everything in it, God knows the beginning and the end. No matter what life may bring, Christians can live secure in the knowledge that God knows our needs and will meet them.

God is faithful. According to Ezekiel 12:25, God promises that the word he speaks will come to pass. God means what he says.

God is love. Everything God does is motivated and energized by love. Because God is love, we can trust that he will take care of us and our loved ones.

God is the God of hope. For the Christian, hope is rooted in the reality that God is constantly working to bring good out of evil, triumph out of tragedy, a crown out of a cross. Thus we can rejoice as we face the future knowing that God is with us.

⚕ *Affirmation for the Day* ⚕
I believe in a power far greater than I am.
I trust in the limitless love and wisdom of God.
Whatever I need will be given to me at the right time.
I rejoice in the knowledge that God is carefully guiding me.
VMP

Reasons Why Fear Conquers Faith

But the people who live there are powerful,
and the cities are fortified and very large.
Numbers 13:28

Consider reading two chapters in the biblical book of Numbers—chapters 13 and 14—to see reasons why fear conquers faith. Of course, our faith should always be greater than our fear, but life can be very intimidating. It is worth noting the experience of the twelve Israelite spies who returned from a forty-day investigation of Canaan. Their initial report was that the new land was indeed "flowing with milk and honey" (Numbers 13:27).

However, ten of the spies were intimidated by the people who occupied the land. Their anxiety is often reflected in the way we face life. As you look closely at the account, notice the clear signs indicating that fear is overcoming faith and ask yourself if you have responded the same way to a challenge:

- *A gross exaggeration of potential problems.* "All the people we saw there are of great size" (Numbers 13:33). Have you ever been guilty of catastrophic thinking?

- *A total reliance on human wisdom.* "The people who live there are powerful, and the cities are fortified and very large" (Numbers 13:28). Like the spies, have you ever forgotten that God helps us meet great challenges?

- *Severely underestimating personal strengths and abilities.* "We seemed like grasshoppers in our own eyes, and we looked the same to them" (Numbers 13:33). Have you ever felt as though a problem was so large and your ability to deal with it so small and limited?

- *An aggressive spread of negative thinking.* "They spread among the Israelites a bad report" (Numbers 13:32). Have you ever been guilty of spreading fear, anxiety, and insecurity?

- *An unrealistic view of the past.* "We should choose a leader and go back to Egypt" (Numbers 14:4). Has fear ever shortened your memory and made you view the past in an overly optimistic fashion?

✎ *Affirmation for the Day* ✎
God sees me for what I will become.
God accepts me for who I am today.
God forgives for what I have been in the past.
VMP

Are You a Functional Atheist?

We have no power to face this vast army that is attacking us.
We do not know what to do, but our eyes are upon you.

2 Chronicles 20:12

"For many years I was a functional atheist," says David. "Do not get me wrong. I have a deep faith in God, and I have believed in God as far back as I can remember," he adds. David also explains he grew up in a Christian home where the entire family was active in their parish. As a young person and later as an adult, he, too, continued that active participation in the Church. He was an avid student of scripture. "Yet I was a functional atheist," David says.

The term "functional atheist" describes people who believe in God but do not pray. They are faithful in living by the dictates of the Christian faith and ethic, attend church regularly, and may even engage intentionally in community acts of mercy. What makes them functional atheists is that they never rely on God's help. They are living the Christian life on their own energy, strength, and ability. Most times they succeed.

That was true of David until he and his wife decided to welcome foster children into their home. When they received three children his life suddenly became extremely challenging. After a few weeks he realized, for the first time in his life, that he was confronted with an issue that he could not manage and succeed alone. As more weeks passed, he began to feel less adequate and more discouraged with the task.

Tempted to give up, he confided in a friend who shared this wisdom: "Parenthood is God's way of showing us exactly where we are spiritually." That statement pierced his heart and mind. David realized his biggest problem was not the lack of parenting skills, but his lack of dependence on God. In the past he had handled everything on his own.

Resolved to be the father these children desperately needed, and to be a better husband, he began spending more time in prayer than he had ever done in his life. "God was faithful and provided the strength, insight, and wisdom to meet the crisis," David says. With that experience behind him, David ceased being a functional atheist and began truly seeking God's graces through prayer.

~⚜ *Thought for the Day* ⚜~

Acquaint thyself with God,
If thou wouldst taste His works.
Admitted once to his embrace,
Thou shalt perceive that thou wast blind before.

William Cowper

Three Simple Ways to Make Time for Prayer

*It is time to seek the Lord, until he comes
and showers righteousness on you.*
Hosea 10:12

Yesterday we considered the fact that some people are "functional" atheists. Today's text is a reminder to pray. We should "seek right thoughts, right attitudes, right decisions.

Here are some easy-to-follow instructions for a stronger, more consistent prayer life:

1. *Plan time to pray.* The major reason many do not pray regularly is because they do not plan the time for prayer. The most effective way to do this is by setting aside a specific time each day when to pray. That way it becomes part of your routine. One woman sets her clock and rises half an hour earlier to pray. "I established how much time I need each morning to shower, put on makeup, prepare and eat breakfast, and then pray. It's my morning ritual." If you are not a morning person, consider using time at noon or in the evening. Be careful you do not plan your prayer time so late that you fall asleep.

2. *Establish a place to pray.* Find a location that is quiet, comfortable, and without distractions. One man describing his prayer location says, "I have carefully selected a spot in the sitting room where the sunlight streams in early in the morning, and that has become my beautiful little prayer spot."

3. *Use pen and paper.* It is easy to become distracted and begin daydreaming during a time of private prayer. Writing out your prayers of praise and concern is an effective way of reducing any distractions. Buy a simple spiral notebook and let it become your prayer journal. Many discover that writing out prayers helps them concentrate better and be more precise in their praying.

⚜ Prayer for the Day ⚜
Gracious God,
I ask for your help in developing a life of prayer.
I ask you to help me cherish,
increase, perfect,
promote, and protect
my daily time of prayer.
VMP

Choosing to Act Rather Than Reacting

When they saw the courage of Peter and John...
they were astonished.

Acts of the Apostles 4:13

Whenever we experience disappointment and setback, there is a tendency to feel doubt and panic. However, those are only initial feelings and should quickly be minimized by establishing a deliberate and careful course of action. Peter and John, early leaders of the emerging Christian faith, acted courageously in spite of opposition. Their stand not only impressed and inspired others but galvanized weaker Christians. When faced with difficulty take courageous and bold steps forward, rather than react in fear and anxiety.

An inspiring lesson comes from Johnny Unitas. Before he was eventually honored in the NFL Hall of Fame as one of the greatest quarterbacks to play professional football, Unitas suffered several major rejections. As a high-school youth he wanted to play college football but none of the larger universities to which he applied wanted him. They said he was too small and too slow. So Unitas went to a small college where he played football and excelled.

Next, Unitas hoped to play professional football and tried out for his hometown Pittsburgh Steelers but was cut from the team early in the process. Rather than accept the verdict that he couldn't play professional football, Unitas responded with a three-point action plan.

First, he found a job in construction so he could support himself. Second, he played in a league that paid him six dollars per game, allowing him to continue developing his skills. Third, he continued to write and phone NFL teams seeking an opportunity to try out. After seven months, he received an invitation from the Baltimore Colts. He was on his way to making sports history.

❧ *Thought for the Day* ❧

Fear causes doubt, hesitation, panic, and withdrawal.
Faith creates certainty, commitment, courage, and boldness.

VMP

Patience Plus Persistence Produce Payoff

I look for your deliverance, O Lord.
Genesis 49:18

God's timing may differ from ours. According to scripture we are to be patient and persistent while waiting in faith for God to act. "I look for your deliverance, O Lord," was the cry of Jacob in the Old Testament. "At the proper time we will reap a harvest if we do not give up," declares Saint Paul in the New Testament (Galatians 6:9).

There are times in everyone's life when it is easy to quit, easy to lower the standard, and easy to abandon the dream. But it is much more rewarding to continue. Those who struggle with circumstances rather than give up are the ones who emerge as winners. Before he entered politics, Harry Truman had a long record of failures.

As a young man he worked the family farm and barely survived. Leaving the farm behind, he made unsuccessful efforts to become an investor in land, in zinc mines, and in oil leases. In spite of being a thirty-eight-year-old bankrupt clothing merchant, Truman ran for political office and won. It was his first career victory. Fundamental to his success was the fact Truman never let the fear of failure discourage or deter him from taking on new challenges.

When tempted to quit, give up, and retreat in the presence of great difficulty and discouragement remember the biblical formula: *Patience plus perseverance produce payoff.*

During hard times remain true to your goals, work hard, and ask God for strength. When the timing is right God will provide "deliverance."

✎ *Thought for the Day* ✎
When the rock is hard,
we get harder than the rock.
When the job is tough,
we get tougher than the job.
George Cullum, Sr.

Diminish Fear by Studying and Facing It

Blessed is the man who finds wisdom,
the man who gains understanding,
                    Proverbs 3:13

Many individuals never fully tap their potential, achieve their dreams, accomplish their goals, or even begin to act on their deepest hopes because they are infected by the deadly trio of *fear, uncertainty,* and *doubt.* Many deprive themselves the opportunity to develop God-given gifts and live an abundant life because of fear.

Rather than be intimidated by the fear of something new or different, take the time to study and analyze it. Information is empowering and liberating. It is impossible for fear and knowledge to coexist.

"It's terribly important at every age to study things that bother you," says television host Sally Jessy Raphael. A lesson she learned as a child contributed greatly to her success in television. Whenever Raphael was frightened by an activity or a situation she would deliberately study it, thereby reducing and even eliminating the fear.

"As a child and teenager, I was consumed by many fears. For a long time I was petrified of the dark, afraid it would engulf me completely. One day I decided to face my fears," she says. "I forced myself to walk into dark rooms and feel my way around until I understood there was nothing in those rooms to fear. You have to be familiar with the enemy, to know what the enemy's next move is, if you want to be a good general."

So look carefully at your fears. Analyze them in order to minimize them.

⊰ *Affirmation for the Day* ⊱
I choose to rise above my fears.
I choose to face my fears with courage and faith.
I am totally willing to take risks and grow.
VMP

Small Actions Have Large Meanings

I made the widow's heart sing.
Job 29:13

Kindness creates a ripple effect, much like a small stone tossed into a pond. Small acts of kindness do have larger meanings. Georgette, an elderly woman, shares a memorable act of kindness extended to her seventy-eight years earlier. Although she was only eight years of age at the time, the memory of kindness remains vivid and fresh.

In 1916 she was attending a Catholic school when the teacher asked which student would like to decorate the church altar with flowers for a special service the following day. Out of the thirty pairs of wildly waving hands, Georgette was selected. However, her family was poor and they lived in a tiny apartment.

After school, Georgette quickly made the rounds of empty lots near her home. There among the rocks, weeds, and rubble, she found three wilted poppies, a sick-looking cabbage rose, and a few fuchsias already shedding their blossoms. She knew her parents could not afford to buy flowers. "Florists' flowers were strictly for funerals," she had heard her mother say. Walking home empty-handed, Georgette dreaded the coming morning. Children could be cruel. Almost home, Georgette heard footsteps behind her and a voice saying, "Why so sad, little one?"

It was a neighbor, a Jewish woman. When she placed her arms around Georgette, the little girl could not hold back the tears. She explained the honor of being selected to decorate the church altar. The woman was quiet and then spoke: "These flowers may perk up if you leave them outside all night in a bucket of water."

Discouraged, Georgette prayed that evening for help with the flowers. Ready for school the next morning, she opened the door to retrieve her flowers. There on the steps was a huge bouquet of beautiful, colorful flowers. A card from the local florist's shop contained this note: "Little one, take these to decorate your church altar."

Looking back, Georgette says: "The anniversary of that day has come and gone seventy-eight times, but no amount of time could make me forget an elderly Jewish woman who changed my life with a small gesture of goodwill."

❧ Prayer for the Day ❧
God of life,
Bless all of my days.
Keep me truly alive and in love with all of life.
Keep me listening, growing, caring, and sharing.
VMP

Where Do We Place Our Trust?

Ahab son of Omri did more evil in the eyes of the LORD than
any of those before him...and began to serve Baal and worship him.
1 Kings 16:30–31

Today's text is one of harsh judgment upon Ahab. His problem: He placed his trust in a false God and a false religion. For that he was soundly condemned. His example should raise in us this question: Where do we place our trust, our faith, our hope? Are we, like Ahab, guilty of placing our trust in a bogus or questionable power?

Consider the insight that comes from this story told by Norman, who is now retired. When he was twelve, an incident took place that nearly ended his life. One hot summer day Norman was playing with a group of boys and girls at a local lake.

An older girl suggested he allow her to practice lifesaving, using him as the "pretend" drowning victim. At the time, Norman did not know how to swim, nor did he have an understanding of the danger he was facing. The girl told Norman to lie on his back in the water. She grabbed him by the hair and began swimming with her other arm out into the lake. Eventually, she was able to pull Norman into water about nine feet deep.

Everything went well until she turned back toward the shore. A wave of water broke over Norman's face. Suddenly, he became terrified. Fighting for breath, he began flailing his arms, breaking her hold on his hair. For a few frantic moments he fought her help. Then, despites the attempts of two other youths, everything went black for Norman.

His next memory was that of lying prone on the beach, getting artificial respiration and spitting out lake water. He had been rescued by a man who heard the cries for help. "I never learned his name, but I am eternally grateful to my rescuer. And I learned to swim the following summer."

That story is a parable of our lives. Where do we place our trust, our faith, our hope? Are we, like Ahab or Norman, guilty of placing our trust in a bogus or questionable power? Is our complete faith in the *corporation* we work for? the *institution* we serve? *science* or *technology*? While some institutions are worthy of receiving our sincere commitment, ultimate trust, faith, and hope must be placed in God. Then, when the waves break over our faces, we will not be paralyzed with fear.

❦ *Prayer for the Day* ❦
Loving God,
Day by day I will reaffirm my complete trust in you.
VMP

The Journey Through Discouragement

*They traveled from Mount Hor along the route to
the Red Sea, to go around Edom. But the people
grew impatient on the way.*

Numbers 21:4

No one is immune to times of discouragement. In today's text the ancient people of Israel "grew impatient," frustrated, and discouraged, even though they were on the way to the promised land. Their journey was time-consuming and difficult. It required physical energy and spiritual faith. Discouragement set in. Our living can parallel the Hebrew experience. Here is a powerful image for dealing with discouragement:

It comes from Jacob Riis (1849–1914), the journalist and social reformer who did so much to improve living conditions for the poor in New York City during the late 1800s.

When asked what he did to rise over his own discouragement and depression, Riis shared his unusual but effective approach. He said that he would go to a place where a stonecutter was working. There Riis would simply watch him. Blow after blow, the stonecutter would bang away at the stone with his hammer and wedge. He might strike it a hundred times with no apparent effect.

But on the hundred and first try the stone would crack.

With that crack Riis realized that the hundred and first blow didn't crack the stone by itself. It was the cumulative effect of the hundred blows before it that brought success.

That's the way the journey through discouragement is accomplished. You work hard for a long time, without seeming to make any progress; then one day there is a "crack in the stone"—a major step forward is taken, a goal is achieved, an obstacle is overcome, the clouds lift, and the sun beams brightly.

When life becomes a more intense struggle and you feel as though you are not making progress, remember that everything you are doing is one more "strike on the stone." Soon it will crack and break, allowing you to shape it. Continue working and believing. Eventually you will pass through the darkness and into the light.

❧ Thought for the Day ❧
Never doubt in the dark what God told you in the light.
Victor Raymond Edman

Thanking God for a Daily Miracle

My Presence will go with you, and I will give you rest.
Exodus 33:14

For eight hours the man has been in an operating room. The anesthetic was readily accepted. He was not feeling well. His symptoms: weariness, irritability, depression. This procedure was necessary for his continued health.

Hour after hour the physician worked on his mind, precisely removing irritants from the brain. Slowly, the poisons and toxins drain away and his tense body begins to relax. He is breathing slowly, rhythmically, sighing and stretching occasionally.

After eight hours the alarm rings. He opens his eyes, blinks, turns the alarm off, and rises. He sits up with a smile. Eight hours later he is a new, cheerful person ready to face the challenges ahead. He is an energetic, youthful man in place of the tired and irritable older man of the previous evening.

Of course, there are no doctors, no tubes, no wires. The room is not in a hospital but is in his home. He has spent the last eight hours sleeping in his bed while the Great Physician performed the daily miracle of a good night's sleep.

The daily miracle of rest is often taken for granted. Only recently have scientists been studying the role of sleep in human life. Among their conclusions: Rest builds and rebuilds the immune system, refreshes the mind, restores energy, increases creativity, and brightens moods.

Some 200 thousand vehicle accidents are related to lack of sleep. It is estimated that sleep disorder results in $16 billion a year in lost income, disability, and poor job performance.

Thus the words of Exodus—"My Presence will go with you, and I will give you rest"—should evoke profound appreciation. Daily we should thank God for the gift of rest.

～ Thought for the Day ～
O sleep, O gentle sleep,
Nature's soft nurse!
William Shakespeare

You Have the Power to Make a Difference

What do you mean by crushing my people
and grinding the faces of the poor?
Isaiah 3:15

"As I view the vastness of world hunger and contrast it with the small-ness of my resources, I become frustrated," says one man in a conversation with friends about helping alleviate world hunger abroad and homelessness at home. It is a frustration experienced by many people. Yet all of us have the power to make a difference. Here's how:

- *Begin by asking the right question.* The crucial question concerning world hunger and homelessness is not "What can I do?" but "When can I start doing it?" Of course, the answer is: "Now!"

- *Identify an organization for your support.* There are many worthwhile organizations that provide emergency assistance, famine relief, food and shelter for homeless persons. Carefully select one you want to support for a one-year period.

- *Establish an amount to give.* Carefully review your finances. Talk with your family, and together decide how much to contribute. And stretch yourself a little. This may mean sacrificing, by reducing the number of times you eat at restaurants or attend sporting or theater events.

- *Be methodical.* During the time you set aside to pay monthly bills, be sure to write a check to that organization. Make these payments monthly just like you pay utility bills month after month.

- *Pray as you give.* Thank God that you have discretionary income that you are able to donate. Pray for those who will distribute the funds. Especially pray for the people who will receive the aid. Be sure to pray not only for their physical health but also their spiritual well-being.

- *Consider ways to get others involved.* A wonderful way to expand your effort is by getting others involved in a similar pattern of giving. Challenge other family members, or those in your community or church, to set up a similar giving plan.

❧ Thought for the Day ❧
The only safe rule is to give more than we can spare. Our
charities should pinch and hamper us. If we live at the
same level of affluence as other people who have our level
of income, we are probably giving away too little.
C. S. Lewis

Walking the True Spiritual Path

To do what is right and just is more acceptable
to the Lord than sacrifice.

Proverbs 21:3

A woman tells of the many learning opportunities she was privileged to receive on her spiritual journey. She attended religious grade schools and was taught by dedicated, loving sisters and priests.

Selecting a religious college, she was further exposed to a substantial education grounded in theology and philosophy, as well as liberal arts. Many of her professors were not only outstanding scholars but exemplary Christians as well.

Over the course of her life, wonderful spiritual reading was recommended and readily available for her. "I read from classics—Saint John of the Cross and Augustine—as well as works by contemporary spiritual writers—Fulton Sheen and Mother Teresa. I read about lives of the saints and benefited by learning more about Teresa of Ávila, Mother Cabrini, and Julian of Norwich." In addition, attending retreats, seminars, and Bible-study groups all inspired and enriched her life.

Recently, however, the woman came upon a new revelation. The great body of learning could be expressed in one simple but profound sentence. In a small craft shop she saw that sentence on a sign posted near the owner's desk. It read: "If you don't live it, you don't believe it."

~≈ Prayer for the Day ≈~
Loving God,
Day by day let
my deeds match my creeds,
my beliefs match my behavior.
Let me faithfully live out what I believe.

VMP

Being a Blessing to the Nation

Righteousness exalts a nation.
Proverbs 14:34

A nation is only as good and as strong as its individual citizens. Therefore, good citizenship begins in the heart and in the home. Here are questions to use for an examination of conscience in order to determine if our "righteousness" will "exalt" this nation.

- Do I respect other members in my family and my circle of friends?
- Do I routinely show acts of kindness to others, both inside and outside my circle of family and friends?
- Do I cooperate with family members and others in the broader community in sharing responsibilities and working for peace and justice?
- Do I show promptness in meeting obligations? Do I keep my word? Am I faithful to my responsibilities?
- Do others view me as dependable? Am I a person who can be counted upon?
- Do I take advantage of my right to vote, voting in every election that comes along—national, state, and local?
- Do I model and exemplify good citizenship for my children, family, friends, colleagues?

Prayerfully review the list of questions grading yourself with either an "S" (Satisfactory) or "NI" (Needs Improvement). Then resolve to make the changes necessary to become a greater blessing to your community and nation.

❧ *Prayer for the Day* ❧
Eternal and loving God,
May I be a great source of
blessing to those around me.
Let my words,
my deeds,
my life be a daily source of
inspiration, comfort, encouragement, and hope.
Let me be a blessing in my community and to my country.
VMP

Making Thankfulness a Daily Habit

Give thanks to him.
Psalm 100:4

Author and educator Leo Buscaglia, Ph.D., tells of an important lesson learned from a Buddhist teacher he had while living in Thailand. The Buddhist often reminded his students that there was always something to be thankful for. As an example, one day he dismissed his class saying:

"Let's rise and be thankful, for if we didn't learn a lot today, at least we may have learned a little. And if we didn't learn even a little, at least we didn't get sick. And if we did get sick, at least we didn't die. So let us all be thankful."

Like the Buddhist teacher, today's Jewish writer of Psalm 100 offers similar instruction: "Give thanks to him." The psalmist does not specify what we are to be thankful for. Perhaps the writer's intent was for us to exercise our own imagination about expressing gratitude.

One way to tap into the power of gratitude is by expressing thanks every time we pay a bill.

For example, when writing a check to the electric or telephone company, pause to be thankful for all the ways in which our lives are made more comfortable by the fact that the company regularly and reliably provides us with its services. Or, when writing the monthly mortgage or rent check, pause to be thankful that we have a comfortable place in which to live; that our spouses and children have shelter and comfort. When paying off the water bill, stop to think about how convenient it is to simply turn on a faucet and enjoy water. It was not that long ago when our ancestors had to pump water from a well in the winter and worry about it becoming dry in the summer.

The Buddhist teacher is quite correct. There are many, many reasons for us to be thankful. Let us take heed and make thankfulness a daily habit.

❧ *Affirmation for the Day* ❧
God is so generous.
I am the recipient of God's great generosity.
God's abundance flows over me every day.
VMP

Wisely Guiding Others

Those who are wise will shine like the
brightness of the heavens.

Daniel 12:3

A noble goal for every spiritual person is the cultivation of wisdom. Our combined life experiences—the good and the bad—should always make us wiser. And when we are, others in a dilemma will often seek us out for guidance. Are we ready to respond with wisdom?

A dramatic and powerful example comes via a Polish couple living through war-torn Europe in the 1940s. One night, a young woman escaped from the Jewish ghetto and knocked at their door. Although she was Jewish and the couple were Catholic Christians, prior to the Nazi invasion the three had been friends. The Jewish woman begged the young couple to shelter her son, Stanley, who was just two.

Because the couple had no children of their own, they knew suddenly harboring a child would be dangerous. It would mean living on the run for the rest of the war. However, they agreed; and the mother left her only son with them, along with three letters. The first was for the young Catholic couple asking them to raise Stanley as a Jew. The second was to Stanley telling him of his parents' love for him and why he had to be given up. The third was to be mailed to relatives in America, should the mother not survive the war. Stanley never saw his mother again. Not surprisingly, after four years of running and hiding, the couple became very attached to Stanley.

In 1946 they learned Stanley's mother perished in a death camp. Because of their love for Stanley, they considered adopting him and having him baptized into their Catholic faith. Still, they remembered the mother's urgent request to have Stanley raised as a Jew. They decided to consult with their new priest, a recently ordained young man who already had a reputation for wisdom and compassion. After explaining the circumstances and being told of the mother's final wishes to have Stanley raised Jewish, the priest said, "Baptizing the boy would not be right." Thanks to the priest's advice, the couple made themselves mail the third letter to Stanley's relatives in America. He was adopted and now lives in the United States. The young priest who listened compassionately and offered wise guidance was Karol Wojtyla.

❧ Thought for the Day ❧
Knowledge is a process of piling up facts;
wisdom lies in their simplification.
Martin H. Fischer

The Power of Faithfulness

Know therefore that the Lord your God is God;
he is the faithful God, keeping his covenant of
love to a thousand generations.

Deuteronomy 7:9

Today's scripture reminds us of God's permanent love for us. However, there are times when we experience this love of God only after we have been faithful to them. Consider the example of Paula, who says she was raised in a large, devout Catholic family. Although she spent twelve years in Catholic schools and attended Sunday services regularly with the family, Paula adopted a different set of values when she went off to college in the early seventies.

On her twenty-third birthday, her mother tried to nudge Paula back into a healthier direction by giving her a Bible. The inscription read: "To our darling daughter, born on the feast of the Epiphany. Read this Bible, use it, mark whatever appeals to you." Though Paula seldom looked at the Bible, the word *darling* left a strong impression. "I was sure that with my present lifestyle, completely at odds with my mother's values, the last thing she could possibly think of me was darling," Paula recalls thinking.

Not much changed in her life until her twenty-seventh year when Paula needed surgery. While recuperating in the hospital, "I heard God call me. More likely, God had been calling me all along. Now, I was finally quiet enough to listen," Paula said. She began to read the Bible her mother had given her four years earlier. Many passages spoke deeply to her. After leaving the hospital she headed to a local Catholic church. That Sunday she heard the priest say, "God loves you as you are, not as you should be."

Those words drew Paula back to the Church. Later she summoned up the courage to go to confession for the first time since high school. In the presence of a priest, she uttered words she had never spoken aloud before: "I have had an abortion." What happened next will be permanently etched on Paula's mind and soul: "The priest laid his hands on my bowed head, and healing poured through my aching soul."

Paula's return to faith began with a Bible inscribed to "darling." That affectionate expression reminded Paula of her mother's faithfulness to her. "Like my mother who called me 'darling,' my God loved me as I was, so I could become who God wants me to be," she now says.

❧ Thought for the Day ❧
Faithfulness in little things is a big thing.
Saint John Chrysostom

It's Not a Sin to Say "No!"

I loathe my very life.
Job 10:1

The inability to say "no" is a problem for many of us. Unwilling to cause offense or let people down, we keep saying "yes" and accepting task after task until we feel weighed down by the burden of life. When we overcommit, we are left feeling frustrated, unhappy, and even bitter. Like Job we exclaim, "I loathe my very life."

It is worth reminding ourselves that it is not a sin to say "no." In fact, many of us could use lessons in the art of saying "no."

Here are some important rules to follow:

- Say no if you feel uncomfortable with the task—lack of interest, lack of motivation, too busy, or just plain weary.

- Say no if you feel uncomfortable with the request, even though you don't understand why. Trust your intuitive sense.

- Say no if the task will interfere with your family or personal life in a disruptive way.

- Say no if it hinders your spiritual growth in some way.

- Say no if you cannot do the task with an attitude of grateful service.

God needs workers, but they should be willing, happy, joyful, workers. When we do say "yes" it should come from a heart eager and enthusiastic about the task.

～≈ *Prayer for the Day* ≈～
Most merciful God,
Help me to make wise choices.
Strengthen my resolve to say no
when necessary and not feel guilty
for doing so.
VMP

Our Invisible Means of Support

So we fasted and petitioned our God about this,
and he answered our prayer.

Ezra 8:23

There is an old joke often heard in religious circles, and it goes like this: David loved to hike and climb mountains. One day as he was out on the trail alone, he got too close to a precipice, lost his footing, and fell over the edge. Desperately, he grabbed a protruding tree root and hung on for his life. But then he felt the root starting to give way.

"Is anyone up there?" David yelled frantically.

Amazingly, a voice called back to him saying, "Yes, what do you want?"

"Help me, please," David cried.

Again the voice responded, "David, this is God. Do you trust me?"

"What does that have to do with anything? Just help me out, please," David pleaded.

The voice asked again, "David, do you trust me?"

David thought for a moment and shouted back, "Yes, God. I trust you."

"Then let go!"

David considered that command but then yelled out, "Is anyone else up there?"

Surely all of us can identify with David's dilemma. When life is moving smoothly and normally it is easy to trust God. But when life begins to unravel, become complicated and unpleasant, it is harder to truly trust God. When difficulties come our way, we must remind ourselves that we are not left alone in the world; that we have, in God, an invisible means of support. This God can be trusted to strengthen, guide, comfort, and lead moment by moment, hour by hour, day by day, and week by week.

❧ Thought for the Day ❧

All I have seen teaches me to trust the Creator
for all I have not seen.

Ralph Waldo Emerson

Encouraging Your Spiritual Leader

Serve one another in love.
Galatians 5:13

Sometimes the loneliest person in a community is the pastor. Being a spiritual leader can be one of the toughest jobs of all. Often the hours are long, the pay minimal, the criticism considerable and constant. This can all combine to create feelings of disappointment, discouragement, and defeat. We must remember that our spiritual leaders are human and can benefit from our support and encouragement. Here are some suggestions:

- *Pray regularly for your spiritual leader.* Ask God to shower your pastor with an abundance of love, hope, joy, faith, peace, power, wisdom, insight, and courage.

- *Express your appreciation in writing.* A compliment spoken is always welcome, but one that is received in writing can be read over and over again. So when you hear a sermon that was especially helpful or you see an act of compassion and caring from your spiritual leader, say so.

- *Use your skills to make their lives easier.* Are you proficient with computers? Help your pastor master the art of computer use. Are you a mechanic? Offer to service the car free of charge or at a reduced fee. Are you a medical professional? Provide your spiritual leader with care.

- *Squelch any gossip that comes your way.* If you hear a negative comment, respond with a positive one. If misinformation is being spread, correct it. Or, if people are gossiping, just walk away.

- *Minister to your ministers.* Take your spiritual leader out for lunch with no agenda except to truly listen. Ask how he or she is doing and to share dreams, goals, aspirations, fears, and frustrations. Respond with as much warmth, understanding, and support as you can.

By engaging in such acts of love, spiritual leaders will not only be encouraged but will feel appreciated, loved, valued , and continue to minister with enthusiasm and energy.

❧ Prayer for the Day ❧
Loving God,
I thank you for sending gifted spiritual leaders into my life.
I praise you for their wisdom, their compassion,
their intellect, and their love for me and others.
VMP

Using Our Power to Encourage Others

*A word aptly spoken is like apples of gold
in settings of silver.*

Proverbs 25:11

The apple is a traditional gift for a teacher. One woman, who has taught twenty-five years, says she has received countless apples but recently received a very special "apple."

It was the end of the school day. She had been the substitute for a group of fifth graders and was sitting at the front of the classroom, making notes for their regular teacher. The students had been dismissed and most of them had left the room. One of the boys was taking his time getting ready to go, and she soon noticed that he was standing beside her chair, quietly waiting.

She looked up and smiled saying, "Yes, Geoff?"

"Ma'am," he replied. "I'd like to thank you for being such a nice substitute teacher. I really appreciated your kindness today."

The teacher was stunned, surprised, and delighted to hear such words from a fifth-grade boy. "I felt a warmth wash over me from my head to my toes as I said, "Well, thank you very much for saying so, Geoff! That was very nice of you."

They spoke for a few moments and then said good-bye. Although it has now been several years since that encounter, the glow of the boy's words remain in the teacher's heart even to this day. Each time she remembers that incident, she recalls the sentence from the Book of Proverbs: "A word aptly spoken is like apples of gold in settings of silver."

We should remember that all of us have a great power to encourage another. Like that fifth-grade boy, we should seize every and any opportunity to pay a compliment, express appreciation, and praise another person.

❧ *Prayer for the Day* ❧
Loving God,
Make me more and more aware
of daily opportunities to encourage others.
Open my eyes and my heart to the lives
of family, friends, and strangers
whom I can encourage this day.

VMP

Banish the Blues

I loathe my very life.
Job 10:1

"Many people find it hard to believe that I go through down times, too…I feel depressed," said Norman Vincent Peale, the well-known optimist and author of the best-selling book *The Power of Positive Thinking*. The truth is that everyone experiences depression and the blues at one time or another. Even great biblical characters had bouts of depression. Caught in the grips of despair, Moses cried out to God, "Put me to death right now…do not let me face my own ruin" (Numbers 11:15, *The New International Version*). And the prophet Elijah lamented: "I have had enough, Lord…Take my life" (1 Kings 19:4). Although experiencing depression is a universal human condition, no one needs to be victimized by those feelings. Here are some simple but effective ways to banish the blues:

- *Count your blessings*. Make a list of your assets—money, talents, skills, friends, family, possessions, etc. You'll come up with a longer list than you might have imagined. Pause to do this right now.

- *Talk back to your blues*. While it is true that there may be some things wrong in your life, remind yourself of the many things that are good. If you are feeling like a failure, remind yourself of your successes.

- *Help someone else*. Reaching out to another person takes the focus off yourself and your pain. It's hard to be sad while you are building up and encouraging another person through your words and actions.

- *Get physical*. Exercise strengthens both the body and the mind. Various studies show that exercise helps the body produce natural "tranquilizers" that lift the mood. Resolve today to begin a regular exercise program. Find something you could enjoy doing four or five times a week.

- *Break your daily routine*. Do something out of the ordinary. Perhaps your depression comes from boredom. Walk through a park and enjoy the natural setting. Observe closely any of God's creatures—birds, squirrels, or swans floating serenely on a pond.

❧ *Affirmation for the Day* ❧
I choose to be happy and healthy.
I choose to create joyful experiences in my life.
I rejoice in the beauty of my life.
VMP

Remaining Open to Hope

You armed me with strength for battle.
2 Samuel 22:40

We are seldom as weak, ineffective, and vulnerable as we sometimes feel. According to today's text, God arms us with "strength for battle" in life. Because that is true, we must always remain open to hope. Often it is when we are the most discouraged that words of hope come our way. No matter how desperate our circumstances, we must remain open to the power of hope. After singer John Denver died in a plane crash, a woman wrote a letter sharing the life-saving impact the singer had on her life a few years earlier. "I grew up in an abusive home and as a teenager in the early seventies decided that my only way out was suicide." Over the next few months she stockpiled pills from her parents' medicine bottles. Carefully she made plans to take them one evening when she knew her parents would be gone and would not find her until the next day.

On the afternoon of the day she planned to end her life, the woman saw John Denver perform for the first time. She explains what happened: "A certain part from one song hit me like a brick. It spoke of loving the life within and feeling as if I'm part of everything in me and around me. For some reason, those words made me realize I could survive my situation. I'm now in my forties, with a loving husband, two great kids and a busy and rewarding life." Although desperately depressed, that woman managed to remain open to words of hope and they came to her via the words of a John Denver song.

Today, remind yourself that God is present in our difficulty and that God has created us with tremendous capacity to adjust, adapt and advance over any circumstances that come your way.

⤙ *Affirmation for the Day* ⤚
I am strong in body and sound in mind.
I approach problems with optimism and creativity.
I have a wide support system of love from family and friends.
I know where to go for help when it is necessary.
I have faith which sustains me in the darkest times.
VMP

Some Important Things to Remember

Do not put out the Spirit's fire.
1 Thessalonians 5:19

Too many times we limit God's power in our lives because we feel unworthy of love or because we feel God is distant and detached from our situation. We are guilty of putting out "the Spirit's fire." To combat that tendency here are some important things we should always remember:

I will remember…
  to depend on God because
    that is what God wants from me.
I will remember…
  there is no limit on God's mercy
    or my privilege to draw from it.
I will remember…
  that God's love for me
    is permanent and unconditional.
I will remember…
  to trust God in the light
    and in the darkness.
I will remember…
  to remain open to God's guidance.
I will remember…
  to be patient,
    knowing that God will act in the right time.
I will remember…
  that God will give me
    all the insight and strength I need.
I will remember…
  that God has promised good to me.
I will remember…
  to live one day at a time.

❧ Thought for the Day ❧

Each of us is perpetually on the razor's edge;
on the one side, absolute nothingness;
on the other, the fullness of the divine life.
Edith Stein

Find Me Faithful...in My Work

Let us not become weary in doing good, for at the
proper time we will reap a harvest if we do not give up.

Galatians 6:9

Even though many jobs are not high-paying or glamorous, we can add dignity to the task and meaning to our lives by doing the work to the best of our abilities. This lesson proved to be pivotal in the life of Ruth Simmons.

Recently she became the president of Smith College, one of the country's most prestigious institutions of higher learning for women. It was an incredible achievement for a woman who is the great-great-grand-daughter of slaves. Simmons began her journey to Smith on a cotton farm in Grapeland, Texas, where her parents were sharecroppers. Later they moved to an impoverished section of Houston, where her father found work in a factory and her mother scrubbed floors for white families.

When asked how such humble beginnings led to a career at the top of academia, Simmons answers: "I had a remarkable mother. She would sometimes take me with her to work when I was a little girl, and the thing I remember vividly is how good she was at what she did. She was very demanding in terms of her own work. 'Do it well, do it thoroughly, whatever you do,' she'd say."

Simmons' mother continues to influence her work even as president of Smith College. "I know the Smith Board of Trustees thinks I'm trying to live up to the standards they set for me, and that's okay," she says. But Simmons has a higher standard: "Every day that I'm here I try to be the kind of person my mother wanted me to be."

Today, let us remember to practice faithfulness in our work.

❧ Thought for the Day ❧

If a man is called to be a street sweeper,
he should sweep streets even as Michelangelo painted,
or Beethoven composed music, or Shakespeare wrote poetry.
He should sweep streets so well
that all the hosts of heaven and earth will pause to say,
"Here lived a great street sweeper who did his job well."

Martin Luther King, Jr.

Find Me Faithful...in Prayer

They should always pray and not give up.
Luke 18:1

In the Gospel of Luke we are told that Jesus taught a parable to convey this one important lesson for his followers: "That they should always pray and not give up" (Luke 18:1).

That teaching about prayer should nudge us to do a careful examination of conscience:

- Do we truly believe in the power of prayer?
- How often do we pray?
- Are we sincere and serious in our praying?
- Do we include those around us who are hurting?

Larry Dossey, M.D., is an unusual physician because he employs the power of prayer in his medical practice. An incident early in his career alerted him to the power of prayer. At the time, Dossey was doing his residency training in Dallas, Texas. There he had a patient with terminal cancer in both lungs. "I advised him on what therapy was available and what little I thought it would do. Rightly enough, he opted for no treatment," Dossey recalls in his book *Healing Words*. Yet whenever I stopped by his hospital bedside, he was surrounded by visitors from his church, singing and praying. *Good thing*, I thought, *because soon they'll be singing and praying at his funeral.*

A year later, when he was working elsewhere, a colleague from Dallas called asking if Dossey wanted to see his old patient. "See him? I couldn't believe he was still alive," Dossey remembered thinking. Studying his chest x-rays, Dossey was stunned. The man's lungs were completely clear—there was absolutely no sign of cancer. The radiologist, looking over Dossey's shoulder, commented that the man's therapy was remarkable. "*Therapy?* I thought. *There wasn't any—unless you consider prayer.*"

⁓ Thought for the Day ⁓

Let our prayers...ascend morning and evening.
Let our days begin and end with God.
William Ellery Channing

Find Me Faithful...in My Commitments to Others

I don't know the man!
Matthew 26:72

Today's text from the Gospel of Matthew contains the disciple Peter's denial that he was ever associated with Jesus. Filled with fear, Peter responds to others who say he was a follower of Christ with the lie, "I don't know the man!"

It is always disappointing and disillusioning when someone we have counted on does not come through. It is a sad fact of life that not everyone who volunteers for a task completes it. Not everyone who says he or she will do a job actually does it. Many find reasons and excuses not to complete their commitments.

Yet life is pleasantly flavored by those who are dependable; those who fulfill what they agreed to do, even when it requires unexpected sacrifices. In 1947 a professor at the University of Chicago, Subrahmanyan Chandrasekhar, Ph.D., was scheduled to teach an advanced seminar in astrophysics. At the time, he was living in Wisconsin, doing research at the Yerkes Astronomical Observatory. He planned to commute twice a week for the class, even though it would be held during the harsh winter months.

But only two students signed up for the class. People expected Dr. Chandrasekhar to cancel rather than waste his time on such a small class. But for the sake of two students, he taught the class, commuting one hundred miles round trip through back country roads in the dead of winter. His students, Chen Ning Yang and Tsung-Dao Lee, did their homework. Ten years later, they both won the Nobel prize for physics. Dr. Chandrasekhar won the same prize in 1983. The professor demonstrated the rare and remarkable virtue of faithfulness: He could be counted on.

✷ Affirmation for the Day ✷
I am loyal, trustworthy, and responsible.
I give love and receive love.
I am faithful in my commitments to others.
VMP

Find Me Faithful...to Myself

Blessed is the man who perseveres under trial,
because when he has stood the test, he will
receive the crown of life that God has promised.

James 1:12

Another arena of life where many experience faithfulness failure is to themselves. When life sends a setback or delivers a harsh blow, too many people give up on themselves. Rather than remain faithful to their dreams and aspirations, they allow themselves a cheap resignation to fate. Rather than look at what remains, they focus bitterly on what has been lost. In so doing, they often become cynical and leave latent talents undeveloped. However, there are those who do not choose the path of least resistance when faced with major life challenges.

Consider the glowing example of Sarah Reinertsen, who was born in 1975 with only part of her left leg. Even that had to be removed at the hip when she was seven. In spite of being an amputee, the little girl was determined to pursue her interest in athletics. When she was twelve, Sarah began working long, hard hours with her track-and-field coach. Together they developed a new way for an amputee to run. Until then, most above-the-knee amputee runners ran by hopping twice on their good leg, then kicking their artificial leg forward. Sarah was the first to use the new step-over-step method in competitions. She runs by taking one step with each leg, the same way people with two legs run. That new method allows above-the-knee amputees to run much faster. Today Sara Reinertsen is the fastest female above-the-knee-amputee runner in the world. Because she was faithful to herself, she holds world records in the one-hundred-meter and two-hundred-meter runs.

⚘ Thought for the Day ⚘

Is your place a small place?
Tend it with care!—He set you there.
Is your place a large place?
Tend it with care!—He set you there.
Whate'er your place, it is
Not yours alone, but his
Who set you there.

John Oxenham

Using God's Words

Man does not live on bread alone,
but on every word that comes from the mouth of God.
Matthew 4:4

Addressing an advice columnist, a person made this practical suggestion on behalf of families who have lost a loved one or have a family
member who is seriously ill: "Preparing food for the grieving family is
one of the ways to show love and concern. However, I would like to
suggest that the food be sent in disposable containers."

That person further explained that "the last thing families need to
worry about is which dish, platter, or bowl belongs to whom, or how to
return it to the rightful owner." The writer suggested that caregivers
pick up inexpensive disposable containers at stores or shop garage sales
for plastic containers that would not need to be returned. "During difficult times, our efforts should be able to make life as easy and uncompli-
cated as possible," the writer concluded.

Initially, that suggestion seems quite practical and wise. However, a
month later another reader wrote the advice columnist responding with a
higher wisdom. "I would like to offer another opinion to the person who
wrote you advising that food brought to grieving people be brought in
disposable containers or garage-sale castoffs rather than in containers
that need to be returned. "Returning the empty container is the important
part," the writer declared. "It becomes a way for the grieving individual to
have contact with the person who sent the food. That subsequent contact
may be more needed than the food that came in the container. People who
are grieving need contact with others, and this is a good way to get it."

In the text for today, Jesus reminds us that we do not *live on bread
alone, but on every word that comes from the mouth of God.* Quickly, let us
ask, "What are God's words?" The answer: compassion, kindness, mercy,
acceptance, and unconditional love. Food meets only our physical needs.
Spiritual and emotional needs are sustained and nourished when we
receive compassion, kindness, mercy, acceptance, and unconditional love
from God and from others. So let us be deeply sensitive to those around
us who are hungry for God's spirit-nourishing words.

⋙ Prayer for the Day ⋘
Holy God,
Let me be a source of encouragement to others.
Let me be a source of hope to others.
Let me use God's words to help and uplift others.
VMP

Living in the Present

This is the day the Lord has made;
let us rejoice and be glad in it.
Psalm 118:24

Much of our anxiety comes from living in the future. Likewise, much of our depression comes from living in the past. The psalmist's words remind us to live in the present. Here are some guiding thoughts on living for today:

Just for today...
I will count my blessings not my burdens.
Just for today...
I will change what can be changed.
Just for today...
I will accept what cannot be changed.
Just for today...
I will adjust to new challenges.
Just for today...
I will do something positive for myself.
Just for today...
I will reach out and touch someone with kindness and compassion.
Just for today...
I will take the first steps toward overcoming life hurts.
Just for today...
I will do something that I have been delaying.
Just for today...
I will be optimistic and hopeful.
Just for today...
I will not dwell on negatives nor entertain despair.
Just for today...
I will remind myself that my cup is half full and not half empty.
Just for today...
I will not magnify problems.
Just for today...
I will imagine a good future.
Just for today...
I will live for these twenty-four hours
and not worry about the future.

❧ Thought for the Day ❧
It ain't no use putting up your umbrella till it rains.
Alice Caldwell Rice

Being Lifelong Students of Prayer

Lord, teach us to pray.
Luke 11:1

Prayer is a lifelong discipline. When we become discouraged with our prayers and our prayer life, let us remember that even the disciples of Jesus began as untutored in the school of prayer. *Lord, teach us to pray,* one asked.

A good place to begin and a good place to reinforce the importance of prayer is to look at the life of Jesus. He is the model of prayer and spirituality. Every great event of his life was first bathed in prayer. Note these examples:

Jesus prayed at the time of his baptism: "When all the people were being baptized, Jesus was baptized too. And as he was praying, heaven was opened up..." (Luke 3:21).

Jesus prayed at his transfiguration: "As he was praying, the appearance of his face changed and his clothes became as bright as a flash of lightning..." (Luke 9:28–29).

Jesus prayed before his crucifixion: "Now my heart is troubled....Father, glorify your name" (John 12:27–28).

Jesus prayed from the cross: "Father, forgive them, for they do not know what they are doing" (Luke 23:34).

Here is the lesson from Jesus' life:

- If prayer was such a profound part of Jesus' life, should it not be just as profound a part of our lives?

- If prayer was such a source of comfort in Jesus' life, can it not become a similar source of comfort in our lives?

- If prayer was such a point of depth spirituality in Jesus' life, will it not also increase the depth of our spirituality?

❧ Thought for the Day ❧
I have been driven many times to my knees by the overwhelming
conviction that I had nowhere else to go.
My own wisdom, and that of all about me,
seemed insufficient for the day.
Abraham Lincoln

Spiritual Attitudes Help Defy Aging

Love your neighbor as yourself.
Matthew 22:39

Recently a major life-insurance company carried out a survey of its policyholders who had lived to be one hundred years or more. One of the questions asked was, "What is the most important thing you've learned in your long life?"

The most frequent answer: *Love your neighbor as yourself.*

Let us examine that response, asking how it relates to the longer life span enjoyed by those who have that spiritual philosophy of life.

First of all, people who live according to that great commandment are almost certain to live longer than those who don't because they have freed themselves from deadly negative emotions, such as anger, hatred, suspicion, jealousy, guilt, anxiety, and so on.

Second, because they are free from those negative emotions, these people are certain to have more vitality, more eagerness, more energy, more joy, and, therefore, increased resistance to disease.

Third, those who truly "love their neighbors" are bound to experience greater life fulfillment, greater meaning, and greater satisfaction than those who do not live by that spiritual philosophy. Again, feeling content and at one with the universe is bound to lead to better health.

Today let us consider how we can intentionally live by Jesus' command to love God and to love our neighbors as ourselves.

⤳ *Thought for the Day* ⤶
If my heart is right with God, every human
being is my neighbor.
Oswald Chambers

Leaving the Land of Look Behind

Do not throw away your confidence.
Hebrews 10:35

Our past need not control our future. Consider the lesson and insight from the following story.

A tourist was visiting the lush, tropical island of Jamaica. In the hotel where he was staying, there was map that hung in one of the hallways. In a corner of the map there was some faint lettering over an almost uninhabited part of the island. Looking closely, the tourist could make out the words *The Land of Look Behind.*

Intrigued, he asked the hotel manager what those words meant. The manager explained they came from the days of slavery on the island. At that time slaves would escape and run away from sugar plantations where they were forced to work long hours in the scorching heat.

Their destination was the uninhabited part of the island. Although they could enjoy relative safety in that wilderness, the runaway slaves were constantly looking over their shoulders in fear to see who was coming after them.

Hence, the name for that part of the island: *The Land of Look Behind.*

Too many of us live in the *Land of Look Behind.* We waste tremendous energies living in a time of past mistakes, regrets, and painful experiences. All that emotional looking back effectively prevents us from looking ahead with confidence, hope, and anticipation of a good future.

Let us remember…our past need not control our future.

Let us be open to new possibilities, rewarding experiences, fulfilling relationships.

Let us know that God is constantly doing a new thing.

❧ Thought for the Day ❧

Look not mournfully to the past
—it comes not back again;
wisely improve the present
—it is thine;
go forth to meet the shadowy future without fear
and with a [courageous] heart.
Henry Wadsworth Longfellow

Turning to Prayer, Not Despair

The Lord will rescue me from every evil attack.
2 Timothy 4:18

No one is ultimately free from pain.

No life journey passes through only calm waters—storms lurk and strike.

Every day someone faces a challenge…

- Health fails
- A baby dies
- A factory closes
- A business folds
- A plane crashes
- A tornado devastates a community
- A wife learns her husband is having an affair
- A bike accident results in permanent paralysis
- A man comes home to find his wife has left him
- A teenager drinks, drives, and dies, leaving behind hundreds of grievers

The list of suffering that comes to people can be endless and raises the question: How do we respond?

Some people turn to despair…but those who know God turn to prayer.

Despair simply accelerates the downward spiral; prayer breaks it and is a motivating force that empowers us to ultimately turn tragedy into triumph.

When a crisis comes our way, let us remember to turn to prayer, not despair.

～ Thought for the Day ～

God whispers to us in our pleasures, speaks in our conscience,
but shouts in our pains; it is his megaphone to rouse a deaf world.
C. S. Lewis

God Knows Our Needs
Before We State Them

Before a word is on my tongue you know it completely.
Psalm 139:4

"Carolyn, you have cerebral malaria." That frightening statement was made by a physician to a missionary serving in Cambodia since 1988.

"I was shocked; but at least I knew then why I was so ill," Carolyn recalls. For days she had experienced spiking fevers, chills, vomiting, and diarrhea. Her strength was waning rapidly and she required constant rest. Carolyn knew she needed medical care, but there were no physicians, clinics, or hospitals in the Cambodian community where she was serving.

However, she knew of an Australian physician in a nearby community and sought his advice. He made arrangements for blood tests the following morning. The first tests were negative for malaria, but positive for amebic dysentery. The doctor gave Carolyn medication, saying she should feel better in a few days.

Instead she got worse. Within two days she could not walk without help. More blood tests were taken. Late that afternoon the doctor came to her home saying she had cerebral malaria. His prognosis was grim. The mortality rate for cerebral malaria is nearly 100 percent. The physician said a new medicine had recently been introduced on the market, but there seemed little possibility of it being available in Cambodia. Carolyn considered an emergency flight to Bangkok, Thailand, but there were no scheduled flights for four more days.

As she considered her limited options, Carolyn remembered that a group of American guests had left a small bag of medicine with her *two months earlier*. Examining the contents she was stunned to discover the very medicine she needed. *How could it be that the newest treatment available for cerebral malaria—not commonly known and very expensive—would be in a bag of medicine left by visitors?* she wondered. "Only God could have made such provision!"

Today's declaration from the psalmist is one of confidence in God. God's presence and power is so pervasive that our needs are known before we state them—*Before a word is on my tongue you know it completely.*

∼ Thought for the Day ∼
God is a circle whose center is everywhere,
and its circumference nowhere.
Empedocles

Placing Our Trust in God Alone

My soul finds rest in God alone.
Psalm 62:1

Recently, a family traveling together on vacation were involved in a serious automobile accident. While the husband and two sons were not injured, the wife was severely hurt. Gail was rushed to the hospital, where for several days her life hung by a thread.

Gail survived the accident. But when she recalled the days afterward, she said that as she lay in the intensive-care unit she could think only of her boys, her husband, Sam, and her God. As her condition worsened and her alertness dimmed in and out, she could think only of Sam and God. Then as her energy dropped even more, in her weakest moment all she could think of was God alone.

Gail's experience brings to mind the words of the psalmist, *My soul finds rest in God alone.* The text continues to read: "He alone is my rock and my salvation; he is my fortress, I will never be shaken" (62:2). The word "alone" is used several more times in this psalm and prompts us to raise these personal, spiritual questions:

- How often do we put our trust in God, plus our job?

- How often do we put our trust in God, plus our lawyer?

- How often do we place our trust in God, plus our insurance plans?

- How often do we place our trust in God, plus our family and friends?

- How often do we place our trust in God, plus our savings and checking accounts?

Of course there is nothing wrong with having a job, insurance, family, friends, and bank accounts. In fact, these are all good and necessary.

Yet the psalmist reminds us that our ultimate hope and trust must be in God *alone*. Family and friends may disappoint us; jobs can be eliminated; insurance may not pay; and financial resources can be depleted.

✑ Thought for the Day ✑
How often we look upon God as our last and feeblest resource!
We go to him because we have nowhere else to go.
And then we learn that the
storms of life have driven us
not upon the rocks but into the desired haven.
George Macdonald

Seeking Out Counsel

In abundance of counselors there is victory.
Proverbs 24:6 (*Revised Standard Version*)

After several years of trying to persuade grocers to carry his new brand of popcorn called *Red Bow*, the creator was deeply discouraged. *Was I, at the age of sixty-three, pursuing a foolish dream?* he wondered as he drove gloomily back to his Valparaiso, Indiana, office. *Were his many years of researching, cultivating, and perfecting the new, better popping corn leading him to a marketing dead end*, he wondered. Whenever he approached a retailer, their comments were always the same: "There are over eighty different brands of popcorn on the market. We don't have room for another, especially when it costs two-and-a-half times as much."

Because every response he got from retailers over the previous four years was negative, he became deeply discouraged. However, the man was a committed Christian and a lifelong Sunday school teacher. In his discouragement he turned to his Bible for guidance. Thumbing through its pages he came across these words from Proverbs 24:6: "For by wise guidance you can wage your war, and in abundance of counselors there is victory"(*RSV*). Those words prompted him to try another approach. This time he asked around for the name of a good marketing company. "A few days later I traveled to Chicago to seek guidance from my chosen counselors," he recalls. After describing his new popping corn to the copywriters at the Chicago marketing firm, they recommended the product be marketed as *Orville Redenbacher's Gourmet Popping Corn*. In addition, they said, his picture should be featured on the label.

Still uncertain, Redenbacher decided to test market their idea. He approached the largest retailer in the midwest: Marshall Field's department store in Chicago. After learning the name of the manager of their gourmet food department, Redenbacher sent a case of the product to his home, but did not enclose a note or return address. A month later he telephoned the manager and asked, "Did you like it?"

"Like it?" the manager responded. "We want to stock it!"

Today Orville Redenbacher's product is the best-selling popcorn in the world. The lesson from his story: *In the abundance of counselors there is victory.* When we don't quite know what to do next, we should seek a second opinion from those with experience and wisdom.

∼≫ Prayer for the Day ≫∼
Loving God, keep my mind and heart open
to wisdom from other people.
VMP

You're Never Too Old to Start an Adventure

There was also a prophetess, Anna...
she was very old.

Luke 2:36

The account in Luke's Gospel speaks of Anna, a prophetess who was eighty-four years old. In spite of her age she was very active with her house of worship and provided spiritual leadership.

Attitude is ageless. Our attitudes are capable of determining whether we will go forward or retreat, continue on or quit, remain open to new opportunities or remain frozen in the past. To achieve success, whatever your age, begin by remembering you're never too old to succeed. History is filled with "old" people who accomplished great things. Motivate yourself by reviewing the lives of people such as

Abraham, whom God called to be Israel's first great leader, was seventy-five when he began his mission (see Genesis 12).

Winston Churchill, who became British prime minister *for the first time* at age sixty-five and assumed the epic struggle against Hitler.

Golda Meir, who became prime minister of Israel at seventy-one.

Cardinal Angelo Roncalli, who became Pope John XXIII at the age of seventy-six and inaugurated major changes in the Roman Catholic Church.

Grandma Moses, who started painting in her late seventies and who had her first one-woman exhibit when she was eighty.

Margaret Thatcher, who became Britain's first female prime minister at age fifty-three.

Sadie and Bessie Delany, who wrote their first book when they were 105 and 103, respectively. Titled *The Delany Sisters Book of Everyday Wisdom*, it was a bestseller.

Samuel I. Hayakawa, who was elected to the United States Senate at age seventy.

Remember that your best years may still lie ahead of you.

❧ *Affirmation for the Day* ❧
I begin every day with gratitude and joy.
I look forward with enthusiasm to this, a new day.
I am capable of accepting new challenges and opportunities.
VMP

Follow Your Dreams

Your young…will see visions,
your old…will dream dreams.
                    Joel 2:28

These words remind us that God is continually giving us new dreams and hopes. Be true to your highest aspirations. Faithfully follow your dreams. Doing so will ensure that you maximize your opportunities and minimize your obstacles. One of the most remarkable individuals of the late twentieth century was Grace Hopper. Born in 1906 she earned a master's degree in 1930 and a doctorate in 1934 from Yale University. Both degrees were in mathematics—and earned in spite of the many voices that assured her she could not work in a "man's field."

In 1943, Hopper joined the U.S. Navy. When the war ended, she tried to remain on active duty but was considered "too old" at age thirty-nine. However, Hopper managed to retain her commission in the naval reserves. Over the next few decades, Hopper did pioneering work designing early generations of computers. By 1955, Hopper created and standardized a computer programming language called COBOL (Common Business Oriented Language). All the while, she continued serving in the naval reserves, harboring a dream to bring the U.S. military into the computer age. A sad day in her life was December 1966, when she mandatorily retired from the Navy at the age of sixty.

However, the United States was engaged in the Vietnam conflict, and the Navy was having problems with the computer systems it was using. Eight months after her retirement, Hopper was "temporarily" recalled to active duty. Her mission: to reorganize in six months all the Navy's computers so they could work smoothly together. Hopper spent the next two decades(!) promoting computer use and educating military personnel in computer functions. Because of her age, every promotion awarded to Hopper took a special act of Congress. She was made captain in 1973. In November 1985, when Hopper was seventy-nine years of age, she was elevated to rear admiral, the first woman to hold that rank. Finally, just before her eightieth birthday, Admiral Grace Hopper officially retired with the satisfaction that her dreams had become a reality.

⚜ Thought for the Day ⚜
Never look down to test the ground
before taking your next step:
only he who keeps his eye fixed on the far horizon
will find his right road.
Dag Hammarskjöld

Just Try Asking

...everyone who asks receives.
Matthew 7:8

We are always under the eye of a loving and kind God. That is why Jesus makes two simple but profound statements: *Ask and it will be given to you* (Matthew 7:7) and *Everyone who asks receives.*

However, many times we fail to follow this simple command. Perhaps pride keeps us from asking. Perhaps we do not truly believe that what we ask for will be given. Yet let us take Jesus at his word and simply ask.

Let us...

- Ask God to guide when we are confused.
- Ask God to provide when we lack.
- Ask God to heal where there is illness.
- Ask God to comfort where there is sorrow.
- Ask God to strengthen for a hard task.
- Ask God to lead where the paths diverge.
- Ask God to watch over our rebellious child.
- Ask God to fortify our relationship with another.
- Ask God to open new doors.
- Ask God to transform a negative into a positive.

⁓ *Thought for the Day* ⁓
God has led.
God will lead.
God is leading.
Richard Halverson

Bouncing Back From Defeat

The Lord gave David victory.
2 Samuel 8:6

Never allow a setback of any kind to disrupt your overall plans and goals. Remind yourself that life is not a straight-line pattern, moving you from success to success. Rather, life is often two steps forward and one step backward. Bounce back whenever you experience a difficulty or defeat.

To find out why some ordinary people often seem to achieve so much more than others, Dr. Alan Loy McGinnis, a corporate consultant and author, interviewed over 190 women and men. He discovered that common to the high achievers is the ability of bouncing back from defeat.

As an example, he cites the case a woman who joined a major cosmetics company as senior director of marketing for European designer fragrances. After only seven months, she was let go as part of corporate downsizing. "It was like somebody had punched me in the nose," she recalls.

A month later, a publishing friend asked for advice on selling advertising to the beauty industry. The woman saw an opportunity to provide the same service for other companies. The result: Within three years she was working out of her apartment, supplying that advice to major companies; and she is making an income similar to what she earned at the cosmetics company. Additionally, she has the pleasure of being her own boss. "Getting laid off forces you to be creative," she says. "It lights a fire under you."

As we face life's challenges, let us resolve to bounce back from every defeat. Let us remember that just as God gave David victory, the same God will give us victories.

❧ *Thought for the Day* ❧
God governs the world, and we have only to do
our duty wisely and leave the issue to him.
John Jay Chapman

Help Bear Someone's Burden

He went to him and bandaged his wounds.
Luke 10:34

When suffering is shared by others, its impact is downsized and re-duced to a manageable level. When suffering is shared by others, the harsh blows of life are softened. The changes and chances of life can be better dealt with when others join in and share the burden.

Let us remember these things about burden-bearing:

- To share a burden is to extend spiritual generosity.
- No burden is too heavy when shared by another.
- Sharing a burden tells the person he or she is known, valued, and loved.
- God demands this level of caring.
- Sharing a burden means transcending human inclinations.

⁓ *Thought for the Day* ⁓
There cannot be a more glorious object in creation
than a human being replete with benevolence,
meditating in what manner he may render himself
most acceptable to the Creator by doing good
to his creatures.
Henry Fielding

The Power of Encouragement

My purpose is that they may be encouraged in heart.
Colossians 2:2

"It had been a day filled with small-scale crises," Janet recalls. Her three children, all under the age of six, seemed to be fighting and crying constantly. As she stepped out of her van to pick up one of the children from preschool, she asked herself, "Was it worth it?"

Janet had a college education and had been working as a reporter with a major newspaper for nearly twelve years when God blessed her and her husband with the first pregnancy. Janet and her husband decided she would stay home to be with the children.

"On many days I felt society was telling me to maintain my independence, to define my self-worth by a paycheck. And yet, here I was, home with three preschoolers. Was I doing the right thing?" she wondered that day.

As those discouraging thoughts raced through her mind, an older woman came up to Janet. Her granddaughter was in Janet's daughter's class and they had spoken briefly on other occasions. The older woman greeted Janet with a large smile saying, "You must be a natural-born mother."

"Just the way she said it lifted my sagging spirits. This woman, a mother herself, saw what was important to me: happy, healthy, well-loved children. God had sent a messenger to remind me and to reassure me that, yes, I was doing the right thing—for my family and for me."

Let us have as our daily purpose to provide sincere words of encouragement to the many people who cross our paths.

~≈ *Thought for the Day* ≈~
Perhaps only a smile, a little visit, or simply the fact of building
a fire for someone, writing a letter for a blind person, bringing
a few coals, finding a pair of shoes, reading for someone,
this is only a little bit, yes, a very tiny bit,
but it will be our love
of God in action.
Mother Teresa of Calcutta

Cultivating the Virtue of Loyalty

A friend loves at all times.
Proverbs 17:17

Some problems cause deep shame and embarrassment. When a person is…

>   forced to declare bankruptcy,
>   abandoned by a spouse,
>   fired,
>   divorced,
>   recently separated,
>   sued,
>   charged with a crime,
>   incarcerated.

Such life events almost always produce great feelings of humiliation. They are the times when people need a friend. Let us reclaim the virtues of loyalty and devotion to friends. Let us resolve not to abandon people in their time of trouble. Let us stand by our friends. In so doing, we will minimize their sense of shame, while creating the emotional climate for their self-respect to grow and flourish.

∼ Thought for the Day ∼
Real friendship is shown in times of trouble;
prosperity is full of friends.
Euripedes

Bending Our Attitudes to Fit the Facts

The discerning heart seeks knowledge.
Proverbs 15:14

During World War II, a young American lieutenant was stationed in England. Their bomber bases, hacked out of the sodden English countryside, were seas of mud. "On the ground, people were cold , miserable, and homesick. In the air, people were getting shot. Replacements were few, morale was low," the man recalls.

However, there was one sergeant—a crew chief—who was already cheerful, always good-humored, and always smiling. The lieutenant was intrigued by his positive attitude and observed him one day as the sergeant struggled in a freezing rain to salvage a plane that had skidded off the runway into an apparently bottomless mire. He was whistling cheerfully. "Sergeant, how can you whistle in a mess like this?" the man asked. The sergeant gave him a mudcaked grin, saying, "Lieutenant, when the facts won't budge, you have to bend your attitudes to fit the facts. That's all there is to it."

The sergeant's words are good advice when we are feeling upset and despondent: *When the facts won't budge, you have to bend your attitude to fit the facts.* Because we cannot always reverse the pains and problems of life, we must adjust our attitudes in order to manage and grow.

⚭ Affirmation for the Day ⚭
I will accept this challenge.
I will vividly examine the future.
I am open to new possibilities.
I am willing to expand, grow, and learn.
VMP

Pushing Back Our Fears

Do not be afraid. Stand firm.
Exodus 14:14

Day after day, James, an impoverished farm boy, sat silently at his desk in the one-room schoolhouse, pretending to be mute, dodging the eyes of his teachers and classmates. When asked a question he would hang his head or respond with a written note—anything to avoid a verbal response. The youth was terrified of speaking in public because of his affliction: stuttering. He lived that way until high school when a teacher asked the students to write a poem. The young man wrote one that deeply impressed his teacher. Applying some psychology, the instructor read the poem with approval, but remarked, "I don't believe you wrote this, James. There's only one way to prove it," he said to the silent stutterer, "recite it from memory in front of the class."

Stung and challenged by the suggestion, the teenager stood and recited the poem aloud—without a stutter and in a voice that stunned his fellow students with its deep, full-throated power. That was the turning point in the life of James Earl Jones. Brimming with a new self-confidence, Jones enrolled at the University of Michigan where he majored in English and theater. He went on to appear in various Broadway productions and became the legendary voice to one of film's most famous villains, Darth Vader, in George Lucas's *Star Wars* trilogy.

Today James Earl Jones is heard all over the world as the voice that dramatically intones, "This is CNN," just before all the cable network's station breaks. Jones found his voice and released the talent locked inside because he accepted a challenge and said "good-bye" to fear.

Many people miss grand opportunities and fail to achieve their potential because they are afraid. There are many fears that can control and squeeze the life out of an individual: the fear of flying, the fear of speaking in public, the fear of change, the fear of education, the fear of commitment, the fear of intimacy, and so on. Fear is a powerful emotion—one that can be a person's greatest handicap.

Yet the Bible makes clear that God's people are not to live in fear—*Do not be afraid. Stand firm.* Let us reflect on those words and claim them the next time we face a fearful situation.

⚜ Affirmation for the Day ⚜
God gives me strength for every task.
God gives me courage for every situation.
God gives me power to persevere.
VMP

Ask Yourself: "Do I Have a Thinking Problem?"

Do not be afraid…I am your shield.
Genesis 15:1

The way we think impacts directly upon our acting and living. How we think can make us courageous, inventive, and expansive or it can make us timid, hesitant, and reluctant. Ask yourself if you are letting fear rule your life and hold you back because you are thinking this way:

- I would like to do it, but I don't have the training.
- I would like to do it, but I don't have the experience.
- I would like to do it, but I don't have the ability.
- I would like to do it, but I don't have the energy.
- I would like to do it, but I don't know the right people.

Each of those statements is a self-defeating attitude. People who conquer fear eliminate such sentences from their thinking. They adopt the view that anything is possible and barriers are meant to be overcome. They live by the deep truth of today's text: *Do not be afraid…I am your shield.*

A good example is Heather Whitestone, twenty-one, who became the first deaf Miss America. Whitestone lost her hearing at eighteen months of age after a reaction to a diphtheria-pertussis-tetanus shot. In spite of her disability, she competed in the Miss America contest, doing a two-and-a-half minute ballet routine.

Although she could not hear the music, she danced by feeling the vibrations, counting the beats in her head, and synchronizing her dance moves to reflect changes in pitch. It was a soaring performance that brought tears to the eyes of many people in the audience. Later she told reporters her mother constantly reminded her as a child that the last four letters of "American" spell "I can."

～ Thought for the Day ～
The most handicapped person in the world is a negative thinker.
Heather Whitestone

Small Steps Conquer Mountains

The Lord is with us. Do not be afraid...
Numbers 14:9

Rather than allowing yourself to be paralyzed by fear, try taking one small step forward.

Consider Alice, forty-three, who had always wanted to earn an undergraduate degree. However, she married right out of high school, had three children, and remained home to be with them.

"All through my thirties I debated with myself about returning to school. After being out for so long, it was terribly frightening to think about being a student again. When my youngest left home for college, I decided it was my time. But I began by taking one class at a local community college. Initially, I was intimidated by the thought of books, teachers, and tests, but quickly established a comfort level. I was thrilled to earn an A in my first course and have continued on to complete a bachelor's degree."

Alice is now finding fulfillment as an elementary-school teacher. It all began because she confronted her fear and took one small step forward.

Conquer fear by taking small steps.

Here are some thoughts that can help overcome fear:

• God is with you.

• Fear is like a bad habit which can be broken.

• Others have faced and overcome fears, therefore, so can you.

⚛ Thought for the Day ⚛
Do the thing you fear
and the death of fear is certain.
Ralph Waldo Emerson

The Power of Words

Let your conversation be always full of grace.
Colossians 4:6

James tells of his mother's great ability to knit. She never attended a meeting without a ball of yarn and a sweater in progress. James remembers the beautiful, bright red cable-knit sweater she carefully made for him the Christmas he was in seventh grade. Delighted and proud of his mother's work, James wore it to school. There a boy looked it over critically and declared, "It looks like a girl's sweater." James never wore the sweater out of the house again.

Patti was in the eighth grade and a member of a very popular group in their junior high school. She and her friends came from affluent families. Every Friday night they gathered at the country club to drink sodas and enjoy dancing. Patti was often the first of her friends calling others before school to see what everyone would be wearing.

One day a teacher asked her to stay after school. When they were alone, the teacher asked Patti if she had ever heard of India's caste system. Patti said no, so the teacher drew some line figures on the blackboard. She explained that a Brahmin, in the top caste, could not even allow an Untouchable's shadow to fall on him. "You and your friends," the teacher said sadly, "remind me of those Brahmins."

Patti showed no emotion at the time, but the teacher's words impacted her deeply. She was shocked to be perceived as a person who *excluded* others. Prior to that conversation Patti never thought about the way she and her friends affected those who didn't belong to the popular crowd. That brief conversation changed Patti's life. Today—twenty years later—she is the most *inclusive* person in her circle of friends.

Our words have great power. They can heal or hurt, injure or inspire, motivate or manipulate. Therefore, it is a vital spiritual discipline that we pay careful attention to how we speak and what we say. The biblical admonition cited above reads this way in *The Living Bible*: "Let your conversation be gracious as well as sensible."

❧ Thought for the Day ❧
Good words are worth much and cost little.
George Herbert

Unclaimed Treasures

Praise the Lord, O my soul, and forget not all his benefits.
He forgives all my sins and heals all my diseases,
he redeems my life from the pit and
crowns me with love and compassion.

Psalm 103:2–4

Because God is a God of everlasting blessings and benefits, mercies and marvels, there is no reason for…

> Needs to be unmet,
>> Hurts to continue festering,
>> Wounds to remain raw,
>> Memories to stay damaged…
> Grace not to be joyfully received,
>> Forgiveness to be withheld,
>> Life to feel unfulfilled,
>> Fear to rule…
> Resentment to grow,
>> Joy to be stifled,
>> The past to be haunting,
>> The future to be fearful…

Claim the power and promise of God to shower you with abundant blessings.

❧ Affirmation for the Day ❧

God's abundant love washes over me.
God's abundant peace flows over me.
God's abundant healing cleanses me.

VMP

Taming the Monster of Impatience

Love is patient...
1 Corinthians 13:4

The humorous story is told of a young woman whose car stalled at a stoplight. She tried to get it started, but nothing happened.

As the light turned green, she sat there frustrated and angry for holding up traffic. The car behind her could easily have gone around her, but instead the driver added to her frustration by blowing his horn constantly and loudly.

Desperately she made several more attempts to start her car. All that time, the driver behind her continued to blow his horn.

Finally, the woman got out of her car walked back to the honker. The man rolled down his window in surprise.

"Tell you what," she said. "You go start my car, and I'll sit back here and honk the horn for you."

That little bit of humor is a good reminder that all of us need to tame the monster of impatience. We need to be much, much more patient with children, spouse, family, friends, and even strangers.

It is worth remembering that patience is a characteristic of God. In Exodus 34:6 we read that God is a "compassionate and gracious God, slow to anger, abounding in love and faithfulness."

Let us resolve to touch others with the divine characteristic of patience.

❧ *Thought for the Day* ❧
Patience is the companion of wisdom.
Saint Augustine of Hippo

Let the Past Be a Guidepost, Not a Hitching Post

One thing I do: Forgetting what is behind
and straining toward what is ahead,
I press on toward the goal.

Philippians 3:14

Today's scripture is a reminder that we should learn from the past, but not dwell on it.

Unhappy people are often prisoners of the past. Psychologically, emotionally, and spiritually they let the past be a hitching post, holding them back rather than a guidepost pointing them to a better future.

However, the movement from sadness to gladness means letting go of the past to live in the present and plan for the future. No matter how difficult or painful your history has been, there are new chapters in your life waiting to be written. Don't waste energy blaming others or yourself for some past deeds.

In her book *Coming Back: Rebuilding Lives After Crisis and Loss,* Dr. Ann Kaiser Stearns cites the following as one trait common to people who survive life's misfortunes:

They accept the responsibility for making their own lives livable and rewarding. Blame may be assigned to others as part of a mourning process, but blaming others, God, or fate for one's misfortune does not become a way of life or an excuse for personal unhappiness. They work to overcome their environment or background or whatever impairs them.

Like the writer of today's biblical text, we should let go of the past and strain toward the future which is full of promise for each of us. Today, think of ways you can release past hurt and pain in order to embrace healing and to enjoy peace.

⤙ *Thought for the Day* ⤚

You can't turn back the clock.
But you can wind it up again.
Bonnie Prudden

The Real Need in Time of Crisis

I cry out to you, O God, but you do not answer.
Job 30:20

Lonely, burdened, and grieving, a man writes these words in his journal: "This can't be real. I know I'm going to wake up from this nightmare. But it is real and the nightmare continues. My wife of less than three years, as beautiful as the day we were married, is gone."

Confiding in his pastor, the man said that when his wife died, "My world crumbled like a house of cards." He told the pastor that these questions haunted him for days and weeks: "Why, God? Why? Where were you when I needed you most?" And, like Job, the man said he cried out to God but did not hear nor feel a response.

Every day men and women of faith come face to face with a tragedy that is overwhelming. It can come via a phone call, a knock at the door, or an announcement from a friend. Suddenly, a neat, orderly world crumbles. Such crises raise the question: What is the most helpful response to hurting people?

Of course, the theology we all know is true:

- God is working to make good out of evil.
- God will provide daily comfort.
- God will bring healing and recovery.
- Prayer helps.
- Dark valleys produce deeper faith in us.

However, the most helpful response is not theological, but personal. What hurting people often need most is someone to share and bear the dark valleys. Those who are reeling from life's cruel blows need to be with sensitive people who can honestly say, "I don't know why this has happened, but let's sit and talk about it." Of course, God can comfort the hurting directly, but frequently God delivers comfort via the love of other people.

~ Prayer for the Day ~
Dear God,
Let me be the instrument of your love and comfort
to those who are hurting. Through my presence
and my love for others, let those who are hurting
experience hope and healing.
VMP

It's Okay to Be Sad at Church

I served the Lord with great humility and tears.
Acts of the Apostles 20:19

Today's brief text is a reminder that tears and piety are not mutually exclusive. The writer, Saint Paul, does not hesitate to share with readers the fact of his tears. Yet, so often when we are in church, we feel the need to shield others from our pain.

This text raises some useful questions for our own spiritual growth. Let us ask ourselves:

- Do we go to church when we are sad but produce a "happy face"?
- Do we go to church when we are hurting but hold back tears?
- Do we go to church when we are weighed down with sorrow but tell those who ask how we are, "I'm fine, thank you."

Probably most of us have hidden our inner feelings from other Christians at church. Perhaps we did not want to burden another person with our troubles; perhaps our pride has prevented us from sharing honestly; perhaps our church has given the subtle message, "Act happy when you're here or don't come."

Whatever the reason we hold back, today's text reminds us that the church is the place to be when we are sad, hurting, pained, grieving, or upset. It is the place to be because members of the faith community are commanded to weep with those who weep.

The text has two applications for us. First, when we are hurting, we should meet with the faith community and share our pains, so they can pray and encourage us. Second, when we see someone at church who is experiencing life's pains, we should reach out with a compassionate heart.

∻ *Thought for the Day* ∻
A church is a hospital for sinners,
not a museum for saints.
L. L. Nash

Ruling Out Despair

I am crushed; I mourn, and horror grips me.
Jeremiah 8:21

Major setbacks usually make us feel vulnerable, even despairing. This is perfectly human and perfectly normal. However, we must continue moving forward, even though despair may be our daily companion. As we steadily continue inching ahead, despair will lose its grip. As this was true for the prophet Jeremiah, it will also be true for us.

Consider the experience of Bernie Marcus and Arthur Blank, two successful entrepreneurs. Bernie Marcus was the son of a poor Russian cabinetmaker and grew up in Newark, New Jersey. Arthur Blank was raised in a lower-middle-class neighborhood in Queens, New York, where he briefly ran with a juvenile gang. He was fifteen when his father died. "I grew up with the notion that life is going to be filled with some storms," Blank says.

In 1978, Blank and Marcus were working at a hardware retailer in Los Angeles when a new owner dismissed them both. A friend suggested they go into business for themselves. "Once I stopped stewing in my misery," says Marcus, "I saw that the idea wasn't crazy." Together, Marcus and Blank began opening the kind of stores they dreaded competing against: hangar-size, no-frills outlets with high-grade service and a huge selection.

Today, their Home Depot is at the top of the rapidly growing home-improvement industry. Because he overcame his own despair, Marcus often asks this question of other entrepreneurs whom he meets: "Was there a point in your life when you despaired?" Marcus notes this response: "I've discussed this with fifty successful entrepreneurs. Forty had that character-builder."

⁓ Thought for the Day ⁓
Never despair, but if you do, work on in despair.
Edmund Burke

Modifying the Negative and Accentuating the Positive

Hope deferred makes the heart sick.
Proverbs 13:12

Whenever you are filled with discouragement and tempted to view yourself harshly, upstage the negatives by reviewing the positives. This means creating a "change of command" in your mind. Replace the negative thoughts with positive ones. Failure to do so will only deepen feelings of despair, as the Bible notes—*hope deferred makes the heart sick.*

Recently one of California's established home builders fell upon bad times. Suddenly shifting economic forces caused the real-estate market to plummet. He was forced into bankruptcy after building over ten thousand single-family residences along the California coast. Sinking into a black, bleak despair, the man sought support and counsel from his pastor.

After listening carefully, the pastor responded with these wise reminders to the man:

"It's true you have been forced to declare bankruptcy, but look at what will remain: The thousands of houses you built will continue to be homes for people over many, many years. Look back and remember the wages you paid out to trade workers and laborers. That money helped them support their families. Some of them even saved money from the wages you paid so that their children, in the future, can get a college education. Because of you some of those children will become the next generation of leaders. They may become doctors, teachers, nurses, social workers, clergy, etcetera."

The pastor responded wisely and with compassion to a hurting man. All of us need to remember the importance of modifying the negative and accentuating the positive.

➴ *Prayer for the Day* ➶

Loving God,
When I experience darkness,
help me see the light;
When I experience bad times,
help me search for the good;
When I experience disappointment,
help me uncover the possibilities.

VMP

Cast Down, but Never Cast Away

Trust in him at all times, O people;
pour out your hearts to him, for God is our refuge.

Psalm 62:8

The writers of scripture were all realists. They never state nor imply that belief in God provides immunity from life's trials.

There are times when we suffer disappointment, endure burdens, carry heartaches, and experience abandonment. There are times when our words are misinterpreted and our actions misunderstood.

But while we may be cast down, we are never cast away by God. That is why the psalmist encourages people: *Trust in him at all times, O people; pour out your hearts to him, for God is our refuge.*

No matter what has happened to us, we are always invited to share our thoughts, feelings, despairs with God. Faith is our lever for moving the world when things are stacked up against us. Prayer is the golden link that binds us to the God who is our refuge and safety.

The psalmist declares his experience that God will never be found lacking. With God there is…

- No need that cannot be met
- No trouble that cannot be relieved
- No problem that cannot be solved
- No crisis that cannot be resolved
- No hurt that cannot be healed
- No fear that cannot be dissolved

❧ *Thought for the Day* ❧

To the Lord unburden your soul. To keep our griefs
to ourselves is to hoard up wretchedness. The stream
will swell and rage if you dam it up; give it a clear
course, and it leaps along and creates no alarm.

Charles Haddon Spurgeon

Five Ways to Let Go of Hurt

Scorn has broken my heart and has left me helpless.
Psalm 69:20

There are times when pain and anger create such tumult inside of us that it threatens to erupt like a volcanic explosion. When that happens, psychologists are quick to note that stuffing or suppressing the anger is unhealthy. However, rather than just erupt at anyone and everyone, there are constructive ways to release the anger.

Here are five ways to let go of hurt:

1. *Write it out.* Draft a letter to the person who caused the hurt. Clearly express your feelings. Pour out every bitter word and feeling which has resulted. Identify the disappointments and frustrations. However, do not mail the letter. The effectiveness is in the writing, not the mailing.

2. *When you feel somewhat purged, walk away from the letter.* It is helpful to step outside, walk through the neighborhood reflecting and enjoying the beauties of nature: trees, grass, flowers, ponds, hill, mountains, and so on.

3. *As you walk, recite healing affirmations* such as these: "Every day I experience healing." "Each day brings me greater peace." "Day by day I grow in wisdom, strength, and forgiveness." Then congratulate yourself on taking these positive steps forward.

4. *Exercise.* Physical activity is highly effective in diffusing anger. Do an aerobic activity, such as jogging or biking. Put on an exercise video and really get into it.

5. *Do something creative.* Plant a shrub, paint a room, refinish an old piece of furniture, paint, sketch, whip up a new recipe. Let this creative activity and its result be the symbol of your letting go of a hurt.

⪻ Prayer for the Day ⪼
Eternal and loving God,
Help me to let go of hurt.
Create in me a new spirit of
forgiveness, wisdom, and understanding.
VMP

God Is With Us in Adversity and Prosperity

I will be with you; I will never leave you
nor forsake you.

Joshua 1:5

"My brother died almost eighteen years ago. Through the years I have grieved often, even though I feel I have accepted his death. However, sometimes when I speak of his death I still experience significant emotional grief. Is there something wrong with me? Am I not trusting God enough?"

The above comments were written to a therapist. Her response was wise and compassionate. Anyone who is grieving a loss—death, divorce, disability, the loss of a job—can benefit from her words:

> Please know that your responses are normal. Grief is elusive. Finding oneself moving back and forth between phases is common. A metaphor that seems helpful to some is that of waves on a beach. At times the waves are strong and regular and at other times quite small and gentle. Our brains hold the memory of the loss and all that took place. At times similar circumstances or situations will trigger the part of your memory that remembers. When we remember, we grieve, and this is appropriate.

I would like to add to her advice the reminder that just as God promised Joshua he would be with him, God is with us in all of our experiences today. Whether we are grieving and sorrowful or cheerful and joyful, God is our constant companion. If we allow him, God lightens our sorrows and heightens our joys.

Let us remember to bring God into our entire lives, whether we experience adversity or prosperity.

～❈ Thought for the Day ❈～

We cannot too often think that there is a
never-sleeping eye that reads the heart,
and registers our thoughts.
Francis Bacon

Living a Sacrificial Life

Greater love has no one than this,
that one lay down his life for his friends.

John 15:13

"He gave his life for me," said a tear-filled former soldier who was being interviewed at the Vietnam Veteran's Memorial in Washington, D.C. "He gave his life for me," the man repeated as he gently moved his finger across his friend's name.

It was an emotionally moving moment to see and hear that soldier. The fact is that sacrifices move people in a way that other acts may not. Compassion, for example, can be written off as the act of someone naive or someone with an ulterior motive. But an act of sacrifice stops people in their tracks. An act of sacrifice prompts people to ask the deeper questions: "Why would you put my interests ahead of your own?" "Why would you go out of your way for me?" Because we live in a time when people are self-absorbed, any selfless sacrifice on behalf of another is notable and inspiring. Here are some ways to follow the example of Jesus:

- *Offer the sacrifice of time.* Because discretionary time is scarce for most of us, this gift is a significant gesture. Ask yourself: "When was the last time I gave someone the gift of time?" Today invite someone over for tea or schedule a breakfast or lunch.

- *Offer the sacrifice of giving money.* Give a needy single parent an anonymous gift of cash.

- *Offer the sacrifice of sharing skills.* If you have a skill or expertise, share your gifts and knowledge with someone in need. Of course, do not charge a fee. All of these will be a great blessing to the recipients. A man I know earns his living working forty to fifty hours per week as a certified electrician. However, on many evenings and weekends, he provides electricians' services free to the many needy families associated with his church.

- *Offer the sacrifice of giving away knowledge.* Perhaps you, dear reader, are an accountant, a lawyer, or a physician. You have many clients who pay you well for your expertise. Why not consider taking on some clients who cannot pay.

✎ Thought for the Day ✎
Self-preservation evolves from our human nature.
Self-sacrifice is the call of faith.
VMP

Caring for the Divorced

When he saw the crowds, he had compassion on them,
because they were harassed and helpless,
like sheep without a shepherd.

Matthew 9:36

A rupture between a husband and wife is one of life's most painful and devastating experiences. With the divorce rate so high, virtually everyone knows someone who is undergoing or has recently experienced a divorce. Today there are "crowds" of divorced people, many of whom feel harassed and helpless. Like Jesus, let us have compassion for them. Here are some effective ways to care for the recently divorced:

- *Listen with the heart.* Resist any urge to offer advice or raise questions— "Have you two been to counseling?" "If you'd have been more attentive, this wouldn't have happened." Such comments only add to the burden. Put yourself in his or her shoes. Listen with compassion. Care about the pain. Cry with the hurting person if you are inclined.

- *Offer to help in practical ways.* Make it easy for the hurting person to accept your help. Rather than saying, "Call me if I can do anything," try being specific and practical. "Let me provide childcare every Saturday afternoon." "Can I come and wash your windows, change the oil, mow the lawn."

- *Encourage his or her faith.* Many divorced people experience deep feelings of rejection not only by a spouse but by other members of their family, circle of friends, and even from those in the church. Reassure the divorced that God loves him as much as ever before. Reassure the divorced that God will stand by her day by day.

- *Pray for the healing of wounds.* Ultimately, healing comes from God. Physicians can't heal a broken bone, and you can't mend a broken heart. The healing for both comes from God. Create the atmosphere that is optimal for healing. Then pray for the healing of wounds as well.

❧ *Thought for the Day* ❧

The light of friendship is like the light of phosphorus,
seen plainest when all around is dark.

Robert Crowell

Expanding Time for Spiritual Growth

Enlarge the harvest of your righteousness.
2 Corinthians 9:10

Most people want to experience spiritual growth. Most people want to have deeper, more fulfilling spiritual lives. Yet most people are very, very busy and cannot block off hours per day for Bible study, prayer, and the reading of religious texts. However, there are some natural ways of expanding daily time to facilitate spiritual growth. Here are ten suggestions to utilize:

1. Schedule a brief, regular (daily) time to offer quick prayers.

2. Say those prayers while in the shower or while commuting to work.

3. While washing and ironing your children's clothing, pray for them.

4. As you do yard work, pray for your family and neighbors.

5. Read a spiritual book while waiting for your children's sports practice to end.

6. Clean house and listen to a tape of your favorite hymns.

7. Take a nature walk during lunch, thanking God for the beauty of creation.

8. Listen to inspirational tapes while driving in the car.

9. Put a "thought for the day" calendar in your kitchen or desk at work.

10. Before retiring read a psalm and imagine resting in God's arms.

After looking over this list, think about other ways you can incorporate spiritual moments in your daily routine.

❧ *Prayer for the Day* ☙

Gracious God,
Lead me to deeper levels of intimacy
with you. Let me develop and
maintain a spiritual fitness plan.
VMP

God Answers Prayer

Your prayer has been heard.
Luke 1:13

Sadly for David, the pilot of a small Cessna airplane, the ground was completely covered with fog. David, a pilot for more than thirty years, was making a routine flight from south Florida to a northern airport, approximately fours hours away.

Six hours later he was still unable to find a landing place due to foggy conditions that covered Florida. All he knew was that he and his two passengers were in total darkness somewhere over Georgia. In addition, the plane was dangerously low on fuel.

As David flew from one small local airport to another, he could see nothing but deep, dense fog. One airport brought up bright runway lights, but David could not see them. Finally, David looked at the fuel gauges and was terrified to see that both tanks were empty.

Calling the nearest air-traffic controller, he explained his desperate situation. The traffic controller said, "Sir, I need to know your name and how many passengers are on board."

Certain that a plane crash was imminent, David's wife and her friend held hands and prayed. Then, David's wife did an unusual thing. She placed her hand over the fuel gauges and asked God to intervene. As soon as she was through with her brief prayer, another air traffic controller called and suggested they head north to the next nearest airport. Feeling it was futile but knowing they had no other choice, David piloted the craft in that direction. Complete silence filled the plane as all three prepared to die, in a fog-covered pine forest over Georgia.

Suddenly, they saw lights shining through a window in the fog. Descending rapidly, David taxied down the runway as emergency vehicles raced to meet them. As soon as they landed, the three looked up and saw the fog closing in again. "God had opened a window just for us," David said. "When we refueled, our forty-gallon-capacity tanks needed forty-one gallons! Indeed, God was with us!"

❦ *Thought for the Day* ❧
If God maintains sun and planets in bright
and ordered beauty he can keep us.
F. B. Meyer

Tips for Strengthening Daily Prayer

But when you pray...
Matthew 6:7

It is worth noting that Jesus expected we would be people of prayer—
But when you pray. Here are some tips for strengthening daily prayer:

- *Choose a regular time for prayer.* Establish a prayer rhythm for your life
by selecting a regular time to pray—early morning, noon, before dinner, at the time you retire. Then resolve to keep that time even if it
means placing it in your appointment book.

- *Find a quiet place where you will not be easily disturbed.* This can be your
bedroom, a guest room in the house, basement, an outdoor patio, or
even the garage.

- *Use visual aids.* I find it helpful to pray before an icon of Saint Nicho-
las. I also have a small cross on the table beside the icon. Both of
those objects create in me an attitude of prayer.

- *Consciously place yourself in the divine presence.* As you pray, speak with
God as you might with a good friend. Speak words of love and praise,
of joy and thanksgiving. Bring to God concerns or needs around the
world and in your community. Include in your prayers those you know
who are ill, grieving, or in need of some aid.

- *Don't be discouraged by distractions.* Everyone who prays is distracted
and can become preoccupied with other thoughts. Whenever you find
yourself drifting away, calmly return to your conversation with God.
Do not be harsh with yourself. To be distracted by other thoughts and
images is quite human and normal.

- *Remain quiet for a few moments.* Take time to say nothing and think nothing. Empty your mind and soul. This is effective for discernment and
discovery of God's will. Listen and respond to the stirrings of your heart.

- *Conclude with praise.* As the time of prayer comes to an end, offer
thanks for God's care, compassion, love, mercy, and kindness.

～ *Prayer for the Day* ～
As I pray, let me remember, O God,
that you are the Root of Life, Holy Wisdom,
Eternal Vigor, Soaring Power.
As I pray, O God, let me be open to you
in all your manifestations.
VMP

Extending Greater Hospitality

Practice hospitality.
Romans 12:18

Here are two heartwarming stories of hospitality:

A Catholic priest visited Israel but when he arrived in that country late on a Friday afternoon, everything was beginning to shut down for the Sabbath. Public transportation was no longer available, and the people he was to visit lived fifteen miles away. Picking up his suitcase, the priest began walking. He did not get far before a family saw him and invited him to spend the Sabbath with them. He accepted their invitation and was received into their home with considerable kindness and courtesy. His time with that family became the highlight of his trip to Israel.

Several decades ago, a Jewish youth was traveling through Spain. It was in the 1960s and he was a long-haired college student trekking through Europe. One night, he got off a train in a village that was already asleep. A little frightened, he approached the only lighted building in the village. It turned out to be a monastery, and the monks received him gladly. After his departure, he discovered they had quietly slipped some coins into his pocket as he slept.

Those stories raise these important questions:

- What would happen in our society today if two such men were wandering through our communities?
- Would they find a safe place to rest?
- Would they be welcomed?

Many social critics feel there is a crisis of hospitality in our society. People—men, women, children, the aged, the very young, the ill, those with handicaps—often find themselves in circumstances in which they do not feel welcomed and are rejected, even shunned.

Today let us reflect on Paul's simple, direct admonishment: *Practice hospitality.*

~≈ Thought for the Day ≈~

The worst sin toward our fellow creatures is not
to hate them, but to be indifferent to them.
George Bernard Shaw

Facing Problems Promptly and Boldly

For to you I have committed my cause.
Jeremiah 11:20

The story is told of an old farmer who lived at the turn of the century. For years he had plowed around a large rock in one of his fields. It was a source of frustration for the farmer because he had broken several plowshares and a cultivator on it. He had grown rather morbid about the rock in the field.

After breaking yet another plowshare one day, and remembering all the trouble the rock had caused him over the years, he finally decided to do something about it. Whatever it took, the farmer was determined to remove the rock out of his field and out of his life.

When he placed his crowbar under the rock, he was astonished to discover that it was only about six inches thick and he could break it up easily. As he carted it away, he had to smile, remembering all the trouble the rock had caused him and how easy it would have been to get rid of it sooner.

That story offers a useful instruction for daily life. A problem is like a rock in our lives. Often there can be a temptation to find ways to avoid the issue. Sometimes we try to bypass the problem by ignoring it or by keeping excessively busy so we do not have time to think about it. Like the old farmer, we can try to "plow" around a problem. Unfortunately, the obstacle will continue to reappear over and over again. The point, of course, is this: We are always better off to deal with our troubles and trials promptly and boldly. And when they appear more than we can handle, we need to remember that God stands with us and will provide the power we need to deal with the matter. Like the prophet Jeremiah, we must trust God and say, "To you I have committed my cause."

❧ Prayer for the Day ❧
Eternal and loving God,
Continue to shower upon me
your love, your wisdom, and your strength.
VMP

The Power of Encouragement

You hear, O Lord, the desire of the afflicted;
you encourage them.

Psalm 10:17

Several years ago Helynn, a twelve-year-old girl who had been crippled by polio four years earlier, was sitting on the steps of the pool at Warm Springs, Georgia. Also present in the pool was President Franklin D. Roosevelt. After he completed his swim program, the president swam over to the little girl. They chatted for a few minutes. He was interested in the child's progress, her thoughts about the Depression, and her impression of the polio treatment center he had built for her and thousands like her. During their conversation the president asked Helynn, "What do you want to do when you grow up?" Crippled by polio and forced to use an iron lung, the girl shrugged and said she wasn't sure she could be anything "but if I had a choice, I'd like to be an archeologist."

Speaking softly but sincerely, President Franklin Roosevelt responded with one sentence that transformed the little girl's outlook and, ultimately, her life. His simple but profound words would return to her time after time, restoring and renewing her sagging spirits and damaged dreams: "Just remember this: If I can be in a wheelchair and be president of the greatest country in the world, you can do or be whatever you want to be."

That life-changing encounter is written by Helynn Hoffa in her book, *Yes You Can: A Helpbook for the Physically Disabled.* Although confined to a wheelchair and an iron lung, Hoffa, inspired and motivated by the president's words, went on to study Egyptology via correspondence courses through the University of Chicago, found employment as a sports reporter, became a magazine editor, a radio show host, has published poetry, and authored a children's book. In spite of major physical challenges, Hoffa has done whatever she set out to do.

Clearly, President Roosevelt was a person who knew how to encourage. A biblical example of another person who knew the importance of encouragement is that of Job, who described himself this way: "I was eyes to the blind and feet to the lame" (Job 29:15). Likewise, today's text reminds us that God is a God who encourages. Let us, in turn, share in that divinelike quality by encouraging others.

⚜ Thought for the Day ⚜
Those who are lifting the world upward and onward
are those who encourage more than criticize.
Elisabeth Harrison

Acting Promptly When We See Needs

Come quickly to help me.
Psalm 22:19

When there is a crisis, do not wait to be asked for help. It is difficult for most people to request aid. Respond promptly and boldly as soon as you become aware of a need. Almost always a response delayed is a response denied.

Consider this touching incident:

Although Burundi is one of the poorest countries in Africa, it has a Rotary Club with a heart. When heavy rains caused flooding and mudslides in Guerneville, California, Carmen McCabe, president of the Guerneville Rotary Club was surprised and deeply touched to receive this letter from Laurent Nzeyimana, president of the Rotary Club of Bujumbura, capital of Burundi.

"In the spirit of Rotary International," the letter read, "a club even as poor as ours wishes to share this modest contribution from the members in response to the flood which has devastated your area. We trust this minute contribution would display our solidarity with you in your time of grief."

Enclosed was a check for $200, an enormous amount of money in that impoverished nation. The lesson from that inspiring story is clear: Don't wait to be asked for help. Act promptly when you see a need.

⧉ Thought for the Day ⧉
He who sees a need and waits to be asked for help
is as unkind as if he had refused it.
Dante

When You Can't Do a Lot, Do a Little

Command them to do good.
  1 Timothy 6:18

Help out whenever you sense a person needs a lift or when you observe someone struggling with life. Although you may not be able to do everything for that individual, you can do something. Often a small act of encouragement yields large dividends by increasing hope, confidence, and courage for the recipient of your kindness. That understanding may have been in Saint Paul's mind when he wrote, "Command them to do good."

Consider this glowing example of a single mother with three children. She wrote an advice columnist to thank people who provided support and encouragement for her and the children during some dark, difficult days.

"Thank you to the grocer who cashed the occasional support checks I received from my ex-husband and held the ones that bounced until I could make them good. Thank you to the parents who took my children with them on vacations I never could afford, even though I worked full time while holding down several part-time jobs. Thank you to the doctor and the dentist who charged me less than their regular rates for my children. Thank you to my principal for paying me to paint the interior of his house so I could buy groceries during the last three weeks of summer before school resumed. Thank you to the farmers who hired my sons to clean their chicken coops and help with harvesting their hay crops. What you paid them was their only spending money."

That single mother concluded her letter saying: "It has been more than twenty years since you opened your hearts to my children and me, but if you could see the two lawyers and Ph.D chemist they became, you'd know we did a good job with the kids."

❧ *Prayer for the Day* ❧
Loving God,
As you are kind, let me be kind;
As you are merciful, let me be merciful;
As you are compassionate, let me be compassionate.
As you are forgiving, let me be forgiving.
VMP

Comfort, Commiserate, and Console...
Through a Note

I long to see you so that I may be filled with joy.
2 Timothy 1:4

The above reading comes from a letter written by Saint Paul to Timothy. Paul's purpose in writing was to commend and further encourage the young minister in his work. Surely, Timothy was delighted to receive such a warm greeting from an important leader of Christianity—*I long to see you so that I may be filled with joy.*

Receiving a letter of encouragement creates one of life's most pleasant experiences. It can raise hopes and reduce fears. Unlike verbal support that is heard only once, a letter or note can be read and reread many, many times. Written encouragement continues to deliver comfort and consolation over many months.

Why not consider becoming a short-note writer with the specific purpose of providing encouragement and support to someone who is struggling. The written word can bring a great deal of consolation when misfortune befalls someone. Here are some harsh events that can be softened through a note of encouragement:

- When someone loses a job...write a note.
- When someone is grieving...write a note.
- When a pastor is discouraged...write a note.
- When someone has an accident...write a note.
- When someone is ill or hospitalized...write a note.
- When someone is separated or divorced...write a note.
- When someone is feeling guilt or remorse...write a note.
- When someone learns they have a serious illness...write a note.
- When someone has a family member in trouble with the law...write a note.

∼ Thought for the Day ∼
God does not comfort us to make us comfortable,
but to make us comforters.
John Henry Jowett

Returning a Past Kindness

This is what the Lord Almighty says:
"show mercy and compassion to one another."
Zechariah 7:9

When British film actor Michael Caine was getting started, the owner of a small theater company on the outskirts of London interviewed the aspiring actor. Although Caine had never performed in public, the owner, Alwyn D. Fox, hired Caine as an extra. For many months, Fox provided the young Caine with encouragement, experience and, most importantly, employment. Eventually Caine left the small theater company, moving on to play larger roles in major films. With the passing of time, he lost track of Alwyn D. Fox but never forgot him.

Many years later when Caine was living in a luxurious home in Beverly Hills, California, he received a letter from a social-security official in London, England. In the letter he explained there was a very sick, old man who was absolutely destitute in one of their hospitals whose name was Alwyn D. Fox. The letter writer further said that Fox had told the hospital staff he once owned a theater and had discovered Michael Caine. The official said no one really believed Fox, but he was writing in case it was true and that if it was, would Caine send a small amount of money to Mr. Fox to buy a few extra necessities to make the last weeks of his life a little more comfortable.

In his autobiography *What's It All About,* Caine says, "I wrote a letter back immediately saying it was indeed Alwyn Fox who had discovered me and given me my first chance as an actor, and I included in the letter a check for five thousand dollars. Two weeks later I got another letter that contained my uncashed check and a note saying that Alwyn had been very happy to receive the letter and had showed it to all the staff. He then went to sleep and died that same night."

As we move through life and progress personally or professionally, let us never forget people from the past who made things a little smoother or provided some desperately needed encouragement and assistance. And, if the opportunity presents itself, as it did for Michael Caine, let us return the kindness gladly and gratefully. This is an important way of fulfilling today's biblical command: *show mercy and compassion to one another.*

⌁ Prayer for the Day ⌁
Loving God,
I thank you for so many who have helped and inspired me.
Let me be one who returns and passes on such kindnesses.
VMP

Taking Nothing for Granted

When you have eaten and are satisfied, praise the Lord your God.
Deuteronomy 8:10

Each afternoon around three o'clock I stop whatever I am doing to sip tea and simply relax. Savoring my favorite green tea, I pause to reflect with gratitude for all that it takes for me to enjoy that pot of tea…

There is the tea leaf, grown carefully for me in another part of the world;
There is the water that is necessary for the tea plant to grow;
There is grower of tea;
There is the picker of tea;
There is the one who dries the tea;
There is the buyer of tea;
There is the supermarket clerk who sells me the tea;
There is the gas stove I use to boil the water.
There is the water I need to steep my tea;
There is the tea pot which holds my tea;
There is the cup from which I sip…

Truly, the list of gratitude for what I enjoy each afternoon is quite extensive. As I sip, I reflect on all that it has taken for me to enjoy my tea and I am truly, truly grateful.

❧ Affirmation for the Day ❧
God always provides.
God always provides so generously.
God is very, very good.
VMP

Be an Angel to Someone

Are not all angels ministering spirits sent to serve...
Hebrews 1:14

A woman is writing to a friend across the country to share a major act of kindness that unexpectedly came her way.

Several weeks earlier her husband had open-heart surgery. Due to an overdose of anesthesia he came home a quadriplegic and lost his ability to speak. Writing to her friend, the woman explained their home had become badly neglected because he could no longer do the work and she was too busy caring for him.

A friend came by to visit and soon realized that several items in the house needed repair—the garbage disposal didn't work nor did the dishwasher. The sliding glass door was off its track, the lock was broken, and the screen had fallen off.

The woman wrote to tell her pen pal that following week, who later returned with her husband and three other couples. The women brought breakfast and lunch for everyone, and the men brought their tools and expertise. For eight hours they donated their hands and their skill.

"It is so nice to have everything repaired and working properly. And, the yard has never looked better," she wrote joyfully.

⚘ *Prayer for the Day* ⚘
Loving and gracious God,
Today I am reminded that an angel is a ministering
spirit sent to serve. Let me serve another in your name.
VMP

Remember Families of the Imprisoned

Remember those in prison as if you were their
fellow prisoners.

Hebrews 13:3

Families suffer terribly when a member is sent to jail. Although the family members have done nothing themselves, often they are emotionally "imprisoned" by others who avoid them, gossip about them, reject them, and even ridicule them.

Listen to Susan's plight. Sharing with a small ministry group in her church, Susan explains: "When a man goes to prison, much is stripped away from him along with his street clothes—his dignity, his pride, his possessions and, all too often, his family. What bothers me more than anything are those who whisper behind my back, won't look me in the eye, and act uncomfortable around me."

Her suggestions for remembering and helping families of the imprisoned include:

- Asking how the imprisoned person is doing.
- Asking how the family is holding up and how to help.
- Inviting the spouse and children to an outing.
- Inviting the spouse and children over for a meal or at a restaurant.
- Asking them to go with you to the library, museum, movie, or even for a walk.
- Calling just to say "hello" and offering a listening ear.

Susan concluded by saying, "Many wives and children of inmates have tremendous financial problems because of the husband's absence and legal fees; they are lonely and experience embarrassment and humiliation. They need good friends. The wife and children did not commit the crime. They need friendship, understanding, and support."

❧ *Prayer for the Day* ❧
Loving and eternal God,
I will be the one to reach out with love, compassion,
acceptance, and comfort when I learn of a family who
have a member in trouble with the law.
VMP

Three Ways of Experiencing God

Let us continually offer to God a sacrifice of praise.
Hebrews 13:15

Our spiritual growth usually comes through one of three ways…

Imperceptible—we are taught the faith from childhood, gradually accept it, and over time experience deeper spiritual growth and maturity.

Gradual—A hunger or thirst for God and spiritual meaning evolves over a period of time. That yearning becomes satisfied as we pray, read scripture, speak with religious leaders, listen to spiritual talks.

Radical—A dramatic conversion whereby we are confronted by the spiritual reality and change the direction of our lives.

However we have come to experience God, let us be glad in it. Our awareness of God and our relationship to the Divine…

Adds meaning to our lives,
Is a source of comfort in time of sorrow,
Delivers strength when we feel knocked down,
Connects us to a consistent flow of love,
Provides us with inspiration for living,
Unites us with other believers in a healthy fellowship.

∾ *Affirmation for the Day* ∿

Divine love fills my life with joy.
Divine love fills my life with hope.
Divine love fills my life with peace.
VMP

For the Sick

In the same way, faith by itself,
if it is not accompanied by action, is dead.

James 2:17

When you learn that someone is ill…

Rock a baby,
Vacuum a carpet,
Wash a floor,
Clean a bathroom,
Bake a pie,
Make a casserole,
Change a bed,
Bring a pitcher of cold water,
Open a window,
Lower a shade,
Give a bouquet of flowers,
Do the grocery shopping,
Answer their phone,
Take messages,
Drive and pick up children at school…
Then pray!

⚜ Thought for the Day ⚜

The greatest works are done by the ones.
The hundreds do not often do much, the companies never;
it is the units, the single individuals, that are
the power and the might.

Charles Haddon Spurgeon

Using the Healing Power of Our Love

Love one another as I have loved you.
John 13:34

One can only imagine the surprise felt by students at Harvard University Medical School when they hear one of their professors extol the virtues of love, kindness, and compassion, saying they have been scientifically demonstrated to contain healing powers.

Yet that is precisely what David McClelland, Ph.D., of the Harvard Medical School tells his medical students. In order to persuade the future physicians to use "tender loving care" with their patients, Dr. McClelland demonstrates the power of love to make the body healthier.

Calling this power the "Mother Teresa Effect," Dr. McClelland showed a group of Harvard students a documentary of Mother Teresa ministering lovingly to the sick. Dr. McClelland measured the levels of immunoglobulin A (IgA) in their saliva before and after viewing the film. IgA is an antibody active against viral infections, such as colds and flus. IgA levels rose significantly in the students who saw the documentary, even in those who were not particularly religious.

In addition, Dr. McClelland was able to achieve the same effect in another way. Discarding the film, he asked his graduate students simply to think about two past events: a time when they felt deeply loved and cared for by someone else; and a time when they deeply loved and cared for another person. On a personal level, Dr. McClelland says he has been able to abort colds using the same technique.

As a result of research and personal experience, Dr. McClelland encourages and even urges medical students to become physicians who approach their patients with love, kindness, and compassion. Speaking to a group of his medical colleagues, Dr. McClelland said, "Doctors, nurses, social workers—all of us—can learn…that being loving to people is really good for their health. And probably good for yours, too."

✎ *Affirmation for the Day* ✎

I live in harmony and balance with everyone I meet today.
I allow the love within me to flow outward, blessing others.
The more love I give, the more I have to give.

VMP

The Adequacy of God

So if the Son sets you free, you will be free indeed.
John 8:36

A pastor tells of taking a youth group from the United States to Holland for a religious conference. One member of the group had a problem with smoking. Each evening he would go alone to a nearby canal where he would light his cigarette. The youth was completely addicted to smoking and had been since he was twelve years old.

During one of the evening-prayer sessions, the pastor spoke to the youth group from the words of Jesus: *So if the Son sets you free, you will be free indeed.* The pastor made this application to the youths: "God, in Christ, can set you free from whatever is binding you, holding you back, pressing you down, loading you up."

Unknown to the pastor, those words had an immediate and profound impact upon the young man addicted to cigarettes. He heard that God in Christ could generate a power within him to overcome his addiction.

As usual, he went to the canal that evening. But for the first time, he went there with a longing to break the habit. He did an unusual thing: He took out his cigarettes and threw them into the canal, one at a time. As each cigarette fell into the water, he repeated those words of scripture that had such a profound impact on him: *So if the Son sets you free, you will be free indeed.*

From that day to this, the youth has never smoked!

❧ *Prayer for the Day* ❧
Eternal and loving God,
Do remind me that...
Whenever I feel inadequate,
you are adequate;
Whenever I feel insufficient;
you are sufficient.
VMP

Learning to Face the Light

Live as children of light.
Ephesians 5:8

One morning a small boy living on a North Dakota farm awoke in great pain. Recognizing their son was deathly ill, his parents were greatly alarmed. Rushing him to the nearest hospital, seventy-five miles away, it was discovered his appendix was ruptured. Peritonitis had set in and poison was spreading rapidly through his body. A tube was quickly inserted into his side to siphon away the deadly toxin. Feverish days turned into frightening weeks.

Miraculously the boy survived. Through the long months of isolation and recuperation in the family's farmhouse, a growing conviction grew within the youth that God had spared him. "It seemed to me that God had given me a second chance at life, and I prayed for guidance to use my life in ways that would please him most," he would later write. To pass the time, the boy began to play sounds on his father's old accordion. The more he played, the more he enjoyed it. Had it not been for the "terrible" experience of a ruptured appendix, the boy might have remained a North Dakota farmer. Instead, he emerged from that experience with a deep faith in God and in himself. Following his interest in the accordion, Lawrence Welk left his North Dakota farm, becoming a gifted musician and host to one of television's most popular programs. Key to Welk's future success was the fact that as a youth he chose to face the light in his life rather than curse the darkness.

Learning to face the light is a spiritual discipline that every Christian should cultivate. Rather than be driven by fear, we should be guided by faith. Although we will experience darkness and difficulty, we live with the brightness of hope, knowing that hard times can be permeated and transformed by God. In times of trial and trouble, we must learn to turn away from the darkness and face the light of God's power and love. Daily this means maintaining faith, trust, and confidence that the clouds will lift, that the darkness will give way to the dawn, that spring follows winter, that resurrection comes out of death and destruction.

❧ Thought for the Day ☙
Light is the symbol of truth.
J. R. Lowell

Growing Through the Darkness

Give thanks in all circumstances.
1 Thessalonians 5:18

At the turn of the century, British naturalist Alfred Russell Wallace (1823–1913) wrote about a lesson he learned by observing cocoons in which moths were developing. He noted one of the larger moths was beating desperately with its undeveloped wings trying to break out of the cocoon. After several hours, Wallace could not bear to watch the struggle any longer. Using a sharp knife, he gently split the cocoon, freeing the moth from its desperate struggle.

However, in the ensuing days, Wallace discovered the moth was not developing naturally. Missing were the beautiful tints and shades of color that should have come into the wings. Also, the wings' growth were severely stunted and they remained underdeveloped. In a few days the moth died, long before its time. Wallace learned that the struggle against the cocoon, which he had interrupted, was nature's way of strengthening and developing the moth's wings.

That same principle is true for us when we struggle in the darkness of a life crisis. Dark times often become our "cocoon," which God uses to strengthen us spiritually and emotionally. Too often we forget when Saint Paul advises—*give thanks in all circumstances*—that his advice includes times of struggle in the darkness. Behind his exhortation is the knowledge that terrible things are not God's will, but God can transform them through redemptive love.

≈ *Prayer for the Day* ≈
Loving God,
I will trust in your love during good times
and hard times,
in the light and in the darkness.
VMP

Being in Partnership With God

The Lord is with me; I will not be afraid.
Psalm 118:6

Clearly and consistently, scripture urges us not to adopt the "victim" posture in life. The writers of the Bible remind us there is a Higher Power that seeks to work for our good. Therefore we do not need to cringe with fear when troubles loom on the horizon—*The Lord is with me; I will not be afraid* is the declaration of faith from the psalm.

That text is an invitation to trust deeply in God. Doing so opens widely the windows of the soul permitting the majestic grace of God to flow freely and creatively in a human life. Facing the light is a way of being in partnership with God. Through that partnership women and men are able to heighten hopes, overcome problems, minimize despair, experience renewal, and be strengthened for dealing with life's larger challenges.

Sadly, when misfortune strikes many people squander their time and energy lashing out at fate. Because they are unable to turn away from the darkness and face the light, they become bitter, angry, hostile, and resentful.

However, faith provides us with balance and perspective when life's trials come. Through faith we enter into a partnership with God. Through that partnership we...

- Can wait patiently and confidently for the storm to pass
- Find a way to gain from our pain
- Become more resourceful, flexible, adaptive
- Seek to solve problems one at a time
- Open ourselves to new opportunities in life
- Decide we want to learn and grow
- Take advantage of available opportunities
- Graciously and gratefully accept help from others

~ Prayer for the Day ~
Eternal and loving God,
Thank you for being my unseen partner in life.
VMP

Making the Right Assumption

...with God all things are possible.
Matthew 19:26

As people of faith, we must always assume that problems are solvable, recovery can take place, physical and emotional "mountains" can be climbed...*with God all things are possible.*

A good example is James R. Jeffreys, born in 1932 with osteogenesis imperfecta—brittle-bone disease. Doctors held no hope for the family predicting the infant would not live more than a year. If by some miracle he survived the first twelve months, he would be so totally disabled that he could never live a productive life. Yet James Jeffreys did live. In order to continue his education, he rolled his wheelchair two miles a day to and from high school. By the age of twenty-one, he opened his own shop, becoming a successful cabinetmaker. Jeffreys was also a prizewinning drag racer as well. Using a car equipped with special hand-held controls, he has won fourteen racing awards.

He married a nurse. They had two natural children and then adopted seven more when they learned there was a fifty percent chance their own offspring could inherit brittle-bone disease. One of their adopted children is blind; one was crippled by polio; one has a spinal disorder; one was born with no legs; and one suffers from diabetes. Four of the children are biracial, and two are Korean. In 1977, Jeffreys was named *Outstanding Adult of the Year* by the American Brittle Bone Society. The governor of New Jersey, where Jeffreys was born and lives, proclaimed a *James R. Jeffreys Day*, declaring that "the life and career of James R. Jeffreys serves as an inspiration and a source of strength to all persons afflicted with physical handicaps."

Jeffreys is a glowing example of someone who made great gains by first making the right assumption. As we face our own challenges, let us remember the words of Jesus...*with God all things are possible.*

✢ Prayer for the Day ✢
Gracious God,
Clarify my thinking,
Fortify my will,
Strengthen my resolve,
Empower me to live by faith.
VMP

Tiny Actions Matter

If you have faith as small as a mustard seed…
nothing will be impossible for you.

Matthew 17:20

Eastern religious leaders often remind their disciples that even a little poison can cause death while a tiny seed can become a huge tree.

For example, Buddha taught: "Do not overlook negative actions merely because they are small; however small a spark may be, it can burn down a haystack as big as a mountain." Similarly, he said, "Do not overlook tiny good actions, thinking they are of no benefit; even tiny drops of water in the end will fill a huge vessel."

Likewise, Jesus emphasized the importance that small acts of faith could yield big results: *"If you have faith as small as a mustard seed, you can say to this mountain, 'Move from here to there' and it will move. Nothing will be impossible for you."*

The practical application of Jesus' teaching is that the "mountains" of life—our heavy burdens, dashed hopes, crushed dreams—can be transported and transformed when we exercise our faith and our will by taking small steps forward. The next time you face what appears to be an insurmountable difficulty, consider taking small actions such as these:

- Praying for guidance
- Consulting with a trusted friend
- Trusting your instinct
- Stepping out on faith
- Thinking and acting optimistically
- Examining every possibility

❧ Prayer for the Day ❧
Loving God,
Help me always to move forward
inch by inch, step by step.
VMP

The Three D's of Faith

But as for you, be strong and do not give up,
for your work will be rewarded.

2 Chronicles 15:7

There are many mountain climbers in the world, but Don Bennet is one who clearly stands out. Bennet is the first amputee to climb Mt. Rainier. It is 14,410 feet to the top, and Bennet did it on one leg and two crutches. On his first try, he got within 410 feet of the top, but a howling windstorm almost blew him off. So he had to retreat back down.

A year later he tried it again and made it to the top in five days. When asked how he did it, he replied, "One hop at a time. When I started to climb, I just said to myself, 'Anybody can hop from here to there,' and I would. When it was the toughest and I was really exhausted, I would look at the path ahead and say, 'You just have to take one more step—anybody can do that.' And then I would."

Discouragement is much like climbing a mountain. The terrain is unfamiliar. Various emotional elements—fear, anger, despair, guilt, regret, and so on—conspire to make the climb difficult and discouraging. Do what Don Bennet did: Move through discouragement "one hop at a time." Like Bennet, study your situation and tell yourself: "Anybody can hop from here to there." Like Bennet, say to yourself, "You just have to take one more step—anybody can do that."

Any problem, no matter now great or complex or seemingly insurmountable, can be shaped and structured when people apply the three D's of faith: *diligence, determination,* and *dedication.* Scripture urges us, when facing great challenges, to exercise those qualities in order to emerge victorious—*But as for you, be strong and do not give up, for your work will be rewarded.*

❧ *Affirmation for the Day* ❧

I am patient with difficulty.
I am determined to overcome.
I am a persevering person.
VMP

Taking Advantage of Adversity

...my power is made perfect in weakness.
2 Corinthians 12:9

Howard Swan was a nationally recognized voice teacher and choral director. Ironically, his success as an educator and choral director came because of a "tragic" event that struck his life. In 1937, at the age of thirty-one, he woke up with a paralyzed vocal cord and no voice at all. It ended his growing career as a vocal soloist. Although he regained the power of speech two years later, he was left with a high, squeaky voice completely unsuited for performance. He regained complete voice control in 1970, when he had a then-new silicone treatment for the vocal chords. "There's a bit of providence in this whole picture," he recalled. "If I had stayed in solo work, I wouldn't have amounted to very much."

Because of the experience of losing his voice, he consulted voice experts, studied every book available, and became an expert on how the voice works. Unable to illustrate with his own voice, Swan had to find words to provide the explanation. "I think this made my pupils a lot more independent. I just didn't sit in a corner and say 'Do it this way' and open up my mouth. I had to find other ways to teach." Thus, out of the ashes of a destroyed vocal career, a new opportunity presented itself to Howard Swan. Making the most of his otherwise devastating experience, Howard Swan became one of the most sought after voice teachers in North America. Among those legions of students were William Olvis, who sang with the New York City Opera Company, and Joy Davidson, who sang in Mila with *La Scala*.

The lesson from his life and today's scripture is this: Make the most of what happens. Take advantage of adversity. Seize the initiative when stormy times come. "There is no object that we see, no action that we do, no good that we enjoy, no evil that we feel or fear, but that we may make some spiritual advantage of all," notes writer Anne Bradstreet.

∽ Prayer for the Day ∾
Loving and gracious God,
Help me see ways to take advantage of every adversity.
VMP

Gratitude is the Cure for Despair

Praise the Lord...all you peoples.
Psalm 117:1

Along with the text above, this well-known advice from Saint Paul reveals profound spiritual and emotional insight: "Give thanks in all circumstances" (1 Thessalonians 5:18). No matter what cruel blow strikes into a life, spiritual maturity means finding reasons to be grateful. Although gratitude may at times be difficult to express or even to feel, doing so transforms our perspective. As we count the blessings that remain and continue to be showered upon us, the present difficulties feel less intimidating and we become more hopeful. Gratitude is always the cure for despair.

During an interview, actress Patricia Neal recalled the tragedies that pounded her life one after another. When her son, Theo, was three months old, his carriage was struck by a taxi running a red light on New York's Madison Avenue. Injuries sustained required eight brain operations and resulted in years of care. Not long after her son recovered, Neal's daughter Olivia died at thirteen, from measles.

Later another blow came; while bathing her other daughter, Tessa, Neal suffered a series of massive strokes that left her semiparalyzed, severely impaired her speech, and confined to a wheelchair. Neal fought back courageously and made a remarkable comeback. The interviewer asked Neal, "How do you manage to retain that warm spirit and glow after all you have been through?" The actress honestly admitted experiencing a "dark night of the soul" following the death of Olivia and during her paralysis. However, she chose to face the light and emerged to declare her gratitude: "The world is fantastic. I thank God I am alive!"

ᕍ *Thought for the Day* ᕬ
Gratitude is not only the memory but
the homage of the heart—rendered to
God for his goodness.
N. P. Willis

Two Ways of Facing the Light

*Let us put aside the deeds of darkness and
put on the armor of light.*

Romans 13:12

A newspaper carried this fascinating account about a woman whose Vancouver, British Columbia, home was burglarized of $400 two years ago. She knew she'd never see the money again. We can only imagine her astonishment one morning when she went out to her driveway to pick up the morning paper. There she noticed an envelope on the windshield of her car. In it she found $400 and an unsigned letter from the thief explaining he was working through his problems with the help of Alcoholics Anonymous. He was making amends to people he had injured. His note explained:

"I realize that I have done more than just steal your money. I have probably robbed you of your sense of security and peace of mind. But I want you to know I'm not like I was two years ago when I stole from you. I am very sorry for causing you grief. Please forgive me." The note was signed: "A Member of AA."

Speaking to a reporter, the woman declared, "I want this person to know I definitely do forgive him. It renews my faith in humanity that there are really good people out there."

That story is helpful in reminding us there are two ways of facing the light. The first is to make amends and do restitution for our actions that have hurt others. The second is to freely and generously offer forgiveness toward those who have hurt us. Those are two ways we can follow Saint Paul's command—*Let us put aside the deeds of darkness and put on the armor of light.*

❧ *Prayer for the Day* ❧
Loving God,
When I am wrong, let me admit it;
When I am wronged; let me forgive it.
VMP

God Knows All the Details

Don't be afraid; you are worth more than many sparrows.
Matthew 10:30

Diane, a homemaker in Toronto, Ontario, keeps an empty bottle of children's medication prominently displayed in her kitchen. It is a strong reminder of God's continual faithfulness. Five years earlier, she and her husband, George, were enduring a stressful time. George had been unemployed for several months and finally found temporary work in another state. That meant she was left alone at home with two preschool children all week. Attempts to sell their home were unsuccessful.

In addition to the financial stress, George and Diane also felt isolated from their community. "We were shocked to suddenly feel we had become invisible to our friends, family, neighbors, and church family," she recalls. "They knew our problems but seemed unwilling or unable to encourage us. We didn't want anyone to pay our way, but we desperately needed emotional support. Feeling we were facing our struggles alone was devastating."

As they sank to their lowest point, George and Diane were surprised by a visit from their pastor and Sunday school teacher who came bringing groceries and encouragement. After the visit, Diane was putting the groceries away when she found that a bottle of nonprescription children's medication had been included. "When I saw those tablets, God's presence was undeniable," Diane explains. Because family finances were so tight, she had put off buying any children's medications. "It was as if God said, 'I love you enough to take care of the smallest detail.'"

In today's biblical text from Matthew, Jesus refers to small sparrows declaring that not a sparrow dies without God being aware of it. Then, Jesus adds this comforting word: *Don't be afraid; you are worth more than many sparrows.* The allusion to birds was Jesus' way of reminding us that God knows all the details of our lives. We should trust that God can and will meet our needs.

∽ Affirmation for the Day ∽
God sees me as beautiful.
God sees me as lovable.
I accept God's love for me regardless of how I feel.
VMP

We're Like a Lost Child

...grasp how wide and long and high
and deep is the love of Christ.

Ephesians 3:18

Our family spent three delightful years living in Virginia Beach where we spent considerable time enjoying the ocean. One day when the beach was crowded, a little girl became separated from her parents and began crying, "Daddy, I want my daddy!" A lifeguard approached her, offering to help find her father. Almost simultaneously, a young man came running toward the lifeguard and the little girl. As he came closer, I could see the distress in his face. "Are you her father?" the lifeguard asked. "Yes," came the reply as the father knelt in the sand beside his daughter. "Michele, are you all right?" he asked, his voice filled with love.

The beauty of that reconciliation was shattered when Michele abruptly threw a handful of sand in her father's face. She was angry because she had gotten lost and blamed him. The father simply brushed the sand from his face and placed his arm protectively around Michele. Soon she reached up, hugged him, and began weeping. He rocked her in his arms for a few moments and then the two stood up and headed down the beach.

That father and daughter's relationship parallels our relationship with God. Like Michele, we, too, can lose our way in life. Instead of reaching out to God for comfort, we first become angry and blaming. The father's love resembles the way God loves us. Like a wise parent, God is patient. God waits for the anger to ease and then responds to us again.

The love of God transcends our human faults, weaknesses, and insecurities. God waits, watches, forgives, accepts, and loves us unconditionally.

⚜ *Thought for the Day* ⚜

God loves each of us as if there were
only one of us.

Saint Augustine of Hippo

Faith As a Revolutionary Act

*...the Lord your God will make you most prosperous
in all the work of your hands.*

Deuteronomy 30:9

"During any time of difficulty, the most revolutionary thing we can do is to have faith." That declaration is made by Susan L. Taylor, the highly creative and successful editor in chief of *Essence* magazine. That awareness comes from a painful but growing experience which took place a decade earlier. At that time she was consumed by worry, anxiety, and fear. Recently separated, Taylor was living on her own with her year-old daughter. She was unable to make her rent payment, the holidays were just around the corner, her car was broken, and Taylor had only three dollars in her wallet.

In despair, Taylor went for a Sunday morning walk, which took her by a church. Impulsively, she entered and sat in the back pew where she heard a simple but life-transforming sermon encouraging her to live by faith. "The preacher said that our minds could change our world. That no matter what our troubles, if we could put them aside for a moment, focus on possible solutions and imagine a joyous future, we would find a peace within, and positive experiences would begin to unfold."

Although the preacher's words seemed simplistic, Susan made a commitment to replace her fear with faith. "Instead of mourning the things that I felt were missing in my life, I began counting my many blessings," she says. "Throughout the day I would pause and give thanks for my life—for breath and health and the fact that I was here. I thanked God for my healthy child, for the part-time job that was keeping a roof over our heads. I gave thanks that I still had my mother and my good friends."

Within days her depression lifted and the pressure in her chest disappeared. And within weeks she received more editing jobs and finally, a full-time editorial position that doubled her salary. Today let us carefully and prayerfully consider Taylor's conclusion: "During any time of difficulty, the most revolutionary thing we can do is to have faith."

～ *Prayer for the Day* ～
Eternal and loving God,
Let me exercise my gift of faith.
VMP

Reaching for Abundant Life

I have come that they may have life,
and have it to the full.

John 10:10

Today conduct an examination of conscience by asking yourself these questions:

- Am I living a life which is dull and dispirited?
- Emotionally and spiritually, do I feel empty?
- Are defeat, discouragement, and depression my daily companions?
- Do I feel as though I am simply going through empty motions each day?
- Is joy absent from my life?

If the answer to many of those questions is "yes," then **today** make the commitment to change.

- Today begin reviewing and reminding yourself God wants your life to be rich in meaning, satisfaction, and fulfillment. I have come that they may have life, and have it to the full, declares Jesus.
- Today harness the dynamic energy of faith and trust in God.
- Today pray asking God to help you change.
- Today allow God's spirit to fill you with joy and delight.
- Today open yourself to love from God and from others.
- Today bless others with your love and kindness.
- Today surrender completely to God and allow the Spirit to guide you.

✢ *Affirmation for the Day* ✢
I fully embrace God's love for me.
I completely give myself to God.
I allow the Divine to guide me this day.
VMP

Cultivate Winning Attitudes

Whatever is noble, whatever is right, whatever is pure,
whatever is lovely, whatever is admirable...
think about such things.

Philippians 4:8

The unhappy and unsuccessful person always projects a bad attitude. Benjamin J. Stein, a former presidential speechwriter and Hollywood scriptwriter, notes:

> The unsuccessful often have a sour, pessimistic outlook. They dislike their work and their world, and assume that everyone around them is dishonest or stupid. They cast a dark pall over everything, and by their own despair and hopelessness infect the people around them. They also betray a lack of confidence in themselves—a deep-rooted belief that they can't do much or do it well. They don't realize they are advertising themselves as losers.

Conversely, the happiest and most successful people always see the best, believe the best, and work for the best. Their outlook is optimistic and hopeful as they move diligently toward their goals. This is a biblical way to live. Saint Paul advised: *Whatever is noble, whatever is right, whatever is pure, whatever is lovely, whatever is admirable... think about such things.*

Throughout this day think about ways you can apply Saint Paul's advice to cultivate and maintain winning attitudes.

❦ Prayer for the Day ❦

Gracious and holy God,
Today...let my eyes see,
let my mind think,
let my lips speak,
let my spirit respond to those things that are
noble, right, pure, lovely, admirable.

VMP

Remaining Grounded by Helping Others

*Serve wholeheartedly, as if you were serving
the Lord, not men.*

Ephesians 6:7

Betsy King is in the Ladies PGA Hall of Fame. For more than two decades, she has had a spectacular and financially rewarding career as a professional golf player.

However, the golf club is not the only object King swings. In between competitions, King can often be found swinging a hammer to help Habitat for Humanity build houses for poor families. Over the last decade King has donated her time and money to construct homes in Arizona, Tennessee, and North Carolina.

Recently, King and some other pro golfers she recruited helped build a house in Charlotte, North Carolina. Not even severe storms could stop King and her friends from completing the task. As harsh wind and severe rains lashed the area, the King crew kept hammering.

"I remember standing in a downpour, putting up siding with Betsy and laughing at the water coming off our heads," recalls Ellen Braswell, a single mother who moved into the house. "I was sorry to see her go."

King explains she is only trying to show appreciation for her eighteen-year, $5 million-plus career. "When I see people who are not as fortunate, it gives me perspective," she says. "I'm less likely to get upset on the golf course about a bad shot."

King's observation is quite accurate. We gain perspective on our own lives when we are involved with others who are less fortunate. Our appreciation for what we have is heightened while any sense of lack or limitation is considerably reduced and marginalized. Let us remember that service to others blesses them and us!

❧ *Prayer for the Day* ❧

Dear God,
Use me to help another.
Use my talents, my experiences,
my wisdom, my insight to bring help
and hope to another person.

VMP

Living by Positive Values

Live by the Spirit.
Galatians 5:16

"To succeed over the long term, you must know what is right and wrong, and you must use these standards of behavior every day in both your business and personal lives. Adhering to a strong code of positive values will make your life productive, fulfilling, and profitable."

The person making that statement is not a member of the clergy or a religious order but prominent management consultant and author Carl Mays. His words reflect the command of scripture that the people of God are to *live by the Spirit.*

A translation of the same verse (Galatians 5:16) by New Testament scholar William Barclay is quite forceful: "Let your walk and conversation be dominated by the Spirit, and don't let the desires of the lower side of your nature have their way." In our daily life we must live by positive values. One way to do that is by flavoring life with spiritual words and deeds. For example...

- Where there is sorrow, we are to bring comfort.
- Where there is hurting, we are to bring healing.
- Where there is cruelty, we are to bring kindness.
- Where there is despair, we are to bring hope.
- Where there is chaos, we are to bring stability.
- Where there is confusion, we are to bring clarity.
- Where there is anxiety, we are to bring peace.
- Where there is conflict, we are to bring harmony.
- Where there is division, we are to bring unity.

～ *Prayer for the Day* ～
Loving God,
Today I willingly make myself available to you and
ask that my walk and conversation be guided by the Spirit.
VMP

Turning Our Pain Into Others' Gain

Therefore, as we have opportunity,
let us do good to all people.

Galatians 6:10

No life is free from pain and suffering.

When hard times come causing anguish of spirit, there is no point in becoming bitter. Those who face the light address their suffering directly and try to turn the pain into gain.

One sad but inspiring example is that of Leland Stanford University near San Francisco. The school is named after the only son of a former governor of California. While on a visit to Italy with his parents, Leland Stanford, Jr., age nine, became ill and died. The grief-stricken parents returned to California and resolved to make some good come out of the tragedy. Their creative and compassionate determination led them to become benefactors of other children, giving them the opportunities they could no longer give to their own son.

Thus they established and heavily endowed the university that bears the name of their son. Today it is a world-renowned institution of higher learning. Generous funding is available for students who might never attend a university because of limited family income. The gift of a university education for many was born out of the anguish of a personal sorrow, which heroic parents converted into a public service.

Of course, not many people have the financial resources to establish a university, but through careful consideration anyone can turn pain into gain and convert sorrow into service through small but important ways. Why not consider opportunities to do good by

- Establishing a modest yearly scholarship at a local college
- Volunteering your time at a suicide prevention hot line
- Befriending a lonely young person
- Raising funds for an organization devoted to helping others
- Leading a small group in your church for study, prayer, and support

❧ Prayer for the Day ❧
Gracious God,
Thank you for leading me through a difficult time.
Now let me seek ways to turn my pain into others' gain.
VMP

Healing Through Helping

Give, and it will be given to you.
Luke 6:38

Much of our anxiety, loneliness, and frustration in life can be greatly reduced when we reach out to help another person. The wonderful reality about life is that we experience healing by helping others. "Happiness is a perfume you cannot pour on others without getting a few drops on yourself," wrote Ralph Waldo Emerson.

Those who are most satisfied and the least lonely in life are women and men who reach out and help others. An inspiring example is that of Myrtle Way. On her ninety-ninth birthday she told friends that she was not lonely and experienced great life satisfaction because two years earlier she volunteered as a tutor for Literacy Volunteers of America. Her first assignment was to help a seventy-year-old Russian woman, newly arrived in this country, with her English. Since then they have spent well over two hundred hours together, meeting twice a week for several hours at a time. "She's my best friend," the student declares. Way has found the experience so satisfying that she recently took on a new student, a woman from China who is an employee in the dining room of her apartment complex.

Today ask yourself:

- Who can benefit from my skills?
- Where can I volunteer some of my?
- How can I utilize my experience to help others?
- Where can I make a difference to someone?

❧ Prayer for the Day ❧
Loving God,
I thank you for the gift of good health,
a fine mind, strength of body.
Help me help others.
VMP

The Power of Determination

Let us run with perseverance the race
marked out for us.

Hebrews 12:1

All of us could learn from Brooke Knapp, a California woman who has almost made a career of facing her fears. That began in 1978 when most of her friends were aviation enthusiasts. Knapp, however, was afraid of flying. She would go to the hangar, see everyone off, and then be left behind. "I didn't like that. I'm a person who likes to participate," she said.

So Knapp decided to take flying lessons. "I was so afraid, I showed up about fifty percent of the time," she recalled. However, she took enough lessons to qualify for her first solo flight. Although crying hard while piloting the plane, she took off and landed successfully. Eight years after that first flight, at age thirty-nine, Brooke continued flying and held 111 world aviation speed records and is chairman of a $7 million aviation management and charter service!

Many places in the Bible emphasize the importance of perseverance and persistence. Scripture reminds us we have the ability to make and act upon decisions in spite of opposition or difficulty. To do otherwise is to invite premature defeat and lingering feelings of frustration. The principle of determination has guided many, like Brooke Knapp, to experience great success.

⇜ *Thought for the Day* ⇝

Everybody has fears.
The world has two kinds of people in it:
those who are paralyzed by their fears
and those who go for it.

Brooke Knapp

Avoiding Mental Paralysis

Be transformed by the renewing of your mind.

Romans 12:2

A Canadian man, who suffered paralysis of his legs, was on an around-the-world journey in a wheelchair to publicize the ability of those labeled "disabled." In Tokyo he was greeted by a large crowd of well-wishers. One American who was present complimented the man in the wheelchair for his enthusiasm and optimism. The man in the wheelchair responded with this great insight:

"It's only my body that is paralyzed. The paralysis never got into my mind."

We all know people who have become bitter, angry, hostile, or withdrawn because of some unpleasant experience in their lives. They have allowed unhealthy thoughts to paralyze their minds. We also know people who refuse to believe in themselves. They, too, suffer from mental paralysis because they feed their minds with thoughts of fear, self-doubt, inferiority, and inadequacy.

The wisdom of scripture reminds us that we have the power to reinvent ourselves. We have the power of choosing to *be transformed by the renewing of your mind.*

Today renew your mind by choosing…

- Faith over fear
- Love over indifference
- Acceptance over judgment
- Mercy over revenge
- Optimism over pessimism
- Praise over criticism

∼ *Prayer for the Day* ∼
Dear God,
Cleanse my mind of all toxic thoughts.
VMP

Maintaining a Sense of Humor

A happy heart makes the face cheerful.
Proverbs 15:13

One of the most beloved personalities of the twentieth century was Pope John XXIII. Among the many reasons for his immense popularity were his dedication, compassion, ecumenism, and humanity, as well as his holiness. Also, Pope John XXIII had a delightful sense of humor that kept him from taking himself too seriously.

One incident reflects both his humility and his hilarity. Following his elevation to pope, his family came from their country village to visit him. They were overwhelmed and intimidated by the pomp and ceremony surrounding their famous relative. Sensing their uneasiness, the pontiff tenderly and humorously said, "Don't be so nervous—it's only me."

The pope's attitude is worth examining and cultivating for ourselves.

Life should not always be a serious, intense matter. We should cultivate and maintain a sense of humor. According to scripture, a *happy heart makes the face cheerful.* Humor cleanses the spirit, lightens the load of life, creates moments of spontaneous joy, and minimizes life's irritants.

As you move through this day, tap into your sense of humor to ease up on stressful or unpleasant situations that may come along. Doing so will allow you to truly have a good day.

❧ *Prayer for the Day* ❧
Gracious God,
Today I will maintain composure,
tranquillity, serenity, and a sense of humor.
VMP

The Importance of Seeking Guidance

Lead and guide me.
Psalm 31:3

After sixteen years of marriage that produced three children, Jennifer, forty, was devastated when her husband admitted to an affair. Additional conflict and a total breakdown of communication resulted in an ugly divorce.

"Suddenly my life went out of control," Jennifer recalls. "Overnight the loss of our joint income plunged me from a comfortable middle-class lifestyle into poverty. I couldn't sleep. For the first time in my life, I had excruciating migraine headaches. I made careless mistakes at work, was demoted, and placed on three months probation. Rapidly, I gained forty pounds. My self-esteem dropped drastically. I became obsessed with self-pity. Fortunately, my pastor persuaded me to see a counselor and the Church helped pay some of the fees. Through counseling, I regained emotional balance and began to function in healthier ways."

Examine that story carefully. Jennifer could have continued her downward spiral, but she prevented it by one wise action—she sought guidance. Through that one small act—confiding in her pastor—Jennifer received three major benefits.

First, the pastor listened and recommended she see a professional counselor. Second, the pastor made arrangements to help pay for some of the therapy. Third, the counseling empowered Jennifer to change the direction of her life.

We all need to remember that when hard times come we do not need to go it alone. In fact, sometimes going it alone amounts to going nowhere. When facing a stormy time don't hesitate to confide in a trusted friend, seek out a gifted spiritual leader, or find a therapist.

✎ *Affirmation for the Day* ✎
I am led to find solutions.
I am given strength for challenges.
I am given wisdom to make good choices.
VMP

Responding Wisely to Life's Challenges

Watch out that you do not lose what you have worked for.
                                                            2 John 8

If life's troubles, trials, and traumas simply came one at a time, almost anyone could cope with them. Unfortunately, the harsh reality is that often problems come one after another. They accumulate, pile up, overlap, causing an emotional overload.

As one problem leads to another, people run the risk of becoming negative, bitter, hostile, withdrawn, and unable to maintain perspective and hope. It is the perfect setup for self-destruction.

Yet, rather than self-destruct, we must learn to respond wisely to life's challenges. The next time you face trouble, trial, or trauma consider...

- Choosing to think positively rather than thinking in negativity

- Choosing to remain confident rather than engage in self-doubt

- Choosing to speak with supportive friends rather than isolating yourself

- Choosing to move ahead with hope rather than living with despair

- Choosing to heal rather than remain wounded

- Choosing to accept help rather than withdrawing

- Choosing to seek God's comfort and strength rather than being angry with God

∼ *Prayer for the Day* ∼
Eternal and loving God,
I choose to live with faith;
I choose to live with hope;
I choose to live with love;
I choose to trust you for all things.
VMP

Recognizing the Enemy Within

Purify your hearts, you double-minded.
James 4:8

For more than a week, a crow was perched on a windowsill of an empty house where he pecked away insistently and angrily at the glass. It was, of course, his own image and it pecked right back at him. The crow kept up the "fight" with his own image for several days hoping to chase away the bird who dared intrude his territory. Realizing his pecking was not deterring the other bird, the crow finally uttered a piercing "Caw" and flew off, never to return.

That crow's drama provides us with insights into our own emotional mirroring and projecting. Today's text is a challenge to look inward and study our motives—do we act out of pure hearts or are we double-minded? When others irritate us, we must question why the irritation exists. And, before reacting and striking out at another with harsh thoughts or words we should ask ourselves:

- Who or what is the image I am threatened by?
- Is it really an intruder, enemy, opponent?
- Or, am I reacting negatively because I recognize parts of myself in the other?

Let us remind ourselves that we are all capable of casting sunshine and shadow over others. Let us strain to see what really is shaping our thoughts, words, emotions, and actions. After doing so, we will be more likely to respond wisely rather than react harshly.

❧ Prayer for the Day ❧
Eternal and loving God,
Let me work toward honest self-evaluation so that
my perceptions are pure and accurate.
VMP

Pray. It Works

Ask and it will be given to you.
Matthew 7:7

Russ, a plant manager tells of a time two years earlier when he experienced great personal and professional problems. "I felt as though my life had come crashing down around my feet. I was going through a deeply painful separation. Simultaneously, my career had hit an all-time low. I felt alone, isolated, betrayed, bitter, and was wondering if God had completely abandoned me."

While driving along city streets, Russ prayed fervently asking God for a sign that God cared about him and his predicament. "I just needed some assurance so I prayed simply, 'Please, God, if you're really there, give me a sign.'" Suddenly the crowded neighborhood gave way to a vacant lot. In the middle of the lot was a tattered billboard which had written in large, bold letters: PRAY. IT WORKS!

Immediately, Russ burst into tears, then laughter. He recognized the billboard as his sign from God. "What a masterful pun. What a rich sense of humor God has," Russ later told a friend. "I asked for a sign and literally got one. I believe God was telling me to lighten up and reminding me that he was with me and would guide me one step at a time."

Today's text is the most basic primer about prayer—*Ask and it will be given to you*. Of course, we must ask wisely and we must be patient, trusting in both God's judgment and God's timing.

❦ *Affirmation for the Day* ❦
I am divinely guided and protected.
I am always safe in God's care.
God knows my needs and desires.
VMP

Winning Starts With Beginning

Through you we push back our enemies.
Psalm 44:5

No matter how serious the trouble, how devastating the circumstance, how complicated the issue, how great the mistake, how hopeless the outlook, begin with the fierce determination to overcome and triumph. Winning starts with beginning!

An excellent example of this principle is singer Gloria Estefan. When her father returned from Vietnam in 1968, he was a broken man suffering a degenerative neurological disease. As a girl, Gloria became his daily nurse while her mother worked to support the family. "Deep down inside I always had a premonition that I would encounter a disaster, just like Dad," she says. In 1990 her tour bus crashed in a snowstorm. "I felt an explosion, then nothing. When I awoke, I couldn't move my legs. The pain was gruesome." Estefan had broken her back.

Remembering her father, Estefan was petrified of becoming a burden to those she loved. Thus she made a commitment to overcome fate. Armed with determination she engaged in a rigorous program of physical rehabilitation. Within a year Estefan released a new album and returned to the stage. Looking back on her trauma, Estefan says, "I wanted to prove you can deal with a problem and get beyond it."

Along with our commitment to overcome, let us commit equally to seeking out God's guidance and strength remembering the psalmist's experience: *Through you we push back our enemies.*

∼ Prayer for the Day ∼
Divine Spirit,
I make the commitment to overcome;
I take my burdens and release them to you.
VMP

Admitting Our Inadequacies

Even to your old age and gray hairs I am he,
I am he who will sustain you.

Isaiah 46:4

Often a major life crisis will set off a chain reaction with more problems erupting at every turn. Such an experience can leave us feeling helpless and hopeless, frustrated and frightened. In those time we must remember the importance of turning to God in prayer and admitting our inadequacies.

Today we are reminded that God remains faithful at every stage of our life's journey—*Even to your old age and gray hairs I am he, I am he who will sustain you.*

During a time of difficulty and dilemma, frustration and fear, let us remember that...

- God's adequacy balances our inadequacies
- God's strength takes over where our weakness ends
- God's hope conquers our fears
- God's peace overwhelms our turmoil
- God's joy pushes back our despair
- God's support limits our anxiety
- God's security reduces our insecurity

❧ Thought for the Day ❧

What God does, he does well.

Jean De La Fontaine

Moving Forward Inch by Inch

He who works his land will have abundant food,
but he who chases fantasies lacks judgment.
                              Proverbs 12:11

Louis L'Amour, popular author of westerns, offers this wisdom: "Victory is not won in miles but in inches. Win a little now, hold your ground, and later win a little more." Today's text conveys a similar theme. It reminds us that the farmer who succeeds is the one who tills the soil, plants the seeds, waters the ground. The successful farmer works faithfully—hour by hour, day by day, week by week. His progress can literally be measured inch by inch. The same is true on the spiritual and emotional level. Our success depends upon our small, faithful, determined actions.

The next time you are faced with a challenge that intimidates and discourages you, tell yourself that you can rise to the occasion. Rather than be stressed out by the issue, tell yourself you will be "successed out" by the challenge. When facing discouragement let the crisis push you up, not pull you down, by thinking these kinds of positive thoughts:

- *I caused this difficulty and I can create a solution.*

- *I won't become angry, cynical, or suspicious but I will be become energetic, creative, and hopeful.*

- *I hold to the belief that every obstacle is an opportunity and every burden can become a blessing.*

- *I have made a mistake, but that mistake will allow me to learn and to grow.*

- *I can overcome.*

～ Prayer for the Day ～
Loving God,
Remind me that the only way to get anywhere
is to start from here I am and
to move forward inch by inch.
VMP

Exorcising the Demon of Fear

Do not be afraid.
Stand firm and you will see the deliverance
the Lord will bring you today.

Exodus 14:13

Fear is often present in our lives. While it is to be expected, fear can strike a crippling blow to one's ability to think clearly and calmly. Once it moves in, fear will try to remain permanently in the psyche, holding a person hostage, canceling hope, obliterating dreams, abolishing reason, and negating faith.

The key to managing, reducing, and exorcising fear is to understand it. To do that, analyze your fears by asking:

- What do I fear about this situation?

- Why am I afraid?

- What previous experiences trigger my fear?

- Am I jumping to conclusions?

- How many "*uns*" contribute to my fear? *un*substantiated stories? *un*familiar ideas? *un*kind accusations? *un*dermined support? *un*due influence to respond in an expected way? *un*balanced and one-sided treatment of an issue?

- How realistic is the fear and what resources can I bring to bear upon it?

- How would Jesus deal with these fears?

- Will I exercise my faith option and trust God to help me triumph over it?

～ Prayer for the Day ～
Holy and loving God,
Your sacred presence is my peace,
my wisdom,
my confidence,
my life.
I thank you!
VMP

The Best Way to Ease Worry

Do not worry about tomorrow.
Matthew 6:34

An area of caution for our family living here in southern California is the rattlesnake. Although we live in suburban Los Angeles, the snakes often come out of the hills at night to enjoy the pavement that is still warm from having absorbed the day's heat. I have gotten into the habit of carrying a flashlight when I need to take the garbage outside or if I need to get something from the car. The flashlight helps me see a rattlesnake that may be lying on my sidewalk or driveway.

I have discovered that the most effective way of using my flashlight is to throw its illumination on the path immediately ahead of me. When I have lifted the light and thrown it far ahead, its beam is soon dissipated and neutralized in the darkness and does not provide me with the light I need to avoid stepping on a snake. Only when I carefully light up the next step or two can I clearly see the path and any objects that may be on it.

The same approach is true of our thinking. If we project our thoughts days, months, and even years ahead, our personal power is dissipated and neutralized. We stumble and struggle without direction through life.

Today's word from Jesus is a reminder to place the force of our thoughts on today and let tomorrow take care of itself. When this day's work is done well, carefully and methodically, we increase the likelihood that the days ahead will indeed take care of themselves.

⁓ Prayer for the Day ⁓
Holy God,
You are forever within me and forever around me;
I live in peace.
VMP

Turning Pain Into Power

Do not be afraid, for I am with you.
Genesis 26:24

Because life brings disappointment and sorrow to everyone, the art of living is to turn obstacles into opportunities, stumbling blocks into stepping-stones and pain into power. Often the difference between success and failure over a life trauma is in the matter of choice. Faced with a monumental challenge, some give up and quit while others choose to adapt, adjust, and advance.

An exceptional illustration is eighteen-year-old Paula White, who recently graduated from her Portsmouth, Virginia, Christian high school as its first deaf valedictorian. Born hearing-impaired, White showed her determination to overcome this handicap as a young child. At age three she began pronouncing and recognizing letters on her own after first seeing them form on the lips of those who read to her.

Refusing to allow deafness to hold her back, White went on to learn how to "hear" others via lip reading and how to speak clearly herself. Today, White views her deafness as a positive influence in her life. She says had it not been for her deafness she probably would not have learned to play the piano, master several sports, speak French, or maintain an A-plus grade-point average throughout her schooling.

White sums up her winning attitude this way: "I'm a very, very proud person. The one thing I absolutely hate is for people to tell me, 'You can't do this.' You wanna bet?"

When facing any disappointment—large or small—let us remember today's scripture promise: *Do not be afraid, for I am with you.*

⁓ *Affirmation for the Day* ⁓
God helps me turn pain into power.
God helps me turn trauma into triumph.
God helps me turn a cross into a crown.
VMP

Learning From Our Troubles

*I have learned the secret of being content
in any and every situation.*

Philippians 4:12

When Ross Perot, former presidential candidate, was addressing the 330-member graduating class at Port Huron Northern High School in Michigan, he expressed this word of caution to students selected as "the most-likely-to-succeed":

"I'm worried about you. My primary concern is that you haven't had to sweat in order to achieve things. That you're not intellectually tough. That you don't know what it is not to finish first."

On the other hand, Perot commended students who struggled to graduate, saying they "have learned from disappointment. They have learned to recover from defeat. They have learned to persevere." The billionaire industrialist from Texas said those attributes are shared by all the successful people he knows.

Life's journey is not always a smooth, easy path. Sometimes there are unexpected dilemmas, detours, and even dangers. As soon as you face a crisis, make an early resolve to learn all you can from it. Let the trauma be your teacher. Doing so will make you a stronger, wiser, healthier, more compassionate, and tolerant human being. It was through difficulty that Saint Paul *learned the secret of being content in any and every situation.*

❧ Prayer for the Day ❧
Loving God,
Teach me how to take the lead of life—
trouble, trial, trauma—
and turn it into the gold of life—
wisdom, compassion, sensitivity.

VMP

Transforming Disappointment Into Opportunity

For you, O God, tested us; you refined us like silver.
Psalm 66:10

The psalmist's words are a reminder that during a traumatic time we encounter both danger and opportunity; a time of testing can produce in us silver *or* lead. You are free to choose your point of focus. Viewing the threat as a challenge opens the door to experiencing the satisfaction of renewal, growth, empowerment, and liberation.

According to health psychologist Kathryn D. Cramer, Ph.D., moving away from threat toward the focus of challenge begins by asking yourself, "In light of my trauma, what are my possibilities and opportunities for growing, for learning, for becoming wiser, stronger, healthier, more loving, and more productive? In essence, what key resources can I seek out of this crisis? What benefits and gains are hidden in my trauma?"

In her book *Staying on Top When Your World Turns Upside Down*, Dr. Cramer cites a client whose wife died in an accident while they were on vacation. Initially deeply depressed and guilt ridden over her death, Dr. Cramer encouraged the man to take an emotional inventory, asking himself what opportunities were present in his tragedy.

The burden of his bereavement was lifted considerably as he responded to the question "What are my opportunities?" with these answers:

- I can learn to be more independent.
- I can celebrate my fortunate past.
- I can search for new ways to love.
- I can find more meaning in my life.

As people of faith, let us seek God's aid in transforming disappointment into opportunity.

❧ *Affirmation for the Day* ❧
Divine love is guiding me now,
Divine love is working through me now,
Divine love is doing its perfect work for me now.
VMP

The Importance of Having a Confidante

When I kept silent, my bones wasted away.

Psalm 32:3

Spiritually, confession is good for the soul. Emotionally, speaking about personal problems is good for the spirit. Talking about the trauma with another person provides the opportunity to become more objective about the issue. Confusing and conflicting feelings, such as fear, disappointment, sadness, depression, rage, and hopelessness, can be sorted out and placed into perspective.

Also, talking relieves the stress connected to the problem, leading to better emotional and physical health. Consider the results of a study in which researchers assigned twenty heart-attack survivors to receive standard monthly medical follow-up, while another twenty-three patients also met every other week in small support groups led by mental-health professionals.

After a year the patients who attended support groups were better off in a number of areas, including blood-cholesterol levels, blood pressure, and weight. Researchers believe the support-group sessions improved cardiovascular health by helping to relieve stress.

So, when fate strikes and leaves you teetering on the edge between confusion and composure, seek out a supportive listener. It could be a family member, a good friend, or professional from the field of social work, psychology, psychiatry, counseling, or the clergy. Or, consider joining a support group that deals specifically with the issue you are facing. Don't hesitate to take whatever steps are necessary to help yourself.

❧ *Prayer for the Day* ❧

Loving God,
Thank you for sending kind, compassionate people into my life
in whom I can confide and share my burdens.

VMP

Allowing Pain to Teach Us

I will refine them like silver.
Zechariah 13:9

Recently, a woman from New York City spoke at the funeral of her sister who died at forty-two, the result of complications from meningitis. Amy, her sister, was born mentally retarded. Although it was a major grief for the family, they all adapted and adjusted to Amy. At the funeral, her sister spoke warmly and tenderly of growing up with a mentally handicapped sister, saying, "I was blessed with Amy in order to learn some of life's most important lessons." Then she cited these three:

1. *Compassion.* "First and foremost, Amy taught us about having compassion—about the importance of helping others and understanding and accepting imperfection," she said.

2. *Patience.* It took Amy many years to learn simple tasks that others could master quickly. Amy learned to swim, ride a bike, and work in a sheltered environment. All were accomplishments that far exceeded what many experts felt she would be capable of.

3. *Responsibility.* "When people ask me how I juggle a demanding job and two children, I think of my sister. I think of how my involvement in her care made me realize I could tackle any task if I approached it with flexibility, resourcefulness, and energy," the woman explained.

Her words point out a crucial life lesson: Painful experiences can be sources of great instruction, and we should allow ourselves to learn from them. Emotionally and spiritually, the mountaintop experiences of life would be greatly diminished if there were no deep, dark valleys to travel. Our joy and appreciation of the light is greatly enhanced because we spend time in the depths of darkness. Take some time to look back over a painful experience. Analyze it carefully. Identify the lessons gleaned from the experience.

❧ Prayer for the Day ❧
Loving God,
Help me learn much from the hard experiences of life
and become a better, wiser, kinder person.
VMP

Yielding to God

The Lord is my shepherd, I shall not be in want.

Psalm 23:1

Our society places a high value on independence, self-sufficiency, and achievement. While these can be positive things, they can also keep God at a distance in our lives. Yet it is usually in the darkness when we let go and turn to God. This is what happened to best-selling author Dan Wakefield, who says he joined a church the week he turned fifty, after studiously avoiding any contact with organized religion since his sophomore year at Columbia University.

During a traumatic year, Wakefield experienced a profound awareness of God's love and peace. Over a twelve-month period both of his parents died, a relationship with a woman he loved came to an end, and his work in television was terminated.

"Faced with a top-ten list of life's greatest stresses, I found myself muttering the Twenty-Third Psalm," he says. "Those words spoke more to my condition as I neared my own half-century mark than anything by Hemingway, Freud, or Sartre."

Wakefield began regularly reading other passages from the Bible, as well as joining with others for prayer and worship. Through those activities, he discovered the God who is present in the pains of life, as well as in the joys of life. He discovered that even in his deepest despair, God's guiding force was present in his life. As we face our own crises from time to time, let us maintain hope and confidence, constantly trusting in God to gently guide and lead us to the light.

❧ *Prayer for the Day* ❧
Eternal God,
As you have led women and men through difficulty in the past,
I trust you to do the same for me today.

VMP

Using Suffering to Heighten Our Compassion

...love one another deeply, from the heart.
1 Peter 1:22

It is worth reminding ourselves that a deep distress can humanize our soul; that we tend to become more compassionate and less judgmental after experiencing our own trial. Those who emerge from a dark and difficult time often have a deeper desire to help others who are suffering. Consider the example of John Penne. In 1973 John and his wife, Wanda, were told they both had cancer. So they sold the Milwaukee business they had run for the twenty-six years of their marriage and set off to make what remained of their lives as comfortable as they could.

Fortunately, John's case was treatable. However, his wife's was not. She was treated with chemotherapy and radiation but died four years later. After Wanda's death in 1977, John, still grieving, felt he wanted to do something in Wanda's honor.

So he approached the local chapter of the American Cancer Society with an idea that came to him during the desperate years of driving Wanda back and forth from the hospital. At that time he was struck by the sight of many cancer patients waiting for rides home. He offered himself as a chauffeur to the American Cancer Society. They provided him with a car and gas money. Since that time John Penne has been driving patients daily "for Wanda." Nothing keeps him from his commitment to make something good come out of his wife's death.

❧ Thought for the Day ❧
It is by those who have suffered that the world
has been advanced.
Leo Tolstoy

Giving God a Chance to Help

Why are you downcast, O my soul?...
Put your hope in God

Psalm 42:5

Amazingly, many people who face difficulty just don't give God a chance to help. Rather than turn to God when they are hurting, many women and men struggle on their own. Yet we must learn to turn to God and ask for what we need, expect, and hope, and then allow God to work.

This was the experience of the country and western singer Naomi Judd. In 1991 Judd was forced into premature retirement from the stage because of chronic active hepatitis. Suffering from that potentially fatal liver disease, Judd could no longer perform. However, she has now returned to her singing career and credits God with granting her healing and recovery.

"I really had to step out in faith and claim my healing," she says. "I was in a wheelchair. I had been in a fetal position in bed. I was a prisoner of my body. Imagine the world's worst case of the flu. Have you ever had a fever that lasted more than a week? It was like that. People can't understand unless they've been there."

In the darkness she opened herself widely to God and discovered that her fear was replaced by hope in God. "Hope has been my constant companion. Hope is what got me through all the struggles," she says. Today let's meditate on the psalmist's words in 42, verses 1 to 6.

❧ *Affirmations for the Day* ❧
Holy God,
I affirm the universe is a beautiful place to be;
I affirm that you always provide;
I affirm divine light and love flow through me now.

VMP

Living by Faith and Not by Sight

We live by faith, not by sight.
2 Corinthians 5:7

A basic biblical teaching is that we are to live by faith and not merely by what we see. Practically speaking, this means turning our lives over to God's care and guidance whenever we face confusion, chaos, uncertainty, or difficulty. We must learn to let go and let God take over.

This is precisely what author Catherine Marshall had to do when she was the young widow of Peter Marshall, a Presbyterian pastor and chaplain to the United States Senate. Because she was left widowed with a young son and very limited financial resources, Marshall decided to work as an author. She began by writing a biography of her husband.

When she submitted her completed manuscript to an editor, she was devastated by his critical comments of her writing. The painful realization of her inadequacy as a writer drove Marshall to tears, but that crisis brought her a major realization.

"In my helplessness there was no alternative but to put the project into God's hands," she recalls. "I prayed that *A Man Called Peter* be God's book and that the results be all his, too. And they were. I still regard as incredible the several million copies of *A Man Called Peter* circulating around the world."

Catherine Marshall went on to become a major writer of spiritual and devotional books in this century. Had she merely lived by sight, Marshall would have been tempted to give up on a writing career. However, she chose to live by faith. She reworked the manuscript, while trusting God to help and guide her struggling career.

❧ *Prayer for the Day* ❧
Eternal and loving God,
I accept the reality you are with me and working
in my life to create miracles, large and small.
VMP

Broadening Our Mercy, Softening Our Judgment

Do not judge.
    Luke 6:37

Truly spiritual people are filled with mercy and devoid of judgmental attitudes. We are called by Christ to broaden our mercy and soften our judgment. Sometimes it is in the dark valley where we begin to fully comprehend Jesus' command—*Do not judge.*

Troubles, trials, and tragedies reveal our vulnerability and weakness. Those times strip us of arrogance, making us less judgmental of others. We become more accepting, understanding, and kind after we have been through a fiery trial. This is what happened to Rod, thirty-nine, a driven, high-achieving executive.

"Previously whenever I learned that another executive was out of work due to a merger or management restructuring I assumed they were laid off because they weren't talented enough or hadn't worked hard enough," he says. "Then, when my company was bought out and the new management terminated my position, I was devastated. I began to see things quite differently. It took me eighteen frustrating and frightening months to find a comparable position. Now I view other unemployed people more compassionately and try to help in any way I can."

While difficulty can indeed teach us to broaden our mercy and soften our judgment, we must not wait for adversity to do this work in us. Today let us begin to view others more gently, more acceptingly, more kindly.

❧ *Prayer for the Day* ❧
Eternal and holy God,
I thank you for teaching me and for showing me the
right way to live in peace and harmony with all.
VMP

Helping by Confronting

When Peter came to Antioch,
I opposed him to his face, because
he was clearly in the wrong.

Galatians 2:11

As difficult as it may be, there are times when the most effective way of helping is by confronting. This is what Paul did to Peter in order to convince the leader of Christianity that he was on the wrong course.

A more recent example comes from the life of popular Christian singer, Amy Grant. In the mid 1980s her life was not as charmed as it appeared. Her marriage was in crisis, primarily because her husband had developed a cocaine habit. Their talk of divorce left Grant in one of her darkest moments. She remembers: "For a few days, I just stayed in bed and mourned my life. The only hope I could seem to see was just junking it all, moving to Europe, and starting everything all over again."

Then her sister came, not to provide encouragement but to confront Grant. She marched right beside Grant's bedside, declaring, "Fine, go to Europe, leave it all behind, start your life again. But before you go, tell my daughter how you can sing, that Jesus can help her through anything in her life, but that he couldn't help you."

Those words of confrontation hit home. Amy remained in America and continued her career as a gospel singer. She and her husband began marriage and personal counseling, slowly rebuilding their relationship with each other and with God. It all began with a confrontation.

When someone we love exhibits behavior that is self-destructive, let us not shrink back. Let us find ways to challenge, confront, and motivate that person to consider other options.

~≈ *Prayer for the Day* ≈~
Eternal and loving God,
Help me to know when to be supportive and encouraging
and when to be challenging and confronting
in order to be a good friend.
VMP

The Importance of Community

I thank my God every time I remember you.

Philippians 1:3

One of the pleasant experiences of living in Virginia Beach was the lack of snow in the winter. Being so close to the ocean, the climate there was very moderate. However, during one February there was an unusual six-inch snowfall. It provided a fascinating lesson in community.

Along a main road stood several large groves of tall pine trees. The branches were bowed down with the heavy snow. They were so low, in fact, that branches from one tree were leaning against the trunk and branches of another.

However, where there was a pine standing alone, the effect of the heavy snow was dramatically different. The branches became heavier and heavier, and since there were no other trees to lean against, the branches snapped under the additional burden of snow. They lay on the ground broken and alone.

The same is true for us. When the storms of life strike us, we need to be in a community—standing close to other people of faith. The closer we stand, the more connected we are, the more we will be able to bear up under our burden.

That was certainly Saint Paul's experience—*I thank my God every time I remember you,* he wrote. Although imprisoned for preaching the gospel, he is sustained by his faith in God and by the support he has received from other Christians.

❧ Prayer for the Day ❧
Gracious God,
I thank you for placing me in a community filled
with kind, loving, supportive people.
VMP

Asking Ourselves: "Why Not Me?"

And I said, "Here am I. Send me!"'
Isaiah 6:8

In April 1995, Craig Kielburger, then twelve years of age, read about the death of Iqbal Masih, a boy his age in Pakistan who spent six years chained to a rug loom working in conditions of slavery. Iqbal escaped and joined a crusade against child labor. He had been shot dead in the street. Craig vowed to keep Iqbal's cause alive.

The Toronto, Ontario, youth started Free the Children, a human-rights group run by kids. Soon Craig felt he had to meet the children he was trying to help so he made a seven-week trip to Bangladesh, Thailand, India, Nepal, and Pakistan. He found disturbing child labor everywhere—a girl bagging candy eleven hours a day, a boy stitching soccer balls. "I met one eight-year-old girl pulling apart used syringes and needles for their plastic," Craig remembers. She wore no gloves and when he asked if she was worried about getting AIDS or other diseases, the girl said she didn't know what AIDS was.

Canada's prime minister, Jean Chretien, was in Asia at the same time; so Craig met with him to talk about child labor. As a result, the Canadian government is expressing official concern and displeasure about child labor to its trading partners. Craig has single-handedly awakened his nation to the suffering of an estimated 200 million children. When he was asked, "Why you?" the youth responded: "If everyone said, 'Why me?' nothing ever would be accomplished. I've read the story of Iqbal Masih. Why *not* me?"

When we see needs and are touched to act, let us respond like Craig Kielburger and, long before him, the prophet Isaiah who said: *Here am I. Send me!*

⁓ Prayer for the Day ⁓
Holy and loving God,
When I see a hurt, let me heal it;
When I see a sorrow, let me comfort it;
When I see a pain, let me soothe it.
VMP

What Does Love Look Like?

My command is this:
Love each other as I have loved you.
John 15:12

Today let us reflect upon Saint Augustine's answer to the question, "What does love look like?"

- It has hands to help others.
- It has feet to hasten to the poor and needy.
- It has eyes to see misery and want.
- It has ears to hear the sighs and sorrows of men.

That is what love looks like.
Today conduct an examination of conscience, asking yourself:

- Does love look like me?
- Do my hands help others?
- Do my feet hasten to the poor and needy?
- Do my eyes see misery and want?
- Do my ears hear the sighs and sorrows of others?
- Does love look like me?

⁓ Prayer for the Day ⁓
Holy God,
Let me be your willing, humble servant
in the spirit and name of Jesus.
VMP

Surrendering Through Prayer

Yet not as I will, but as you will.
Matthew 26:39

A German legend offers an important insight into prayer. Centuries ago villagers were troubled with poor harvests, so they made this prayer: "Lord, for one year promise us that you will give us exactly what we ask for—sun and rain when we ask for it."

God agreed to their request. When they called for sun, God sent sun. And when the villagers called for rain, God sent rain. Never did the corn grow taller, nor the wheat so thick, as it did that season. Likewise, fruit trees bloomed abundantly. As the harvesttime approached, their joy turned to sadness when the farmers saw to their shock and dismay that the cornstalks had no corn, the wheat stalks produced no grain, and the leafy fruited trees bore no fruit. "Oh, God," the villagers prayer in despair, "You have failed us."

God replied, "Not so my children. I gave you everything you asked for."

"Then why, God," they cried, "have we no fruit or kernel or grain?"

"Because," God answered, "you did not ask for the harsh north wind." Without the winds, of course, there was no pollination.

The lesson: We must pray, be specific, make our needs and hopes known, but leave the final answer in God's hands. That is the way Jesus prayed, "My Father, if it is possible, may this cup be taken from me. *Yet not as I will, but as you will.*"

❧ *Affirmation for the Day* ☙
God knows what is best for me;
God's love for me is perfect;
God acts for my highest good.
VMP

Just Face Life's Storms

Put your sword away!
Shall I not drink the cup the Father has given me?
John 18:11

A Wyoming cowboy said he learned one of life's most important lessons from Hereford cows. All his life he worked cattle ranches and saw firsthand how winter storms took a heavy, deadly toll among herds of cattle. Freezing rains, bitter winds, and plunging temperatures often combined to create harsh weather and enormous blizzards.

The cowboy noted that when such conditions emerged, most cattle would turn their backs to the icy blasts and slowly drift downwind, mile after mile. Finally, intercepted by a boundary fence, they would pile up against the barrier and die by the scores.

However, Herefords acted differently. This breed would instinctively head into the windward end of the range. There they would stand shoulder to shoulder facing the storm's blast, heads down against its onslaughts. "You almost always found the Herefords alive and well," the cowboy explained. "The greatest lesson I ever learned on the prairies—just face life's storms."

That is precisely what Jesus did. Rather than have Peter defend him, allowing Jesus to flee from authorities, Jesus ordered Peter to put down his sword. Jesus chose to face his life's storm. He is a model for us. When life's harshness strikes at us, we must face the storm with courage, dignity, and great trust in God.

❧ Prayer for the Day ❧

Eternal and holy God,
Deepen my trust in you,
Heighten my faith in you,
Increase my confidence in you...
So that I can face life's storms confidently.
VMP

The Greatest Gift

For God so loved the world that he gave his one and only Son.
John 3:16 (read John 3:16-21)

Newspapers in Florida carried a sad but moving story about a seven-teen-year-old boy named Jason. He was a high-school honor student who was close to his mother, his wheelchair-bound father, and his younger brother. Jason was also an expert swimmer who loved to scuba dive.

He left home one morning to explore a spring and underwater cave near his home. His plan was to return that evening in time to celebrate his mother's birthday by going out to dinner with the family.

Jason became lost in the cave. Seeking a way out, he apparently became wedged in a narrow passageway. When he realized he was trapped, he shed his yellow metal air tank and unsheathed his diver's knife. With the tank as a tablet and the knife as a pen, he wrote one last message to his family: I LOVE YOU MOM, DAD, AND CHRISTIAN. Then he ran out of air and drowned.

That final message—something communicated in the last few seconds of life—is something no one could be indifferent toward. It touches the heart and moves the spirit. In a similar way, God's final words to humanity are etched on a Roman cross. They are blood red and scream out to be heard. The message from God is like Jason's: I LOVE YOU.

⚔ Prayer for the Day ⚔
Holy and kind God,
Because of your love for me
I live with gratitude and joy;
compassion and kindness.
VMP

Christ Is Our Guide Through Life

I am the way and the truth and the life.
John 14:6

The story is told about a missionary who once became lost in the African jungle. When, at long last, he came to a primitive village, he asked one of the villagers to lead him out. After more than an hour of hacking their way through thick jungle growth, the missionary said to his guide:

"Are you sure this is the way. Where is the path?"

His guide responded, "Sir, in this place there is no path. I am the path."

That story links us to the words of Jesus: *I am the way and the truth and the life.*

Let us remember that ultimate meaning of Christ's life, death, and resurrection was to reveal the God who…

- Makes a way out of no way

- Turns tragedy into triumph

- Creates something new from the old

- Generates light in the night

- Frames victory out of defeat

- Produces hope where there is despair

- Causes good to come out of evil

- Brings life out of death

∼ Prayer for the Day ∼
Eternal and holy God,
I thank you for Jesus
and I affirm that the Christ within me
is working and creating miracles
in my own life.
VMP

God Lovingly Knows All the Details of Our Lives

You know when I sit and when I rise.

Psalm 139:2

A young business owner had experienced considerable success and was opening a second branch office. One of his friend's decided to send a floral arrangement for the grand opening. She carefully selected a wreath made up of beautiful, colorful flowers.

When she arrived at the opening, she was dismayed to find that the card attached to her wreath was inscribed Rest in peace."

Upset, she complained to the florist. The florist apologized for the error and offered her a free bouquet of flowers to take home as a token of his apology. After apologizing, the florist tried to inject this humor into the situation:

"Look at it this way," he told the woman. "Somewhere a man was buried under a wreath today that said 'Good luck in your new location.'"

Of course, as human beings, all of us can and do make mistakes. Sometimes those are the result of inadequate attention to details.

Today's psalm declares that God notes the smallest details of our lives. There is never a mix-up, because God watches over us with infinite love and infinite concern. God can be trusted to guide us through every and any dilemma.

❧ *Thought for the Day* ❧

The very word God suggests care, kindness, goodness;
and the idea of God in his infinity is infinite care,
infinite kindness, infinite goodness.

Henry Ward Beecher

Faith Means Believing "It Is Possible!"

Everything is possible for him who believes.
Mark 9:23

A highly effective way to beat back feelings of self-defeat is to assume "it is possible."

This was a technique endorsed by Jesus—*Everything is possible for him who believes.*

When facing a major crisis too many people give up prematurely because they are convinced "it is impossible." However, those who overcome great trials do so because they operate from the conviction that "it is possible." In the presence of a great personal trial, or when dealing with a serious professional setback, build up your confidence by reciting positive affirmations such as these:

- It is possible for me to find a solution where none is apparent.
- It is possible for me to create a path where one does not now exist.
- It is possible for me to discover a breakthrough.
- It is possible for me to explore every alternative.
- It is possible for me to find people who can help.
- It is possible for me to respond with creativity and energy.

⚬ *Prayer for the Day* ⚬
Loving God,
Help me to take seriously
and literally the words of Jesus:
Everything is possible for him who believes.
Let me see that all disappointments and challenges
contain positive possibilities.
VMP

Recognizing Life's Wake-Up Calls

Blessed is the man whom God corrects.
Job 5:17

Mistakes, errors, and failures characterize the "classroom" of life. But we can learn great lessons from our mistakes. Errors are often life's wake-up calls, challenging us to take a second look at ourselves, our behavior, our lifestyle, and so on. The writer of Job is aware that these wake-up calls can be a time of considerable spiritual and emotional growth— *Blessed is the man whom God corrects.*

A good example of someone who learned from failure is Anne Busquet. After working hard in the corporate world, Busquet was rewarded for her effort when American Express made her general manager of its Optima Card unit. However, when five of her two thousand employees were found to have deliberately hidden $24 million in losses, she was held accountable. American Express officials did not fire her but demoted Busquet, offering her a position managing one of the company's smaller businesses. Although her self-esteem was shaken, Busquet realized the Optima failure was her wake-up call.

Looking back at what happened, she realized that her intense perfectionist impulse was intimidating to her employees. Her personal style may have made subordinates so fearful of reporting bad news that they tried to disguise the losses.

"I never realized the impact I had on people. I realized I needed to be much more understanding," she says. Busquet went to work on herself, learning to be more patient and a better listener. She made it clear that she was open to receiving all information, good and bad. "I question why profit numbers are good as well as why they're not. If I had done this before, I might have uncovered the Optima problem sooner," she says. Busquet is now an executive vice president. She learned from failure and has emerged stronger, wiser, more mature, and a better executive.

⚜ Thought for the Day ⚜
Anyone may make a mistake;
none but a fool will persist in it.
Cicero

Tapping Into the Therapy of Humor

Do not grieve, for the joy of the Lord is your strength.
Nehemiah 8:10

Recently I attended a funeral of a young man in his thirties who died from cancer. Expecting the service to be filled with sorrow, I was pleasantly surprised as several friends spoke and shared humorous events from the young man's life. It was inspiring to hear the entire audience laugh frequently at the things this young man once said and did. Even the immediate members of his family were laughing and seemed to be comforted by the humor. Some of their tears were the direct result of laughter. Observing them, I was prompted to recall these words from the prophet Nehemiah: *Do not grieve, for the joy of the Lord is your strength.*

When we are criticized, misunderstood, put down, neglected, or hurt in other ways, it can help to put a humorous spin on the words or actions.

Humor was effectively used by pianist Liberace. As his career began to move forward, Liberace had a concert scheduled at Madison Square Garden, New York, in June 1954. Although the auditorium was filled with wildly enthusiastic fans who thoroughly enjoyed the performance, the critics loathed Liberace. The reviews were scathing. Rather than allow the criticisms to drain his enthusiasm, erode his self-esteem, or erase his achievement, Liberace brushed off the comments by telling his critics, "What you said hurt me very much. I cried all the way to the bank."

Let us try to utilize the therapy of laughter to soften some of life's unkind blows.

❦ *Thought for the Day* ❦
Humor simultaneously wounds and heals,
indicts and pardons,
diminishes and enlarges;
it constitutes inner growth at the expense of outer gain,
and those who possess and honestly practice it
make themselves more through a willingness to make themselves less.
Louis Kronenberger

Ministering to a Sick Friend

Pray for each other so that you may be healed.
James 5:16

Joyce was driving her two boys to soccer practices, volunteering at school and church, working evenings and managing her busy household. With alarming speed, her body began to betray her. This energetic, vivacious woman who toiled sixteen hours daily suddenly found her energy dropping. Soon, she was unable to maintain daily activity beyond three hours. She spend most of the time resting. A series of tests determined she had Systemic Lupus Nephritis, the type that affects kidneys. Fortunately, high quality medical care enabled Joyce to regain her health. During the five weeks she was limited to home and bed, friends found ways to help Joyce and her family. Here are some:

- *They provided a "break" in her illness.* When it seemed there was no life beyond her condition, a friend called and invited Joyce out for lunch. "Doing something so normal was a refreshing diversion," she says.

- *They sent words of encouragement.* Cards and notes that arrived in the mail daily were of enormous support. "I found myself looking forward to the daily mail. Often I read the cards over and over."

- *They gave books and magazines.* Joyce received a stack of used magazines, best-selling novels, and many inspirational books to keep her spirits up. "Being bed-bound meant I had a lot of time to read. Not only did I learn a lot during my illness, but I was able to read novels I would never normally have had time for," she says.

- *They prepared and delivered meals.* "My friends were very thoughtful about meal preparation. Most people called ahead to find out what we would enjoy eating and to be sure they were not duplicating meals others were sending."

- *They gave gifts of money.* Illness creates financial stress. Joyce was unable to work at her part-time job, and there were medical expenses not covered by insurance. Anonymous envelopes of cash were frequently left at her home.

- *They prayed for her recovery.* Faith plus medical skill resulted in a positive outcome for Joyce. Friends constantly reassured Joyce they were praying for her. Her church remembered her every Sunday.

⁓ *Thought for the Day* ⁓
Friendship is in loving rather than in being loved.
Robert Seymour Bridges

Reaching Out to a Stranger

I was a stranger and you invited me in.
Matthew 25:35

More than two decades ago, a fourteen-year-old girl in Cleveland became so angry with her parents that she ran away to New York City. Cold, hungry, penniless, and without a friend, she was shivering on the street corner when a cab pulled up. As some party-goers got out, a man in the group noticed the girl and, asking if she needed help, insisted that she join them for dinner in a nearby restaurant.

After hearing her story, the man took the teenager to the train station and bought her a ticket back to Cleveland. Before they separated, the man gently reminded the girl, "Whatever your desire, if you want it enough, you can make it happen." Then he gave her twenty dollars and his address and telephone number. If she ever needed anything, she was to call him.

The teenager returned to her family. Although she often thought of the man, she could not find the paper with his name and number. After high school, the girl attended college, graduated from medical school, and became a surgeon. Happily married to another physician, she was soon the mother of two children. When her daughter was fourteen she asked for some vintage clothes and props for a school program. As mother and daughter searched trunks of old school things, the lost paper fell out of a diary. It took months of inquiries before the mother finally located her benefactor.

Twenty-five years after the two met, Ralph Burke received a letter and a check for three hundred dollars. The woman asked that he accept it with the love and spirit in which it was sent, explaining it wasn't to repay a "kindness that has no price." Rather, she hoped he would come meet her family. Accepting the invitation, Burke was welcomed like a long-lost uncle. Burke said he always believed everyone should perform simple acts of kindness whenever one can. "Some time, some way, they always come back to you," he says.

Let us reflect on this amazing story and link it to the words of Christ—
I was a stranger and you invited me in.

⁓≷ Prayer for the Day ≷⁓
Loving God,
Open my eyes that I may see
the needy stranger in my presence.
Then, open my heart so that I may respond
with wisdom and compassion.
VMP

Kindness Delayed Is Kindness Denied

May the Lord make your love increase and
overflow for each other and for everyone else.
1 Thessalonians 3:12

Don't delay, defer, or deny an opportunity to be kind. Act kindly whenever possible, as soon as possible. Kindness delayed is kindness denied. Respond as soon as you see a need, even if it is inconvenient to do so.

A father recently received an emergency phone call from a stranger who told him their family dog had been hit by a car at a nearby, busy intersection. The father and his eleven-year-old son ran to the street corner to find the dog lying completely still, with feet outstretched. Because the boy was distraught, the people who had called remained there to comfort him. Before long it was evident that the dog was just in deep shock and was not seriously hurt. He was soon sitting up, licking the boy's hand.

The young couple explained they witnessed the dog being struck by a car and stopped to pick up the animal from the busy road. They found the phone number on the dog tag and called the family. They were not the people who hit the dog. The person who hit the dog did not stop. This young couple saw it happen and took the injured dog from the busy street so that oncoming cars would not hurt him more. In their act of kindness these strangers obviously saved the dog's life. Father and son will never forget their kindness.

The lesson in that story: Kindness delayed is kindness denied.

❧ *Thought for the Day* ❧
A kind heart is a fountain of gladness,
making everything in its vicinity
freshen into smiles.
Washington Irving

Be Kind to an Enemy

If your enemy is hungry, feed him;
if he is thirsty, give him something to drink.
Romans 12:20

Most of us can find ways to be kind to family members, friends, neighbors, colleagues, and even strangers. Perhaps the great test of our kindness is whether or not we can be kind to those to have hurt us by their words or deeds. Expand the boundaries of your soul by reaching out with kindness to an "enemy."

In September 1965, Bill Schiebler was a twenty-four-year-old officer in the army and on his way to Vietnam. Before leaving the country he visited his grandfather in Appleton, Wisconsin, to say good-bye. It was an emotional farewell because both knew they might not see each other again. As Schiebler left, his grandfather offered these parting words: "Now, you remember, Bill, be kind to your enemies. God loves them just as much as he loves you."

Later that year, the grandfather's admonition came back to Schiebler during a tense trek behind enemy lines. Schiebler and his unit had captured two North Vietnamese prisoners and were trying to make their way back to the safety of their camp. It was an exhausting hike in the darkness, particularly for one prisoner who was barefoot. "In the glow of our flashlight, I looked at his feet; both were a bloody pulp. Even though he was grimly stoic, it was clear he would have great difficulty making it back. For a moment I hesitated," Schiebler recalled.

"Already I had seen too many good friends die at the hands of the North Vietnamese." However, Schiebler impulsively picked the man up, flipped his body across his back, and carried him through the thick jungle. "As I trudged along, a faint weeping sounded from the man on my back," Schiebler said. "I pretended not to hear it until he began to sob. Without thinking, I gave his body a slight squeeze of reassurance." When they finally reached the camp, word of Schiebler's act of kindness to an enemy spread, which prompted others to respond compassionately to their prisoner. "Our medic went out of his way to give him some antibiotic salve to ward off infection," Schiebler said.

⤳ Thought for the Day ⤳
What do we live for, if it is not to make life
less difficult to each other?
George Eliot

Using Our Influence to Encourage Others

You are the salt of the earth.
Matthew 5:13

A woman simply signed as "Carol" wrote to an advice columnist to share not a problem but a joy that surprised her life. In the early 1990s the woman saw the movie *Crazy People*, starring Dudley Moore. The film was about people with mental illness who banded together to become productive citizens in their community. The writer felt the movie sent a clear and positive message to the public about people struggling with mental illness.

"Since I suffer from clinical depression and have for most of my life, I wrote a letter to Dudley Moore telling him how much this picture helped me," she says. To her surprise, a few months later, her phone rang and she heard, "May I speak to Carol? This is Dudley Moore calling."

The actor called simply to express support for Carol in her struggle with clinical depression. Carol described the actor as modest, sincere, and extremely caring. "I can't tell you what a big help it was knowing that someone of his fame still cares for those who fight a daily battle with mental illness. It made my day," she concluded.

Today's words from Jesus are a reminder that we have influence. Like salt, we flavor life by what we say and do. While most of us are not famous actors and actresses, all of us have influence over someone—a child, a spouse, a relative, a friend, a neighbor. Perhaps, because of our profession or standing in a community, we have a larger sphere of influence. Whatever the case, we should, like Dudley Moore, use our influence to help others.

⚜ Thought for the Day ⚜
Your influence is negative or positive,
never neutral.
Henrietta Cornelia Mears

The Power of Determination

...stand firm in one's spirit.
Philippians 1:27

Country and western singing star Dolly Parton will never forget the day everyone laughed at her when she was a teenager. It happened during graduation ceremonies at her small high school. Graduating students were invited to stand up and announce their plans for the future. "I'm going on to junior college," one young man announced. "I'm getting married," declared a young woman.

When it was Parton's turn to speak she walked to the microphone and said simply, "I'm going to Nashville to become a star." The entire auditorium erupted in laughter. "I was stunned," Parton recalls. "Somehow, though, that laughter instilled in me an even greater determination to realize my dream. I might have crumbled under the weight of the hardships that were to come had it not been for the response of the crowd that day."

Parton's experience is an invaluable lesson for everyone. Parton could have allowed her dream to die because of the audience's disappointing response. However, she was able to use a moment of humiliation and convert it to inspiration.

This story provides us with an ideal opportunity to reexamine the power of determination. Those who enjoy the fruits of success and satisfaction in living are able to take personal disappointments, hurts, rejections, and mistakes and employ them as the raw material to create greater energy and motivation for moving forward. The spiritual term for determination is standing firm.

ᘏᕔ *Prayer for the Day* ᕔᘏ

Dear God,
Do not allow me to give up prematurely.
Do not allow me to accept easy defeat.
Do not allow me to lower my standard.
Strengthen my will; empower my resolve;
and fortify my determination.

VMP

Winning Starts With Beginning

What you decide on will be done,
and light will shine on your ways.
  Job 22:28 *(New International Version)*

Here is a basic truth about life: Doing activates, while not doing inhibits. Taking a first small step often opens the door to larger opportunities. And today's scripture offers this reminder—What you decide on will be done, and light will shine on your ways.

A good example of someone taking the first step is Mary Jane, a thirty-one-year-old Chicago school administrator. When she began to feel bored and restless with her work, a childhood dream of being a lawyer re-emerged. "I wasn't sure I had the ability or the stamina to handle the vigorous course of study leading to a law degree," she says. However, Mary Jane began by purchasing a book to help her prepare for the law-school entrance exam. "I worked my way through the exercises most evenings for a year before taking the exam. To my pleasant surprise I earned a high score." Fortified by that positive experience, she applied to a law school, was accepted, and awarded a $10,000-a-year scholarship.

To enjoy the fullness of life spoken of in scripture, we need to take the first step. We must be willing to accept the risk of failure. Winning starts with beginning!

❧ *Thought for the Day* ☙
What you can do, or dream you can, begin it.
Boldness has genius, power and magic in it.
Only engage, and then the mind grows heated.
Begin, and then the work will be completed.
  Johann Wolfgang Von Goethe

Determine Your Own Destiny

We have different gifts, according to the grace given us.

Romans 12:6

Remind yourself that with God's help you do have the power to control your own world regardless of what others may think and say about you. Those who have made the most notable achievements in our lifetime were often discounted by authority figures in their lives.

Consider these:

Thomas Edison. When he was seven years old, a teacher regarded him as a slow learner. In his presence she told a school official that Edison was "addled," meaning easily confused and distracted. She remarked that it was useless for Edison to continue his education.

Amelia Earhart. The pioneer aviator was also dismissed by a significant adult. "I am very concerned about Amelia. She is bright and full of curiosity, but her interest in bugs and other crawling things and her daredevil projects are just not fitting for a young lady. Perhaps we could channel her curiosity into a safe hobby."

Woodrow Wilson. The future president and professor at Princeton University was regarded as a poor student who learned slowly and laboriously. "Woodrow is a unique member of the class. He is ten years old and is only just beginning to read and write. He shows signs of improving, don't set your sights too high for him," noted his school officials.

Jacqueline Susann. When the aspiring writer submitted her manuscript *Valley of the Dolls*, one editor wrote this scathing evaluation: "She is a painfully dull, inept, clumsy, undisciplined, rambling, and thoroughly amateurish writer. She wastes endless pages on utter trivia, writes wide-eyed romantic scenes that would not make the back pages of *True Confession*. Most of the first 200 pages are virtually worthless and dreadfully dull." (*Valley of the Dolls* become one of the highest-selling novels in publishing history, with nearly 29 million copies sold.)

Clearly, these achievers took charge of their own life.

❧ *Thought for the Day* ❧
Every human being is intended to have a character
of his own; to be what no others are, and to do what
no other can do.
William Ellery Channing

Exploring Fears to Overcome Them

Don't be afraid of them. Remember the Lord,
who is great and awesome, and fight...
                                    Nehemiah 4:14

Fear is one of life's emotional poisons. It infects the personality creating a paralysis of insight and action. Often fear is the result of ignorance and lack of information. Thus the most effective antidote to fear is to study it. Fear explored is fear exposed and diminished. Under careful scrutiny, most fears will evaporate.

It has been reported that among his many personal problems and phobias, Michael Jackson suffered from a fear of flying. When Michael P. Schulhof—chairman of the Sony Corporation of America, for whose *Epic* label Jackson records—heard about the entertainer's flying problem he invited Jackson to fly with him. Schulhof, a licensed commercial pilot, asked Jackson to join him in the cockpit of one of Sony's jets. There he demonstrated the plane's safety features and showed Jackson how the jet operated. Schulhof's effort to demystify the experience of flying worked, says Sandy Gallin, Jackson's agent, and "was instrumental in helping the entertainer overcome his fear of flying."

Today, examine your life, asking, "What fears are holding me back?" Perhaps you have wanted to return to college, switch careers, enter the workplace for the first time in many years, reach out and establish new friends, start your own business...but you are hesitant out of the fear of failing. Carefully examine your fears. Do not let them hold you back. Ask God to help you overcome them and broaden the horizons of your life.

～ Affirmation for the Day ～
As I take risks, life unfolds with joy and delight.
As I face my fears, my fears recede.
All is well with my life because God loves me.
VMP

Look for the Good in the Bad

For our light and momentary troubles are
achieving for us an eternal glory that far
outweighs them all.

2 Corinthians 4:17

Because life brings all of us unexpected and unpleasant events, we must learn how to deal with them. One way is to train ourselves to look for the good in the bad. The fact is that there is a silver lining in every crisis and catastrophe.

Only after a serious automobile accident ended his hopes of becoming a soccer player did Julio Iglesias find his true calling. While recovering from injuries in a Madrid hospital, Iglesias taught himself to play the guitar and sing. He discovered a new gift and, more importantly, that his talent brought pleasure to others. He began performing whenever an opportunity presented itself. Five years later he won an international singing contest and has gone on, establishing himself as one of the world's most popular vocalists.

When bad events come into your life begin to manipulate your way through them by expressing and exploring these thoughts:

- *I will find the good in the bad.*
- *I will respond courageously and boldly.*
- *I will triumph over this tragedy.*
- *I will be open to new possibilities.*
- *I will allow this event to be my teacher but not my master.*
- *I will be the master of my universe.*

Factor into your thinking the words of Paul that our problems are *light and momentary* and can be used to achieve greater things for us.

≈ *Thought for the Day* ≈

Troubles are usually the brooms and shovels
that smooth the road to a good man's fortune;
and many a man curses the rain that falls upon
his head, and knows not that it brings abundance.

Saint Basil

Scars of the Heart

With his mouth the godless destroys his neighbor.
Proverbs 11:9

This is sad but true: Upon leaving a community pool, a mother was overheard shaming her child who had apparently been afraid to put his face in the water during a swim lesson. "You little coward," the mother hissed at him. "I'm am ashamed of you."

"The little coward," the three-year-old boy, began to sob. The mother stared coldly at him and then proceeded to shame him for crying!

We're quickly shocked and outraged whenever we hear of flagrant physical or sexual child abuse, but many people wound others with words every day and never give it a second thought. Shaming words leave emotional scars on the human heart as surely as physical abuse leaves scars on the body. Shame sabotages self-esteem. It assassinates the human spirit. Gradually, shaming statements undermine the victim's healthy sense of self, leaving him or her feeling worth less than nothing.

There are many shaming statements used every day—by ourselves, as well as others. We should think before saying things like

> You should have known better!
> Didn't anybody teach you any manners?
> You idiot!
> That was a stupid thing to do!
> What's the matter with you?
> You should be ashamed of yourself!
> Can't you do anything right?

A good way to make yourself more aware of shaming words and deeds is to practice this exercise for one day. Whenever you feel a flush of shame or embarrassment, ask yourself, "What was said to me? Did it make me feel diminished, hurt, rejected?" Once you become more aware of what shame sounds and feels like, you will more readily recognize shaming language and behavior.

With God's help we can arrest this unhealthy behavior in ourselves and stop others from trying to dump it on us.

⚜ Prayer for the Day ⚜
Loving God,
Help me, always, to use words that help, inspire, and heal.
Help me to avoid words that hurt, injure, and destroy.
VMP

Ten Rules for a Happy Day

Do not store up for yourselves treasures on earth...
but store up for yourselves treasures in heaven.
Matthew 6:19–20

1. *Today I will not strike back.* If someone is rude; if someone is impatient; if someone is unkind... I will not respond in like manner.

2. *Today I will ask God to bless my "enemy."* If I come across someone who treats me harshly or unfairly, I will quietly ask God to bless that individual. I understand the "enemy" could be a family member, neighbor, colleague, or stranger.

3. *Today I will be careful about what I say.* I will carefully choose and guard my words, being certain that I do not spread gossip, slander, or malign anyone in any way.

4. *Today I will go the extra mile.* I will find ways to help share the burden of another person. I will find ways to make life more pleasant.

5. *Today I will forgive.* I will forgive any hurts or injuries that come my way.

I will also work to forgive injuries that have been inflicted upon me in the past.

6. *Today I will do something nice for someone, but I will do it secretly.* I will reach out anonymously and bless the life of another person.

7. *Today I will treat others as I wish to be treated.* I will practice the golden rule—do unto others as you would have them do unto you—with everyone I encounter.

8. *Today I will raise the spirits of someone who is discouraged.* My smile, my words, my expression of support, can make the difference to someone who is wrestling with life.

9. *Today I will nurture my body.* I will eat less; I will eat only healthy foods; I will thank God for my body.

10. *Today I will grow spiritually.* I will spend more time in prayer; I will begin reading a spiritual book; I will find a quiet place and listen to God's voice.

❧ Thought for the Day ❧

Life is a quarry, out of which we are to mold
and chisel and complete a character.

Goethe

Spiritual Lessons Via Physical Therapy

Let us not give up meeting together,
as some are in the habit of doing,
but let us encourage one another.
Hebrews 10:25

A friend recently underwent minor surgery after he injured his knee playing soccer. Initially, he lived with the pain for several months, believing it would pass. When the pain remained, a doctor advised surgery to correct torn cartilage. He spent several months in physical therapy. My friend reflected on the experience and came up with these three spiritual applications:

1. *Some problems won't go away.* At first he believed his knee would heal unaided, but it did not. In life there are problems that require intervention for healing to take place: past physical or emotional abuse, damaged relationships, deep psychological scars. While it may be tempting to ignore such issues, the pain will stay and possibly even cripple us if we don't seek help.

2. *Lose quickly but gain slowly.* My friend discovered how quickly muscle mass can be lost without the ability to properly use his leg. One leg was decidedly larger than the other. After three months of physical therapy, the gap was diminishing but the difference was still noticeable. What's true in the physical realm is also true in the moral and spiritual. A reputation for honesty can evaporate in a moment of weakness. A marriage can be injured, almost beyond repair, by a careless action. It can take a long, long time to recover.

3. *We can use help from others.* My friend could not heal alone. He needed skills from a surgeon and, later, from a physical therapist. In our spiritual lives we need to be in fellowship with others who share our values and vision. *Let us not give up meeting together, as some are in the habit of doing, but let us encourage one another,* advises the writer of Hebrews. With people of like mind, we receive instruction and inspiration.

❧ Thought for the Day ❧

Be united with other Christians. A wall with loose bricks
is not good. The bricks must be cemented together.
Corrie Ten Boom

Going the Extra Mile

If someone forces you to go one mile,
go with him two miles.

Matthew 5:41

Before the advent of cellular phones, a salesman who had been on the road for nearly a week stopped at a pay phone to call home. He had only a few coins and knew he would not have long to talk with his wife, so they spoke right until the moment the line went dead because he had used up his allotted time with the money he had inserted.

As he was walking away from the phone booth, he heard it ring and turned around to answer it. Thinking he would be asked by the operator for more money, he was pleasantly surprised when the operator said: "I thought you would like to know that just after the line went dead, your wife said, 'I love you.'"

There are always two types of people and two ways of doing a task. One type of person does it with minimal effort and concern. Often such a person makes it clear that he or she dislikes the job and does it as quickly and as minimally as possible. The other type of person will do a task to the best of his or her ability. This person often does the task with a smile, a gracious courtesy, and does the task very well.

Today's word from Jesus is a reminder that we are to be like the telephone operator. We are to be as helpful as possible, even when the demand for assistance comes from someone who may be rude and unreasonable.

❦ *Prayer for the Day* ❦
Eternal and gracious God,
Help me to think deeply about ways
that I can go the extra mile for someone.
Then, help me to do it!

VMP

Called by God to Share Suffering

Remember those in prison as if you were their fellow prisoners,
and those who are mistreated as if you yourselves were suffering.

Hebrews 13:3b

During the 1950s, Bill lived and worked in racially tense Alabama. His job was that of a shoe buyer for a chain of shoe stores. On some trips he would be accompanied by a black employee of his firm named James.

On one overnight trip Bill and James pulled into a motel to spend the night. They walked to the front desk and requested a room for the two of them. Looking at Bill, a white American, the desk clerk said, "I can give you a room, but I will not give one to him," pointing to James.

"If he can't stay then I won't stay," Bill said calmly but clearly.

The two men walked outside. In the parking lot, James told Bill, "Why don't you just go ahead and take the room. I'll sleep here in the van. I'll be all right."

"No," replied Bill. "If they won't let you stay in that motel then I won't stay there either."

Both James and Bill spent the night in the van.

Bill fulfilled eloquently the command in today's scripture—*Remember those in prison as if you were their fellow prisoners, and those who are mistreated as if you yourselves were suffering.* Bill not only shared James' suffering but affirmed that James was a human being who deserves respect and dignity.

❧ Thought for the Day ❧

Among those who stand, do not sit;
Among those who sit, do not stand;
Among those who laugh, do not weep;
Among those who weep, do not laugh.

Jewish Proverb

Deep Roots Help Us Survive Trials

His roots dry up below and his branches wither above.
Job 18:16

Trees show us how to survive the storms in our lives. Only when a tree establishes deep roots can the tree grow tall and upward, withstanding storms and surviving fires. Sometime ago, a forest fire raged in the Ozark mountains along the Arkansas border. A man who owned several dozen acres that contained an oak forest was greatly disturbed to know the fire was ravaging his trees.

To his astonishment, when he went to investigate the damage after the fire, he discovered that only the dead and diseased trees had burned. They were the trees whose roots did not run deep. On the other hand, the growing, healthy trees remained unharmed. Their root system was deep and extensive, permitting them to survive the fire.

That lesson from nature should nudge us to reflect on our own root system. We must ask ourselves what we are doing to be certain that we are properly grounded and growing in healthy ways, spiritually and emotionally. Here are some ways to develop and maintain deep roots:

- Regular worship and fellowship with others
- Reading from spiritual and inspirational books
- Bible study, both privately and in a group with others
- Frequent and regular prayer and meditation
- Confessions offered to God with the request for forgiveness
- Asking for forgiveness from others
- Extending forgiveness to others

~≈ *Thought for the Day* ≈~
The weaker we feel, the harder we lean on God
And the harder we lean, the stronger we grow.
Joni Eareckson Tada

I Have to Forgive...

If you hold anything against anyone, forgive him.
Mark 11:25

A woman whose daughter died from a rare form of cancer learned this important lesson: "One of the things we must do before we can move ahead in any situation is to completely forgive whatever wrongs, real and imagined, that have been done to us."

In her case, this is what she says she has to do:

I have to forgive the doctors and nurses whose training had not prepared them either to deal with a child whose illness they couldn't understand or how to be supportive of her grieving parents and sister.

I have to forgive the people who stayed away from us because they had never been taught about the needs of a bereaved person.

I have to forgive the people who tried to "cheer us up" or "take our minds off of it." They, too, were baffled by the horror of it all, and were, in their own way, trying to be helpful.

I have to forgive the people who told us Linda's death was God's will. They were trying to comfort us.

I have to forgive myself for so many things... I have to forgive myself for the times I was cross or demanding; for all the situations I handled badly as Linda was growing up...

Today, make this woman's forgiveness exercise your own. Take out a sheet of paper and begin completing sentences that begin with the words *I have to forgive...*

❧ *Thought for the Day* ❧
A little understanding makes forgiving a lot easier.
Lewis B. Smedes

Being Aware of Our Sins of Omission

Defend the cause of the weak...
Psalm 82:3

In a letter written to advice columnist Ann Landers, a person tells of having dinner at the home of some new friends. Seated at the table were a neighbor, the host and hostess, and their two teenage children.

Halfway through the meal, the neighbor turned to the hosts' teenage son and asked, "Why do you wear your hair like that? Are you trying to advertise the fact that you are antiestablishment or what?" The man continued to lecture the youth whose face turned a bright red from embarrassment.

The writer said, "I'm sure it took a lot of self-control for the boy not to lash out in anger. He kept looking at his plate and did not respond." The man continued harassing the youth for another ten minutes until, finally, the host was able to change the subject. The writer concluded the letter to Ann Landers saying, "by then, I had indigestion," and asked for Ann Landers' view.

Her response is noteworthy: "Was that the best you could do—sit there and get indigestion? Why didn't you tell the man that the boy's haircut was his own business and he was out of line? File this one under 'sins of omission,' and the next time you are in such a situation don't just sit there—speak up."

We can wrong people and injure them by failing to speak up when they are being oppressed and mistreated. Let us not be guilty of the "sin of omission." Let us adhere to the psalmist's admonition—*Defend the cause of the weak...*

⚛ Thought for the Day ⚛

To sin by silence when they should protest
makes cowards of men.

Abraham Lincoln

God Works in Mysterious Ways

He performs wonders that cannot be fathomed,
miracles that cannot be counted.

Job 5:9

This story of the sole survivor of a shipwreck has a useful spiritual lesson…

In the seventeenth century, a sailing vessel crossing the Pacific was battered and broken by a fierce typhoon. The one and only survivor managed to land upon a small uninhabited island. He was able to do this by desperately clinging to a wooden beam from his ship.

After much trouble and considerable effort he built a crude hut where he placed all the belongings he had saved from the sinking ship that had washed ashore. Each day he prayed to God for deliverance, and he continually scanned the ocean horizon to hail any ships that might happen to pass by.

One day, upon returning from a search for food, he was horrified to find his hut in flames. Everything he had was gone. The man felt this was the worst that could happen, so he looked up toward the heavens and cursed God. About three hours later, however, a ship arrived and the captain said, "We saw your smoke signal!"

The spiritual application of that story contains a minor and major theme. The minor theme is this: *Sometimes help comes our way in unusual and unexpected ways.* The major theme is this: *God works in mysterious ways.* Because we cannot anticipate how God will respond to our prayers, we must be open to God's responses, which may come in surprising ways. Let us not miss out on recognizing God's activity on our behalf because of rigid expectations.

❧ *Thought for the Day* ❧
Were the works of God readily understandable
by human reason, they would be neither
wonderful nor unspeakable.
Thomas à Kempis

A Large Lesson From a Little Girl

The Lord is good, a refuge in times of trouble.
He cares for those who trust in him.

Nahum 1:7

A prominent neurosurgeon in his city was seated beside a pastor at a banquet. During their conversation, the pastor asked, "Doctor, what was the greatest operation you ever performed?"

"I'm not really sure because many operations I have performed required all my skills. Perhaps the one that meant the most to me was the time I operated on a little girl who was given a less than 10 percent chance of survival. I remember her being so sweet and so pale when she entered the operating room." The physician added that at the time he was experiencing serious personal problems, which included a deteriorating marriage, as well as major difficulties with his teenage son.

As the surgical staff was preparing to administer the anesthetic to the little girl, she asked the doctor if she could say a prayer, explaining that every night before she went to sleep she said a prayer. "Of course you may pray," the doctor said, "and include me in your prayer if you don't mind."

In a sweet voice the child offered up her evening prayer:

Jesus, tender Shepherd, hear me,
Bless thy little lamb tonight;
Through the darkness be thou near me
Keep me safe till morning light.

"And, dear God, please bless the doctor," she added. Then the girl assured the doctor she was ready for surgery, saying, "I'm not afraid because God loves me and is right here, and he will bring me through this okay."

"I was blinded by tears and had to turn away and do another wash-up before I could start the operation," the doctor said. Then he prayed quietly: "Dear God, if you never help me save another human being, help me save this little girl." He operated, and the miracle happened. The girl lived and is now a healthy, growing child. However, as he left the hospital that day, the doctor told the pastor, "I realized I was the one who had been operated on, not just the little girl. She taught me that if I take all my problems and put them in the hands of God, he will see me through."

❧ Affirmation for the Day ❧
God is great. God is good.
God is the unfailing and unlimited source of all I need.
VMP

When You're Under Attack

Deliver me from my enemies, O God; protect me from those who rise up against me. Deliver me from evildoers and save me from blood-thirsty men. See how they lie in wait for me! Fierce men conspire against me for no offense or sin of mine, O Lord. I have done no wrong, yet they are ready to attack me. Arise to help me; look on my plight!

Psalm 59:1-4

During a fourteen-day period, the pastor of a large church received more criticism than normal.

There was an anonymous phone call from someone who labeled him the "scum of the earth" because his church opened a daycare center, which drew many African-American children.

There was an angry church member who threatened to quit because of a disagreement with the pastor's leadership.

There was a letter from a second-time visitor who criticized the pastor for preaching about money. (It was the yearly stewardship-emphasis Sunday in his church.)

There was a complaint from an important church lay leader who felt the pastor was not doing enough for the church youth.

While clergy do receive routine criticism, that was a rough fourteen days for the pastor. His consolation came from this prayer in Psalm 59. "Reading it I realized David [the author] didn't just have critics—his enemies were plotting to kill him. They wanted him dead and were working toward that goal," he remembers thinking. The pastor was encouraged by David's faith in God's goodness and protection.

"When I'm under attack, it helps me to remember David's courage. He trusted in God's protection and justice. And, when I'm under heavy criticism I do the same!"

⚘ Thought for the Day ⚘
Lord, help me to remember that nothing
is going to happen to me today that you and I
can't handle.
Popular American Prayer

The Mending of a Life

*Those who suffer... should commit themselves
to their faithful Creator.*

1 Peter 4:19

No matter how bad your life is, it can be repaired. Here are some suggestions:

1. *You are not alone in your brokenness.* Moses fled the country after killing an Egyptian guard. Yet God called on him to lead the people of Israel out of slavery and into freedom. In the New Testament, Peter was the one who denied ever knowing Christ, yet this same man was used by God to preach a powerful sermon on the day of Pentecost. The fact is that most people experience brokenness at some time in their lives. Broken lives are the rule, not the exception.

2. *Broken lives can be rebuilt.* No matter how far you have fallen, you can be raised. No matter how tattered your life is, it can be repaired. No matter how many pieces your life has crumbled into, you can be put back together again.

3. *Begin the mending by asking for God's help.* You may need to make major changes—ask God to empower you. You may need to turn from one way of life to another—ask God to empower you. You may need to refocus your life—ask God to empower you.

4. *Live like a person who is loved by God.* Don't replay past tapes and rehearse past failures. Remind yourself that God is redeeming, guiding, and empowering you. God has forgiven you and you must forgive yourself.

5. *Let others help and support you.* An experience of brokenness is a heavy burden to bear alone. Confide in wise people—a pastor, a counselor, a spiritual leader, a trusted friend.

⚜ Thought for the Day ⚜
He that so much for you did do,
Will do yet more.
Thomas Wasbourne

Taking All Human Hurts Seriously

My soul is downcast within me.
Psalm 42:6

There are too many in too much pain. A great deal of human suffering could be reduced if we chose to take every human hurt seriously and respond with compassion and love.

Consider the plight of a woman writing anonymously to an advice columnist to share this painful experience from the past: "I was barely sixteen when I found out I was pregnant. I miscarried when I was about ten weeks along. I was amazed how many people told me how lucky I was. How could I be lucky? The emotional conflict I endured was incredible. I was mourning the loss of a child." She went on to say that if she had been twenty-five and married, no one would have dared say she was "lucky!"

Today, that woman is a national award-winning teacher and has a beautiful one-year-old son. "As I look at him I know I was given another chance. However, when I miscarried my baby at sixteen, all I wanted was to be treated as a grieving mother." She concluded her letter by reminding the advice columnist and her readers that a mother's grief is boundless and ageless. When she lost her baby she needed the love and support of her friends and family.

Let us use that story to sensitize us to the hurts of others regardless of their age or circumstance. Let us be the ones who touch their lives with kindness, empathy, compassion, and love.

❧ *Thought for the Day* ❧

Quiet and sincere sympathy is often the most welcome
and efficient consolation to the afflicted. Said a wise man
to one in deep sorrow, "I did not come to comfort you;
God only can do that;
but I did come to say how deeply and tenderly
I feel for you in your affliction."
Tryon Edwards

Acting As a Person of Faith

The weapons we fight with are not the weapons of the world.
On the contrary, they have divine power to demolish strongholds.

2 Corinthians 10:4

Two tragic incidents clearly demonstrate how people of faith respond during a time of personal crisis:

In the first one, a four-year-old girl had fallen under the wheels of a school bus and was killed. Emergency workers had to help the distraught bus driver—herself a young mother—away from the scene. The following day that bus driver received a message from the mother of the child who was killed. She said simply, "I do not blame you for what happened."

While suffering the trauma of losing a child, the woman tapped into her faith, which taught her to be considerate and to be forgiving. It was a powerful act of human compassion in a moment least expected.

In the other incident, a sixteen-year-old high-school track team member died after being struck in the head by a discus. After being kept alive by life support, it was evident the youth would not survive. The family prepared for the worst by filling out organ donation forms. He died twenty hours after being struck. When interviewed by reporters, the father and mother shared these words of praise:

"We're grateful that his organs will be able to be used to help seven other people," the father said.

And, the mother told the reporter: "We're thanking God for the good times we had with him. It was a good sixteen years. We don't understand this accident, but we trust God has a plan for us."

The lesson from those grieving parents is this: Whenever any crisis comes into our lives we should act as people of faith. We should respond spiritually to the crisis. It may mean extending forgiveness. It may mean finding reasons to be grateful. It will always mean trusting God to help us and guide us. Responding spiritually frees us from being caught up in blame, despair, or bitterness.

❧ Prayer for the Day ❧
Loving and eternal God,
As I pray,
As I read scripture,
As I worship,
As I listen to sermons,
May my faith and trust be quietly growing.
VMP

How God Can Lift a Depressed Spirit

He came to a broom tree, sat down under it and prayed that he might die. "I have had enough, Lord," he said. "Take my life."

1 Kings 19:4

People who believe in God are not immune from depression. The prophet Elijah is a good example. After a successful ministry came some resistance to his message. The entire chapter of 1 Kings 19 reveals ways in which God can lift the human spirit and restore us back to energetic service. Notice these divine methods:

1. *God let Elijah rest.* Sheer exhaustion depletes our physical, mental, and spiritual energies. The simple task of rest renews our spirits, restores our energy, and refreshes our outlook.

2. *God listened to Elijah complain.* There are two important aspects here: First, Elijah poured out his frustrations in prayer and God listened. It is appropriate to tell God exactly how we feel, without censoring our language. God can handle our anger and frustration. Second, the depressed need to be listened to. They benefit by expressing and exploring their feelings. Depressed feelings can be reduced and even eliminated when the depressed have someone they can talk to, and be listened to, without judgment.

3. *God refocused Elijah's attention.* There was a powerful windstorm, a destructive earthquake, and a threatening fire that consumed Elijah's attention. As Elijah took the focus off himself, he began to see things differently and feel better.

4. *God gave Elijah a new challenge.* God did not resolve all of Elijah's issues. He sent the prophet back to Damascus with a special task: He was to anoint two kings and a prophet. When depressed, often a new challenge can give us a renewed sense of purpose for our lives.

5. *God gave Elijah a friend.* God sent Elijah an understudy, Elisha, who moved from being a student to a personal friend. Often, when we are depressed, we tend to isolate ourselves, but the company of one faithful friend can ease the pain and lift the burden of depression.

❧ Prayer for the Day ❧
Gracious God,
Whenever my spirit is engulfed by darkness,
let me patiently trust you to meet my needs
and lead me through the night into the light.
VMP

God Still Loves the Rebel...the Skeptic...

This is the one I esteem:
he who is humble and contrite in spirit,
and trembles at my word.

Isaiah 66:2

A father tells of learning that one of his teenage sons had done something seriously wrong. The youth knew he had flagrantly violated one of the basic principles of his home. It was an inexcusable indiscretion, but what made matters worse was the youth did not disclose it. The father found out through another source. Angry, he confronted his son.

However, when confronted the son was not belligerent or defiant. He didn't shout, "I hate this house," or "I hate those rules," or "You're too strict." Rather, he admitted his violation, saying humbly and quietly: "It's true, and I'm sorry I did it."

Then the father gave what he knew was a painful punishment: The youth would not be permitted to get his driver's license the following month as planned. That was a rite of passage the youth had looked forward to for years.

Instead of exploding into a rage about the consequence or storming from the room in anger, the boy simply burst into tears saying, "I understand, Dad. I'm really sorry!" By then, the father was also in tears and embraced his son, assuring him of his love. "When I later thought about that incident, it struck me as strange that although it was just minutes after learning of his rebellious act, I felt closer to my son at that point than ever before," the father recalls. "His spirit of brokenness, honesty, and transparency made me love him even more."

That father-son confrontation is like our relationship with God. God still loves the rebel, the cynic, the skeptic in us. And perhaps God's love for us is more sensitized when we come seeking help, comfort, forgiveness. In today's scripture, God is reported as declaring, "This is the one I esteem: he who is humble and contrite in spirit, and trembles at my word.

⊰ *Prayer for the Day* ⊱
Eternal God,
I thank you for your
love when I am honorable, noble, good and kind.
I thank you also for your love
when I am less that I ought to be.

VMP

When God Seems Far Away

O my God, I cry out by day, but you do not answer.

Psalm 22:2

There are times in life when there is nothing more difficult than the absence of God's presence. In the midst of physical or emotional pain, we cry out to God and wonder if God hears or even cares. A good lesson for dealing with the absence of God comes via the great Elizabethan poet and preacher, John Donne. He had more than his share of suffering.

In fact, his life was one tragedy after another. His father died when he was four years old. He was denied a degree from Oxford University—a degree he worked hard to earn—because he was Catholic in a time of Protestant political power. Then, in 1601, Donne married Anne More, the love of his life. Through a series of circumstances beyond his control, Donne lost his job and was blacklisted from any further employment.

To find peace of mind and soul, Donne switched religious loyalties, becoming part of the Church of England. At age forty-two, he sought ordination as an Anglican priest. Just as things were beginning to look a little brighter his wife died, leaving him in deep grief and the single parent of seven children.

In spite of his grief and home responsibilities, Donne worked hard in his vocation and, in 1621, became Dean of Saint Paul's Cathedral. Two years after he came down with a mysterious illness that lasted for nearly two months. He was so ill that friends maintained a "death watch" over him. During that difficult time of great pain, Donne took pen and paper and cried out to God. The result was *Devotions Upon Emergent Occasions*.

That powerful book provides a model of what to do when God seems far away. Like the biblical figure Job, Donne wrestles with God, argues and shouts at God, asks questions of God but always affirms that in spite of his very human feelings of pain and abandonment, God is a God who cares and who is in the process with him. "God's hand is in every translation; and his hand shall bind up all our scattered leaves again," he wrote.

Let us remember that in the midst of pain and when we feel God is absent, it is appropriate to question, cry, complain, and even argue with God. God alone is our audience, and he is not far off.

❧ Affirmation for the Day ❧

God made me.
God loves me.
God keeps me.
VMP

A Spiritual Lesson From a Father and His Son

The Lord is my strength.
Psalm 118:14

A father watched through the kitchen window as his young preschool-aged son played in the backyard sandbox. The boy was trying unsuccessfully to lift a large rock out of the sandbox. No matter how hard he tried, the boy could not do it. Sensing his son's frustration, the father went outside and said, "You didn't use all the strength you had."

"Yes, I did," the boy protested. "I tried as hard as I could. I just couldn't lift it!"

"No, you didn't use all the strength you had available," the father insisted. "You didn't call on me to help you."

Do you have a burden in your life which you can't lift today? Admit your inadequacy and ask God to help you. Don't get caught up in pride and resist seeking out God's help.

Sometimes there are problems we just can't overcome on our own. Those may be alcohol, drugs, food, abusive and destructive relationships, life-threatening illness, or even the prospect of death.

Let us always remember that God is a God of love, compassion, and mercy.

～≪ *Prayer for the Day* ≫～
Eternal and holy God,
Strengthen and save me.
Guide and direct me.
Renew and restore me.
VMP

Managing Family Conflict

*It is harder to win back the friendship of an offended brother
than to capture a fortified city.
His anger shuts you out like iron bars.*

Proverbs 18:19, *The Living Bible*

A family is not abnormal or dysfunctional just because conflicts emerge from time to time. Today's scripture refers to the reality of family strife. *It is harder to win back the friendship of an offended brother than to capture a fortified city. His anger shuts you out like iron bars.*

Within every family there are differences of opinion, approach, style, and expression. Often children test limits and assert their independence by acting in ways parents find disagreeable or unacceptable. Such acting out is normal and should be viewed as simply one aspect of a child's maturing and learning process. An expectation that there will be no conflict within a family is unrealistic and naive. That view will only result in disappointment. Even parents who have strong and loving rapport with their adult children experience conflict from time to time.

One example is that of the mother-daughter singing team of Naomi and Wynonna Judd. While their relationship is warm and strong, there are moments when harmony is absent. Naomi Judd explains, "Before a show in Denver, Wynonna and I were fighting because she had forgotten her outfit. We were mere minutes from showtime, and I opened fire with both guns. 'You stupid kid,' I screamed. 'Aren't you ever going to grow up and get your act together?'" Immediately, the daughter declared she would not sing with her mother that night. As the two shrieked at each other, their manager stepped in saying, "Ladies, there are several thousand people out there who've paid money to hear you tonight. You must decide whether you're going to rise to professionalism or be a disappointment to everyone, including me."

His comments evoked a mature response from both women. They quickly resolved the conflict, made amends and went on to sing. The point: Even the closest of families experience conflict from time to time.

When such conflicts arise within the family, let us work to resolve them for the common good.

⊱ Prayer for the Day ⊰
Eternal and gracious God,
When a conflict arises in my family,
let me be quick to listen, slow to judge,
eager to understand, gracious in my response.
VMP

Separating the Person From the Behavior

Neither do I condemn you.
Jesus in John 8:11

In healthy relationships, a person is always accepted even when the behavior is unacceptable. Jesus' words—*Neither do I condemn you*—must have been a great gift to the woman who was caught in the act of adultery. Religious leaders brought her to Jesus believing he would judge her harshly. His response was one of loving acceptance of her without condoning her behavior.

We must learn to separate the person from the behavior we find objectionable. This means learning to speak appropriately when there is a confrontation. Saying "I'm upset that you came home an hour past curfew because I was very worried something might have happened to you" is more appropriate than angrily declaring "Late again! I'm not surprised because you are so irresponsible and immature. You'll never amount to anything!" The first response is a simple statement of fact, which faults the behavior, while the second response erodes self-esteem by demeaning the individual.

Separating the person from the behavior is a form of unconditional love because it conveys this important message: "I love you with no strings attached, regardless of how you behave. This doesn't mean I always accept your behavior, but it does mean I always accept you as a person."

∼ Thought for the Day ∼
Don't condemn the sinner! We are, or we were,
or we could be, as this man is.
An old abbot to his monks

Being the Right Kind of Friend

I am worn out from groaning; all night long I
flood my bed with weeping and drench my couch with tears.

Psalm 6:6

Sarah had a devastating experience when her fifty-four-year-old husband died suddenly from a heart attack. "When Jimmy died I was devastated and angry at God for this 'injustice.' Although I had not attended church regularly, I called the pastor. He was extremely helpful, reminding me that it was okay to be angry. He assured me that God could handle my anger. The pastor encouraged me to vent my feelings. He listened sensitively and compassionately. Gradually, my faith deepened and became a sustaining power in my life. As I became more spiritually connected, I felt my anger diminish and give way to acceptance and peace."

That encounter raises this important question: Could I be the right kind of friend when someone who is devastated by loss came to speak with me?

Here are characteristics of people who truly help others during a time of personal crisis:

- They listen more than they speak.
- They do not pass judgment on you or your feelings.
- They do not tell you how to feel.
- They don't change the subject when you talk about your loss.
- They are accepting of you.
- They do not respond with clichés, such as "He's in a better place now."
- "It was God's will." "You can get married again."
- They do respond with supportive, sympathetic statements, such as "I'm sorry." "How can I help?" "What can I do?" "This must be very painful." "Tell me more."

⤜ *Prayer for the Day* ⤛
Eternal and loving God,
Let me be the friend who
consoles and consoles,
strengthens and stabilizes,
those who hurt from life's blows.
VMP

Managing a Personal Crisis With Wisdom

I will give you words and wisdom...
Luke 21:15

When a major crisis looms and threatens to take over your life, take these steps:

- *Begin with the faith that God is present.* Although the darkness may seem all-consuming, God will pierce the darkness with light.

- *Explore and express your feelings.* Crisis creates many unfamiliar, intense feelings. Do not be afraid of them. Do not run away from them. Express and explore them through journal writing, in a support group, with a sensitive spiritual leader.

- *Join with others in a similar experience.* "The people most able to give us encouragement in facing such sorrows and fears, not surprisingly, have been those who have been through similar grief," says one man grieving the loss of his twenty-four-year-old daughter who was killed in an auto accident. Try joining a support group. If there is not one in your community, connect informally with others who have had a similar loss. That can be done through telephone contact or conversations over coffee.

- *Ask for specific help.* Extended family and friends will offer their assistance, but often it is vague—"Let me know what I can do!" Review your circle of acquaintances and then call on them when specific issues arise.

- *Turn to God and ask for daily wisdom.* Remember the words of Christ—*I will give you words and wisdom...*

⟳ *Affirmation for the Day* ⟲
God knows me and loves me.
God gives me confidence.
God gives me strength.
VMP

Pressing Forward

Why is the Lord bringing us to this land
only to let us fall by the sword?
Our wives and children will be taken as plunder.
Wouldn't it be better for us to go back to Egypt?

Numbers 14:3

When the Spanish explorer Hernando Cortez landed at Veracruz on the Gulf of Mexico in the sixteenth century, one of the first things he did was burn his ships.

His goal was to conquer this new land by pushing west to the Pacific. By burning his ships he eliminated the possibility that his men would lose heart and sail back to Spain. The presence of the ships gave Cortez's forces an alternative if they lost the fight that lay ahead. Burning the ships gave the men a powerful motive to win. Convinced they could not turn back, they were better able to focus on the goal and do what had to be done to reach it.

Sadly, many people never achieve that focus. They have realistic goals, but never seem to make much progress. Many have good ideas, but fail to execute them. They waste time, take detours, postpone actions, and just don't move forward.

If you find yourself in this dilemma, make a firm commitment to your goal or idea. Then, burn your "ships" and keep moving forward. Do so in the sure and certain hope that God will bless your commitment and help you on the journey.

✎ *Thought for the Day* ✎
Life without a goal is like entering a jewel mine
and coming out with empty hands.
Japanese proverb

An Amazing Answer to Prayer

You will call and the Lord will answer.
Isaiah 58:9

Peg, a retired person, lives in a beautiful planned community surrounding a lake. A spring storm had blown down and partially severed two enormous branches from the willow trees on her lakeside property.

Hundreds of smaller branches still attached to the larger ones were mired in the mud along the shoreline. Knowing she was responsible for keeping her area neat, Peg knew she had a huge mess to clean up. But the branches were not accessible from land. "I knew I'd have to hire a tree surgeon with a boat. And since I'm a widow living on social security I worried about the expense," she said.

One day while surveying the scene, she prayed simply and desperately, "Dear God, what am I going to do?" Then her prayer was interrupted by the sound of some beavers who were busy felling small trees on the other side of the lake.

The next morning Peg looked out of her window and gasped. The beavers had discovered the half-downed branches. She watched as they severed each branch, chewed off the bark and then headed down the lake with the naked white sticks in their mouths. "The urge to go out and cheer them on was strong, but I stayed inside so I wouldn't frighten them away," she recalled.

All week those beavers worked, and when they were finished the troublesome branches were gone. In an answer to her prayer, God sent some of his very best tree surgeons—a few eager beavers!

❧ *Thought for the Day* ❧
Prayer always makes a difference.
John Bowker

Asking God for Daily Wisdom

But the wisdom that comes from heaven is first of all pure;
then peace loving, considerate, submissive, full of mercy
and good fruit, impartial and sincere.

James 3:17

Watching her father die from a struggle with cancer, Kathryn struggled to find the words to comfort him. She wanted to reassure her father he did not need to fear death, but was unable to get the words out whenever she was visiting him.

One day, as she entered the hospital elevator, a woman carrying a bunch of bright balloons got on, too. That woman said she was visiting a friend and was saddened to learn that Kathryn was in the hospital to visit her dying father.

Upon leaving the elevator, the woman spontaneously turned to Kathryn and said, "You know, I just returned from India where death is such a natural process. It made me think there's only one thing you can do for a friend whose dying—just help them not be afraid." With that she got off the elevator.

This time, when Kathryn was with her father, she was able simply to tell him not to be afraid. "I could almost feel something relax in him," she recalls. "It was such a gift. It helped him a lot. I felt that woman on the elevator was an angel sent to me with a message of wisdom."

As part of our daily prayers, we should ask God to give us wisdom for the day—wisdom to respond appropriately to the many encounters that come our way daily. Let us ask God to fill us daily with *the wisdom that comes from heaven.*

⚜ *Prayer for the Day* ⚜
Loving God,
Fill me so much with your divine spirit
that my words and my actions
will enrich the lives of those around me.
VMP

Prayer Produces Efficiency

The Lord is near. Do not be anxious.
Philippians 4:5-6

The busier you are, the more you need to pray. The more hectic your life, the more time you need to spend in prayer. "I am so busy now that if I did not spend two or three hours each day in prayer, I would not get through the day," said Martin Luther.

The fact is that prayer produces efficiency. Here's a simple but true illustration. A man was replacing a burned-out bulb in the taillight of his car. When attempting to put back the lens, he noticed that he had lost a little screw in the grass beside the driveway. He had an urgent appointment and not much time to spare. He searched for the screw, but to no avail.

Seeking to enlist more help to find the screw, the father called his six-year-old son and his three friends to come over and look. In childlike faith, the man's son said, "Dad, have you prayed about finding the screw." The father admitted he had not. So the boy offered this quick prayer: "Heavenly Father, dad needs to find that screw badly. Help us to find it. Thank you. Amen."

As soon as the boy completed his brief prayer, the father placed his hand down in the tall grass, moved it briefly, and then retrieved the screw.

Some would say that was a mere coincidence. However, those who are spiritual understand it was providence that led the father to the missing screw. Prayer produces efficiency. Try offering a prayer the next time something is misplaced and you are unable to find it. Or, try offering a prayer the next time you have a full schedule and are feeling overwhelmed by the day's activities.

∼ Thought for the Day ∼
I am so busy now that if I did not spend
two or three hours each day in prayer,
I would not get through the day.
Martin Luther

The Priority of Praise

Praise be to the God and Father of
our Lord Jesus Christ!

1 Peter 1:3

"The first thing I do when I wake up is pray. It's a time of solace in which I take a few moments to appreciate all I have and to think about my expectations for the day. What do I have to accomplish in order to feel that I've made the most of the gifts I've been given?"

The person making that statement is not a priest, minister, or rabbi. It is Oprah Winfrey, the well-known television personality. Praise and prayer are very important aspects of her life. She prays not only first thing in the morning, but prior to taping her daily program. "Before I go down to tape the show, I do the same thing [pray]. I make it a point to be alone so that I can say thank you for this opportunity and to clear my head of my own stuff in order to get into what my guests and my audience have on their minds," she says.

Feeling grateful is spiritually and emotionally healthy. It is the sign of a mature person. Gratitude is the opposite of being self-centered, indifferent, and arrogant. Expressing gratitude to God and to others is a way of widening our love and spreading our joy. Saying "thank you" is a very positive thing to do.

Consider taking on the spiritual discipline of gratitude. This can mean...

- Being kind to everyone you meet day by day
- Saying "thank you" for every kindness that comes your way
- Expressing profound gratitude to God for the gift of daily life
- Accepting people just the way they are
- Counting up blessings and not tallying up burdens...

❧ Thought for the Day ❧

If you're feeling sorry for yourself and are ungrateful
about life, try to change your attitude.
List all your blessings.
Then offer thanks.

Malcolm Boyd

Keeping Focused

Let us fix our eyes on Jesus, the author and perfecter of our faith,
who for the joy set before him endured the cross,
scorning its shame, and sat down at the right hand
of the throne of God.

Hebrews 12:2

Gelindo Bordin, Italian marathon runner at the 1988 Olympics in Korea provides a useful example of keeping focused. When he went to the Olympics in 1988 he wasn't considered a serious medal contender. His best record placed him eleventh among the 131 entrants. In addition, no Italian had ever won the Olympic marathon race.

However, as the twenty-six-mile race progressed, one by one, the runners dropped out due to the heat and the grueling race. At the halfway point, only fifteen runners were still competing and Bordin was leading. At the twenty-four-mile mark, two runners broke away and surged ahead of Bordin. Another runner was close behind. If that one surged, Bordin knew he would lose any chance of picking up one of the three medals—gold, silver, or bronze.

Bordin's strategy was to stay focused on the runner ahead rather than the runner closing in on him. A mile and a half remained. Bordin pushed himself harder and passed the number two runner. The front-runner glanced back and became worried. Bordin surged ahead of the lead runner and won the race, earning the gold medal.

Spiritually, life is like that race. We race best when we focus on God in Christ, not on the negatives behind us. "Let us fix our eyes on Jesus," instructs the writer of Hebrews. Let us remember all he had to go through on the cross. When problems come our way and it looks as though you can't go on, remember Jesus finished the work God gave him, even when it meant death on a cross.

⚶ *Prayer for the Day* ⚶
Dear God,
Help me to remain focused on you,
your power,
your peace,
your love.
Then, and only then, can I live with
quiet trust in your wisdom.
VMP

Purging Ourselves From the Sin of Omission

Anyone, then, who knows the good he ought to do and doesn't do it, sins.

James 4:17

The concept that there is a "sin of omission" comes from James' simple, straightforward statement: *Anyone, then, who knows the good he ought to do and doesn't do it, sins.*

Today, let us purge ourselves from the sin or omission by conducting this examination of conscience:

— This week, did I have an opportunity to do something good, but failed to act?

— This week, did I have an opportunity to take a stand for the right, but did not?

— This week, did I have an opportunity to speak out for justice, but chose not to?

— This week, did I have an opportunity to show compassion, but let the opportunity slip away?

— This week, did I have an opportunity to express love, but hesitated and did not?

— This week, did I have an opportunity to provide comfort, but chose to let someone else do it?

— This week, did I have an opportunity to promote peace and goodwill, but was too intimidated to speak up?

Be profoundly honest in answering these questions to yourself. Where there is a shortcoming, ask God's forgiveness and seek God's power to respond more appropriately the next time.

⚜ *Thought for the Day* ⚜
Mediocre—most Christians are mediocre!
A. W. Tozer

Helping Ourselves by Helping Others

Let us not love with word or tongue
but with actions.

1 John 3:18

Shirley, whose beloved husband of twenty-one years died from cancer, tells how she was able to get beyond the excruciating pain of grief. Her family lives on the east coast of the United States and she lives on the west coast. Consequently, there was not much family support beyond phone calls.

However, local friends—along with a grief-support group—were very encouraging. But what really helped Shirely was her focus on giving back to society by volunteering her time at the very hospital where her husband died.

"Since I work five days a week, I could do this only on Saturday or Sunday, so I am now the receptionist for four hours every Saturday in the intensive-care unit," Shirley explains. "It has been such a rewarding experience. I have been able to take the edge off my own grief by helping others. At the end of my shift I feel so very, very good," she says.

The wonderful thing about reaching out to others is that…

In helping, we are helped.
In comforting, we are comforted.
In giving, we are given.
In supporting, we are supported.
In consoling, we are consoled….

In soothing, our pains are soothed.
In healing, our hurts are healed.
In strengthening, our lives are strengthened.
In encouraging, our troubles are lessened.
In caring, our problems are sized down.

Remember that the good you do comes back to you.

❧ Prayer for the Day ❧
Holy and loving God,
Enable me to be…
Helpful to those in difficulty,
Kind to those in need,
Sympathetic to those whose hearts are sore and sad.
VMP

When We Can't Understand, We Must Trust

As the heavens are higher than the earth,
so are my ways higher than your ways and my
thoughts than your thoughts.

Isaiah 55:9

Today's text from Isaiah was a great source of comfort to Dale, a young husband whose wife, Kathy, committed suicide while he was away on business. Kathy had suffered from schizophrenia since she was in her early twenties. She heard audible, frightening voices and had nightmarish visions and severe thought disorders.

Prior to the schizophrenia, Kathy enjoyed life. She was a cheerleader in high school, immensely popular and attractive. She was homecoming queen. Also, she was a committed Christian who was very active in her church.

As the first symptoms emerged, Dale prayed for her healing and introduced Kathy to a series of trial-and-error episodes with doctors, hospital stays, and medications: Haldol, Navane, Prolixin, Clozaril, Lithium, Ativan, Buspar, Trazodone, and others. Prolixin helped Kathy enough to lead a seminormal life, but the frightening hallucinations never stopped.

Dale's prayer for healing was never answered. When he returned home from a two-day business trip, he found his wife who had shot herself. He has since been left with grief, guilt, and unanswered questions. "I offer no platitudes as a result of my experience with schizophrenia. It was a deeply painful experience for Kathy and myself," he says. "The only thing I can offer is that it is possible to love despite it and that there is comfort in scripture, and in knowing a finite mind can never fully comprehend God's big picture—*my ways higher than your ways and my thoughts than your thoughts.*"

When our understanding fails, we must simply trust in God.

⚞ Thought for the Day ⚟
Praise God for all that is past.
Trust God for all that is to come.
Joseph Hart

Emerging From Hardship
Wiser and Stronger

But he knows the way that I take; when he has tested me,
I will come forth as gold.

Job 23:10

Since problems come to all of us, it is vital that we emerge from such hardship wiser and stronger, rather than bitter and timid.

On October 26, 1967, Senator John McCain was shot down over North Vietnam. Although he ejected safely out of his Navy jet, he landed in the midst of an angry Vietnamese mob who attacked him. McCain suffered two broken arms, a shattered knee and shoulder, and received bayonet wounds on his legs. He was in such horrible physical condition that the first American POW to see McCain said, "I didn't think he was going to live out the day." McCain himself acknowledges, "I was the worst injured of any POW who survived the war."

Although he spent five-and-a-half years in a prisoner of war camp without receiving medical treatment, McCain managed to survive and leave a stronger human being. "I don't recommend the treatment, but I am a far better person for having undergone it," he says.

Fortunately, most of us will never be prisoners of war, forced to live under harsh physical and emotional conditions. Yet, sooner or later, everyone faces his or her own time of trial. It may be the result of an injury, disability, divorce, job loss, litigation, the death of a loved one, the birth of a child with handicaps, whatever. When troubles and traumas come, some people crumble and collapse. Others, like John McCain, emerge stronger and wiser. The Bible reminds us that God is with us in hard times and that God uses life's bruises for our advantage—"I will come forth as gold," was Job's declaration over his trials.

When we face difficulties, let us ask ourselves:

- What can I learn from this experience?
- How can I make this experience deepen me as a person?
- What would I do differently in the future?
- How can this pain become a point of growth and learning for me?

～ Thought for the Day ～
The world breaks everyone,
then some become strong at the broken places.
Ernest Hemingway

Embracing God's Divine Love

Cast all your anxiety on him
because he cares for you.
1 Peter 5:7

Today's scripture is one of the clearest and most comforting in the Bible. Because God loves us deeply and cares about us, we are told simply to…

• Turn all of our anxieties over to God

• Express all of our fears to God

• Respond to life's trials by trusting God…

Here are some ways of following Saint Peter's instruction and embracing God's divine love:

In times of darkness…
  ask God to pierce that darkness with light.
In times of despair…
  ask God to give you hope.
In times of weakness…
  ask God for strength.
In times of fear…
  ask God for courage to conquer.
In times of confusion…
  ask God for clarity and a sense of direction.
In times of emotional turmoil…
  ask God for peace.
In times of suffering…
  ask God for the grace to bear it with dignity.
In times of illness…
  ask God for patience.

✎ *Thought for the Day* ✎
He giveth more grace when the burdens grow greater;
He sendeth more strength when the labors increase;
To added affliction, he addeth his mercy,
To multiplied trials,
His multiplied peace.
Annie Johnson Flint

Letting Adversity Energize Us

But as for me, I will always have hope.
Psalm 71:14

The truth is that a crisis can either sedate or motivate us. We can face the challenge, no matter how large and intimidating, or we can immediately give up in defeat. When faced with a major difficulty one person will succumb while another refuses to surrender.

Be the person who refuses to surrender and use adversity, whenever it comes your way, to energize yourself.

An inspiring example is that of Maria Luna Brem. She survived breast cancer, but her marriage failed and her cancer returned two years later. She hit rock bottom—divorced, broke, and unable to feed her kids or pay for her next surgery. Wearing a wig to hide chemotherapy-induced baldness, she began desperately knocking on doors looking for work. The first seventeen potential employers said no. Finally, she was hired to sell cars at a Dallas, Texas, dealership.

Her determination to survive and support her family paid off. Brem became a top sales person, winning one award after another. With her cancer in remission, she began saving money to open her own dealership, which she did in 1989. Today her Chrysler-Plymouth dealership in Corpus Christi is among the three largest Chrysler dealerships in the state of Texas.

⚜ Thought for the Day ⚜

Times of calamity and confusion have ever been
productive of the greatest minds. The purest ore
is produced from the hottest furnace, and the brightest
thunderbolt is elicited from the darkest storm.
Rev. Charles Caleb Colton

Exercise to Strengthen Yourself Emotionally and Spiritually

Do you not know that your body is a temple of the Holy Spirit…?
1 Corinthians 6:19

Today's reading reminds us that our body is the temple of the Holy Spirit. Thus it makes sense we are to look after our bodies and not abuse them by overeating and a lack of exercise. Not only are there physical benefits to exercise, but an increasing number of studies clearly indicate that physical activity strengthens our emotional and spiritual hardiness in these ways:

- Creating more energy
- Relieving tension
- Strengthening the body's stress-coping mechanisms
- Clearing the mind and improving concentration
- Building a more positive self-image
- Developing self-confidence
- Improving sleep
- Alleviating depression

If you feel you are too stressed out to engage in a regular exercise program, consider again Senator John McCain (cited in the reading for October 2):

"As soon as I could, I started exercising," he says. "I started out just doing situps because that was all I was capable of doing with a bad leg and two broken arms. Then I started doing push-ups, which were incredibly painful at first. And even though my leg would bend only a few degrees, I began running in place in my small cell. It was a funny looking hop, but it kept my muscles from atrophying. Other injured POWs who didn't exercise often came out of the camps badly disabled."

✎ Affirmation for the Day ✎
I thank God for the gift of my body.
I treat my body with respect.
I recognize my body as a good friend.
VMP

Surround Yourself With Supportive People

It was good of you to share in my troubles.
Philippians 4:14

Life flows much more smoothly and trials are weathered more grace-fully when we are surrounded with supportive people. Keep in mind that often those who can be most supportive during a time of crisis are ones who have had a similar experience. So, if you are facing a time of unemployment, spend time with those who have been unemployed. Or, if you face a life-threatening illness, join a support group made up of similar people. During times of adversity, fellowship with others stimu-lates the will, encourages the heart, and fortifies resolve.

Here is one unusual but highly inspiring example. On December 19, 1944, Lt. Robert King and a number of other American servicemen were taken prisoner by German troops during the Battle of the Belgian Bulge.

While imprisoned, Lt. King felt that he and the other men needed a way of banding together for mutual support so he formed a Toastmaster's Club in the prison camp. Their first meeting was held on February 6, 1945, and, when conditions permitted, the club met every Tuesday and Friday afternoon.

In addition to giving short speeches that were critiqued, the members made presentations before club members on topics such as these: "How I Would Run a German Prison Camp in the United States," "If I Were Made Mess Officer of This Prisoner of War Camp," and "How I Handle My Monday Bread Ration." On May 2, 1945, Lt. King and other surviv-ing men were liberated. Looking back at the POW Toastmaster's club, King says that the club was effective in maintaining soldiers' morale and preventing their will from being broken.

～ Thought for the Day ～
Because of a friend, life is a little stronger,
fuller, more gracious thing.
Arthur Christopher Benson

Always Use Your Power of Choice

Prepare your minds for action.
1 Peter 1:13

Rather than be limited by problems, intimidated by circumstances, or defeated by difficulties, make the choice to challenge the issue. Rise to the occasion.

Here is a useful insight from the world of elephants. In Thailand, when elephants are captured an iron band connected to a heavy chain is secured around each elephant's foot. The elephant is also chained to a large tree. At first, the elephant lifts its leg and pulls, trying with all its strength to break the chain or uproot the tree, but nothing ever happens. An elephant will try this day after day, until it finally gives up. Whenever this powerful animal lifts its leg and feels just a slight tension, it drops its foot back on the ground in complete submission.

After that time of taming, it is easy to control the giant animal. The elephant is then taken out to work and is tied only to a small stake. The elephant could, through minimal effort, easily break the chain or pull out the stake and run free. However, the elephant is trapped because it believes it can never break free. The creature is imprisoned simply because it perceives the situation as impossible.

This is the application for daily life…

Do not allow yourself to be chained by events, no matter how catastrophic they may appear to be. Choose to conquer events rather than be conquered by them.

❧ Thought for the Day ❧
Nonachievers stay home because they are frightened
to try and to fail…
successful people feel the same way as they do—
they're frightened too. But they try.
They go to work frightened…
they go to social situations frightened…
they go to meetings frightened….But they go.
Irene Kassorla

Maintaining a Gratitude List

Give thanks to the Lord, for he is good.
Psalm 118:1

A crisis, whether personal or professional, always sabotages our view of things. Troubles and traumas distort our perception. The corrective is to create a gratitude list.

Begin with a blank sheet of paper and ask yourself this simple question: "What are the good things in my life just now?" Then list everything that comes to mind. A gratitude list can include things like…

- Enjoyable music heard over the car radio
- The love of a friend, spouse, children, or parents
- Health
- Prosperity
- Education
- Meaningful employment
- A mentor at work
- A teacher who took a special interest
- A spiritual leader who deeply impacted your life
- A good book
- An unexpected kindness
- A compliment freely and sincerely offered
- An achievement that brings you pride

No matter what your circumstances are at the present moment, creating a gratitude list will show you that there are many more blessings flowing in your life than you would have thought.

❧ *Thought for the Day* ❧

Expressing gratitude ignites the light within us
and is a sure path to joy.
Gratitude is one of the highest vibrations of energy
we can create, it's free.
Charlotte Davis Kasl

Respond to Life's Trials With Action

*So we continued the work... from the first
light of dawn till the stars came out.*

Nehemiah 4:21

Those who survive the major tests of life are those who respond actively and aggressively. They do not give up. They do not accept defeat. They do not engage in negative thoughts such as these:

- *I don't have a chance.*
- *I'll never get over this.*
- *It's no use.*
- *I'm doomed.*
- *It can't be done.*
- *There's no way.*
- *It's impossible.*

Journalist Linda Ellerbee sadly tells this story about her mother. "After my father died, my mother gave up on life. She refused friends' invitations to go out until they stopped asking her. Then she stopped traveling, first outside of the city then outside of her house."

Whenever Ellerbee invited her mother to join her for shopping or coffee at a restaurant, the mother declined. Three years later she died. "As much as I love my mother, I'm still angry at her for giving up, because I believe it led to her death. The less she did, the less there was of her," Ellerbee declares.

The lesson: Do not take a weak, timid, indecisive approach to life's trials because it only breeds inertia, failure, and disappointment. Respond boldly, positively, and forcefully to a crisis and it will soon begin to shrink in the face of your efforts.

⊰ Prayer for the Day ⊱
Loving God,
I thank you for being my unseen partner in life.
Give me the power to face all of
life's challenges boldly and courageously.
With your help, I can and will overcome.
VMP

Tomorrow Doesn't Have to Be the Same As Yesterday

Though your sins are like scarlet,
they shall be as white as snow;
though they are red as crimson, they shall be like wool.

Isaiah 1:18

Tomorrow doesn't have to be the same as yesterday. We can be regenerated and renewed by God's spirit. This glorious truth is cited repeatedly in scripture. Some examples include:

Ezekiel 36:26: "I will give you a new heart
  and put a new spirit in you."
Isaiah 1:18: "Though your sins are like scarlet,
  they shall be as white as snow;
  though they are red as crimson, they shall be like wool."
Titus 3:5: "He saved us through…
  renewal by the Holy Spirit."

Consider the example of Jane, a woman who is widely respected in her community for her work with underprivileged children. To see her today one would never suspect that God transformed her life in the bathroom of a New Jersey county jail. At the time, she was a teenager who had been mainlining heroin into her veins for five years. One by one, a panel of authorities—a psychiatrist, psychologist, social worker, physician, and even her attorney who walked out on her in court—declared her hopeless.

Alone and desperate, she encountered a Christian who read to her from the words of Isaiah 1:18: "Though your sins are like scarlet, they shall be as white as snow." After hearing that sentence, Jane says, "I began to believe there is hope. I cried, 'God, I failed living!'" She asked God to help her turn away from a life of self-destruction. God's spirit touched her deeply that day in jail and gradually she began to experience hope and renewal.

As a result of her encounter with God, Jane today is committed to working with poor children. "I see hopelessness in their eyes that I knew as a teenager. I want to impart something from God, leave them with the hope that was given to me," she says.

⊰ Thought for the Day ⊱
God hugs you.
Saint Hildegarde of Bingen

Everywhere on Earth, Peace Is in Search of Makers

Blessed are the peacemakers.
Matthew 5:9

Everywhere on earth peace is in search of makers. Jesus said, "Blessed are the peacemakers." His words are a command that those who follow Christ engage in working toward harmony and goodwill among all people.

Everywhere on earth peace is in search of makers. We do not need to be international diplomats ending wars. Life provides all of us with ample opportunities to work for peace in our families, neighborhoods, schools, towns, wherever.

Here is an outstanding example of one peacemaker. At 2:00 a.m. in the parking lot of a 24-hour supermarket, a taxi cab raced into the lot. There, the driver jumped from the cab running into the store, his irate passenger in hot pursuit. Soon a bizarre scene of angry accusations and gestures had developed. Angry words could soon escalate into physical violence.

Apparently, the passenger tried to pay the cabdriver with a second-party check. The cabdriver had driven to the store to see if he could cash his protesting patron's check but had been turned down. The cabdriver was now refusing to chase all over looking for a place that would cash it. Instead, he held on to it, in lieu of payment for the $7 fare. The second-party check was for an amount more than the fare.

A small crowd had formed, the police were called, and a frightened night manager was desperately trying to reduce the tension. Just when the situation seemed as if it might come to blows, a man stepped out of the group of spectators and asked the cabdriver if he would return the check to his passenger if the fare were paid. The driver assured him that was all he wanted—the money for the fare. The stranger calmly took $7 from his wallet and paid the driver. The check was returned to the astonished passenger. Since no crime had been committed, only an explanation to the police was needed. The spectators dispersed, no one was injured, and peace was restored.

⤳ Affirmation for the Day ⤲
God's peace flows through my life right now.
I am an ambassador of God's peace for others.
I respond to others with a deep sense of peace.
VMP

An Example of Turning the Other Cheek

If someone strikes you on the right cheek,
turn to him the other also.

Matthew 5:39

There are many ways to put into practice Jesus' teaching on turning the other cheek. Here is one example, which took place at an airport.

A traveler, between flights, went to one of the airport shops and purchased a small package of cookies. Then she sat down and began reading a newspaper. Gradually, she became aware of a rustling noise. From behind her paper, she was shocked to see a neatly dressed businessman helping himself to *her* cookies. Not wanting to make a scene, she leaned over and took a cookie herself.

A moment or two passed, then came more rustling. He was helping himself to another cookie! By this time, they had come to the end of the package, but she was so angry she didn't dare allow herself to say anything. With only one cookie remaining, the man broke the last one in two, pushed it across to the woman, ate his half, and left.

Still fuming over the incident, the woman later opened her purse to pull out her ticket for the flight and was shocked to discover her pack of unopened cookies. The stranger was eating his cookies, not hers. When she reached over and took a cookie out of his package, he "turned the other cheek" and offered her more.

❧ *Prayer for the Day* ❧
Loving God,
Let me find gentle, creative ways
to "turn the other cheek" whenever
opportunities arise.
VMP

Kindness Is Expected From Christians

Always try to be kind to each other and to everyone else.

1 Thessalonians 5:15

Earlier in this century, a missionary was teaching a class of Chinese girls in a Sunday school. She was telling them about Jesus and described how his life was spent doing kind deeds and making people happy.

In the middle of the talk, an eight-year-old Chinese girl, who was attending the Sunday school for the first time, raised her hand and said, "I know Jesus. He lives on my street."

Amused, the missionary explained that Jesus lived many years ago and again explained his ministry of compassion. At the end of the class, the little girl reiterated her claim: "I know Jesus. He lives on my street."

The teacher asked for more information and the little girl explained that on her street lived a man who was kind and loving, just like Jesus. This man spent his time doing good deeds.

Upon further inquiry, the teacher discovered that the man referred to by the little girl was another missionary who did, indeed, live on the girl's street. The teacher's description of Jesus' kindness made the little girl think of that man.

There is a historical link to that incident. In the early days of Christianity, the Romans often confused the Greek work *christos* or Christ with the word *chrestos*, which means kind. Linguistically, one can see how the confusion could arise. But spiritually, the link between being a Christian and being kind should be there naturally.

❧ *Thought for the Day* ❧

Each one of us is bound to make the little
circle in which he lives better and happier.

A. P. Stanley

Living With Our Eyes Open

Then their eyes were opened and they recognized him.
Luke 24:31

Jesus asks us to see the Christ in the needs of other people (Matthew 25:35). We need to live with our eyes and hearts wide open if we are to do this. Consider the story told by a man who was visiting Switzerland. While sitting at a crowded bus stop he saw a boy about six or seven years old walking toward the crowd.

The youth appeared to be walking aimlessly without a care in the world. Then, he looked behind him and realized that he had become separated from his parents and was walking alone. Fear came over him and he began to cry out, "Somebody! Somebody!"

As he came closed the visitor noticed that the boy was a Down's syndrome child. The louder he called for "Somebody!" the wider the people parted to avoid this child. "The youth began to look around at the people almost as if he were a cornered animal with an attacking force surrounding him," the visitor recalls. "Somebody! Somebody!" he continued to scream as his face grew whiter with fright.

"Somebody ought to do something," the visitor thought to himself. Finally the bus pulled up and people started to get on while the boy kept yelling "Somebody!" Then, out of the crowd came a young woman who answered "Somebody." She gathered the boy up in her arms, held him tightly, and quieted him by whispering, "Somebody. Somebody." The visitor was impressed with the young woman's response and comfort.

However, he was even more impressed as a second scene emerged. He saw another woman running toward the lady holding the little boy. At that moment the visitor realized that this woman was the mother of the child and the other young lady was just a kind person who saw someone hurting and in fear so she reached out in love.

～ Prayer for the Day ～
Loving God,
I ask myself this question for today:
Am I living with my eyes open?
If not, help me to do so and see the Christ
in others who are hurting.
VMP

October 15

Getting Involved

If there is a poor man among your brothers in any
of the towns of the land that the Lord your God
is giving you, do not be hardhearted or tight-fisted
toward your poor brother.

Deuteronomy 15:7

A local newspaper staged a traffic accident to see how people would respond. A driver rammed a car over the curb and onto a busy sidewalk, then slumped against the steering wheel, apparently unconscious. For nearly an hour dozens of people walked around the car, ignoring the apparent tragedy.

Had this incident not actually taken place, we would never believe people could be so detached. Yet, on another level, the same thing happens every day. There are wrecked people whose lives feel broken, and they are ignored by the majority. For example, there are people...

• With broken hearts

• With crushed spirits

• With wounded bodies

• With damaged emotions

• With shattered souls

• With injured memories

In addition there are...

• People uprooted by war and civil strife

• Children impacted by divorce

• Families victimized by discrimination

• Men and women living under the crushing weight of poverty

Too often such individuals are simply ignored by the majority of us as we go on our daily tasks.

～ Prayer for the Day ～
Eternal and loving God,
Sensitize me toward the needs and hurts of
others so that I will not be hardhearted or tight-fisted
toward those who are hurting.
VMP

Kindness Has a Price Tag

Do not be afraid; do not be discouraged.
Go out to face them tomorrow, and the
Lord will be with you.

2 Chronicles 20:17

When he was in his seventies, the American Industrialist and first President of Bethlehem Steel Company, Charles M. Schwab, was the victim of a frivolous lawsuit. The sum for which he was being sued was extremely large. Schwab, who could have settled for a fraction of the amount out of court, refused to do so.

Letting the case run its legal gamut, he won it easily and, before leaving the stand, asked the court's permission to say a few words not concerned with the matter at hand. His message was this:

"I'd like to say, here, in a court of law, and speaking as an old man, that nine-tenths of my troubles are traceable to my being kind to others. Look, you young people; if you want to steer away from trouble, be hard-boiled. Be quick with a good loud no to anyone and everyone. If you follow this rule, you'll be seldom molested as you tread life's pathway. Except, you'll have no friends, you'll be lonely, and you won't have any fun!"

Schwab's observation is worth further reflection. Kindness has a price tag. Not everyone to whom we extend a kind act will respond gratefully. We can be judged and criticized for our efforts. Gossip and rumors can be stated about us and our intentions. Yet we must not allow ourselves to become discouraged and quit. In spite of resistance and negative responses, we must continue to reach out and touch our world with kindness and compassion.

~ Prayer for the Day ~

Gracious God,
Harden me against myself so that
I do not become discouraged in doing good.

VMP

An Act of Faith

The ways of the Lord are right.
Hosea 14:9

In 1985, Val, a missionary educator, and her husband took their three children, aged seven, nine, and eleven, to live in a war zone in northern Namibia. Because of apartheid, the family was forced to live in a "white-only" security district. After fifteen months of petitioning, they were given permission to live outside with the Owambo people.

On the first weekend they moved, Laura, their seven-year-old, ran in with a national girl. With faces beaming, they asked if Laura could spend the night at the house of her new friend, Mona. Her mother had given permission. Would Val consent as well?

"I thought Mona's mother worked in the school cafeteria, but I knew nothing of her father. In America I would automatically have said no until I could check out the home," Val explains. "But I knew that a national's willingness to open her home to my daughter could be an open door to ministry with the Owambo. I couldn't risk being seen as a foreigner who had crusaded to move next to them but who really wished to live separately."

Val breathed a quick prayer "telling the One who gave Laura to me in the first place that I was reentrusting her to his care that night." Mona and Laura became dear friends and for weeks people who didn't know Val's name called her "Laura's mother." The entire neighborhood came to know Laura and, as a result, accepted the entire family.

When we are divided in mind and tugged in separate directions, let us turn and trust the One who knows what is right.

❧ *Affirmation for the Day* ❧
Wherever I am, God is!
The love of God surrounds me.
The light of God guides me.
Wherever I am, God is!
VMP

Some Things to Remember and Some to Forget

But do not be afraid of them; remember well what the
Lord your God did to Pharaoh and to all Egypt.

Deuteronomy 7:18

Our mind can become our greatest asset or our greatest liability. With our thoughts we can sculpt a life that is positively engaged with others or we can create a life that is lived timidly and hesitantly. In today's text the ancient Israelites were urged to change their way of thinking—they were not to be afraid of their enemies but rather remember the power of God for them while they were slaves in Egypt.

Here are some ways to make the mind work for our good. Let us…

Remember our potential
   but forget our limitations;
Remember our strength
   but forget our weakness;
Remember our ability
   but forget out disability;
Remember our talents
   but forget our liabilities;
Remember our joys
   but forget our griefs;
Remember our friends
   but forget our enemies;
Remember our opportunities
   but forget our obstacles;
Remember our blessings
   but forget our burdens;
Remember our faith
   but forget our doubts;
Remember our goodness
   but forget our weakness;
Remember our hopes
   but forget our fears.

⚘ Affirmation for the Day ⚘
I learn in joyous ways.
I live in joyous ways.
I live with gratitude and joy.
VMP

Hidden Strength

He is like a tree planted by streams of water,
which yields its fruit in season and whose leaf does not wither.

Psalm 1:3

Ingrid Trobisch is a popular Christian writer and the author of numerous spiritual books. She tells of being impressed by her mother's reaction when she had to call her to tell the mother that their father died suddenly in Tanzania, Africa.

At the time, Ingrid was at a religious boarding school in Nebraska and her mother was in Springfield, Missouri, with the other younger children. The father, a missionary, had gone back to Africa alone, leaving his family behind because it was the peak of World War II. For some reason, a telegram conveying the man's death was sent to his daughter in Nebraska rather than directly to the mother in Missouri.

"Mother," Ingrid said, "I have some bad news for you. Are you strong?"

"Yes, Ingrid," she said slowly. "Tell me what it is."

Ingrid read the telegram from Africa, which stated simply the father had died on March 18, 1943, from heart failure following malaria.

After a long moment of silence, the mother asked Ingrid in a calm voice, "How are you and how is your grandmother? How is she taking the news of her eldest son's death?"

When Ingrid tried to comfort her mother, the mother said, "The future is not dark. The Lord has helped us up until now. He will continue."

Have you ever observed a person—like this mother—going through a crisis with courage, dignity, grace, and confidence and wondered what gives that person such enormous strength in trial? Where does such hidden strength come from? According to the writer of today's psalm, such hidden strength is a gift from God. It is given to those who trust God and live in faith. When we need the strength it will be given. We will be like a tree planted near water whose leaves will not wither.

❧ *Prayer for the Day* ❧

Loving and gracious God,
I thank you because...
When I am weak, you make me strong;
When I am wounded, you bring me healing;
When I am frightened, you give me courage.

VMP

Just Be There!

*He who refreshes others will himself
be refreshed.*

Proverbs 11:25

Recently I conducted a funeral for a forty-seven-year-old man named Gary. Two years earlier he was seriously injured in an automobile accident. Because his spinal cord was severed, he suffered paralysis from the waist down and could only move via a wheelchair. Gary spent most of the previous two years recovering from his injuries and battling various ailments. His death was the result of heart failure, which physicians felt was related to the accident.

When I met with his wife to discuss the funeral service, she commented sadly, "Although Gary was a highly regarded executive in the community, after his accident most friends fell away. He spent most of the last two years feeling isolated. Only his family, and one or two friends, remained faithful to him. It was an additional burden for him to realize that his friends seemed to have forgotten about him."

Unfortunately, Gary's experience is not an unusual one. Many people who have been injured by life—experiencing a separation, divorce, the loss to death of a loved one, and so on—report a falling away of friends, people they were counting on to be there.

The lesson: Give as much love and support as possible to someone going through a tough time. Be there as soon as you hear about a hardship. Continue to visit, phone, and send encouraging notes. Your presence and support will contribute greatly to the individual's physical, emotional, and spiritual survival.

❧ *Prayer for the Day* ❧
Loving God,
Day by day give me sensitivity to others
combined with insight to respond wisely,
compassionately, and graciously to their needs.
VMP

Keeping Hope Alive

You will be secure, because there is hope.
Job 11:18

We must always remember to kindle the small spark of hope. Where there is hope, there is endeavor and accomplishment.

Consider tri-athlete and race-car driver Pat Rummerfield. In 1974 a nearly fatal automobile accident left Rummerfield, then twenty-one, fully paralyzed from the neck down. His profound anger and grief were diminished when he discovered he could move his left toe.

"I would visualize myself playing basketball every day, even hearing the ball bounce on the wooden court," he recalls. Although it took sixteen months of rehabilitation before Rummerfield could tie his shoelaces, he persevered. Today he is one of the few fully recovered quadriplegics in the world, and his once useless body is capable of impressive athletic performance. After finishing several mini-triathlons, Rummerfield qualified to compete in the Ironman Triathlon World Championship in 1992. He is also the first recovered quadriplegic to obtain a professional racing license.

When you are faced with a crisis or if a friend is faced with crisis, here are some attitudes to maintain that will keep hope alive:

- I refuse to be defeated.
- I will take advantage of every opportunity.
- I will not assume the mentality of a victim.
- I will learn new things.
- I will grow through this experience.
- I will rise to the challenge.

❧ *Thought for the Day* ❧

Hope is the best possession. None are completely wretched but those who are without hope.
William Hazlitt

Watch Your Language

He who guards his lips guards his soul.
Proverbs 13:3

The language we use to describe ourselves can either build or erode the quality of our living. Today's text, *He who guards his lips guards his soul,* is filled with wisdom and truth.

Consider Sherry's experience. "When I was diagnosed with breast cancer, family and friends began quietly whispering that I had a *terminal illness* and that I was a *cancer victim,*" she recalls. Deeply discouraged, Sherry attended a cancer support group. In relating her story, Sherry described herself as being a "cancer victim" and having a "terminal illness."

Members of the support group quickly suggested she use less dramatic terms. After hearing from other people in the group, Sherry was greatly encouraged. "I couldn't believe how wrong I was," she later confided in a good friend. "My doctor told me I would probably recover and yet I became convinced I was a terminal cancer victim. After just one group meeting I no longer felt terminal nor victimized. What a relief!"

The change came because Sherry learned to speak of herself in different, more hopeful ways.

When we encounter difficulty and hardship let us guard our lips and be careful about how we describe the situation. Our words can either erode or build our confidence.

❧ *Thought for the Day* ❧
The essence of worry...
is the absence of thought,
a failure to think.
D. Martyn Lloyd-Jones

Feed Your Mind Healthy Thoughts

The mind controlled by the Spirit is life and peace.
Romans 8:6

We are what we think. That is why it is important that we indulge ourselves in activities that are inspiring and uplifting. We must always take actions that stimulate, boost, energize, motivate, and charge up our minds. Consider buying a book of meditations and commit to reading one each morning. Or, pick up a book filled with inspiring, hopeful thoughts.

"Whenever I feel my spirits sinking and depression coming on, I purchase books that are inspirational and motivational," says Judy, an art dealer in San Diego. "I have them in various rooms of my home and turn to them whenever there is a free moment. Not only do they have an immediate and positive impact on my mood, but they always leave me saying 'I can' rather than 'I can't.'"

Or consider David, a skilled neurosurgeon. "My work is extremely high stress. I do surgery on a daily basis on the brain and the spinal column. It's very, very high risk and I am constantly aware of those risks. Every morning as I drive to the hospital I play inspirational tapes by various motivational and spiritual speakers. I find their words and insights calming and confidence-building."

⤖ *Prayer for the Day* ⤖
Loving and eternal God,
Whenever I am frightened or confused
renew my mind so that I can focus upon
those things that are lovely, admirable,
excellent, noble, pure.
VMP

Listing the Positives

Test me in this," says the Lord Almighty, "and see if I will not throw open the floodgates of heaven and pour out so much blessing that you will not have room enough for it."

Malachi 3:10

When troubles come and depression sets in, we tend to view everything else in a highly negative light. Setbacks and letdowns become greatly magnified while the positives are scarcely noted. Balance your perception by making a list of the many positives in your life.

Author and minister Norman Vincent Peale often recommended this simple task to people who were depressed. On one occasion, Rev. Peale was counseling a man who was going through a difficult divorce. In deep despair, the man began drinking heavily, which, in turn, caused him to lose a good job. The man told Rev. Peale he was considering suicide.

Promptly, Rev. Peale suggested, "Let's draw up a list of your assets." The man was surprised by the list of positives that quickly emerged. They included a healthy, strong body; good mental ability, a supportive extended family, and friends who would stand by him.

As the man viewed his life a little more positively, his depression lifted and the downward spiral of his life was halted. "This story ends happily," Dr. Peale recalled. "The young man now has a fine job. After the divorce he became engaged to a wonderful woman; he is rebuilding his life."

～ Thought for the Day ～

When upon life's billows you are tempest tossed,
When you are discouraged, thinking all is lost,
Count your many blessings—name them one by one
And it will surprise you what the Lord hath done.

Johnson Oatman, Jr.

See the Good, Expect the Best

"I know the plans I have for you," declares the Lord,
"plans to prosper you and not to harm you,
plans to give you hope and a future."

Jeremiah 29:11

Your mind is a powerful tool. Don't waste it brooding over what you don't have, aren't experiencing, didn't receive. That kind of negative thinking will only leave you feeling more discouraged, depressed, and dissatisfied. A healthier approach is to see the good and expect the best. Apply to your experience the promise of God spoken through the prophet Jeremiah: "I know the plans I have for you,"…"plans to prosper you and not to harm you, plans to give you hope and a future."

The famous actor Kirk Douglas employed this successful technique for seeing the good and expecting the best—a technique he often employed when his career appeared to be stalled. Early in his career, Douglas had been out of work and desperately needed a role. Although he managed to land a part, he found the role extremely difficult to play. No matter how hard he tried, Douglas felt he delivered the lines poorly and that he brought no life or energy to the part. Finally, he found a simple but effective way to motivate himself: He focused on how the role would provide him with a salary as an actor and keep him from being a waiter!

Like Kirk Douglas, all of us will experience times when our zest for life is low. It is often a time when strength is diminished, energy is reduced, creativity is hindered, and every undertaking is laborious. During those emotional lows it is easy to magnify our faults and minimize our talents.

Let us find small, simple ways to break out of such sluggish times. And, let us remember and be renewed by the divine promise of scripture—*"I know the plans I have for you," declares the Lord, "plans to prosper you and not to harm you, plans to give you hope and a future."*

∼ Thought for the Day ∼
God is love and God is sovereign.
His love disposes him to desire our everlasting welfare.
A. W. Tozer

Shed an Old Skin

As surely as the sun rises, he will appear.
Hosea 6:3

"In times of dryness and desolation we must be patient…putting our trust in the goodness of God. We must animate ourselves by the thought that God is always with us, that he only allows this trial for our greater good, and that we have not necessarily lost his grace because we have lost the taste and feeling of it," wrote Ignatius of Loyola.

Those words of wise counsel reflect the reality every Christian experiences in times of spiritual dryness. It is a subjective feeling that God is distant, aloof, and even absent. During a time of spiritual dryness, prayers feel empty, hymns are sung without energy, sermons are lifeless, and scripture appears to have no power over daily life. Often called the "dark night of the soul," it is a time when the absence of God's presence is greatly and painfully felt.

Even individuals in scripture experienced moments when clouds of darkness descended on the spirit or God seemed hidden and uncaring. On one occasion Moses shouted at God, "If this is how you are going to treat me, put me to death right now" (Numbers 11:15, *New International Version*). Similarly, Elijah found himself so discouraged and frustrated he prayed: "I have had enough, Lord…Take my life." And the psalmist lamented, "Why have you rejected us forever, O God? Why does your anger smolder against the sheep of your pasture?" (Psalm 74:1).

During such times of spiritual dryness and frustration, we must learn to be patient. Also, a time of darkness can be the signal that we have reached the end of one chapter in life and must begin a new one. Let us be flexible enough to turn over a new page. Let us patiently wait for God to act, recalling today's scripture, "As surely as the sun rises, he will appear."

❧ Thought for the Day ❧

We must be willing to get rid of the life we've planned, so as to have the life that is waiting for us. The old skin has to be shed before the new one can come.

Joseph Campbell

Always Choose Faith Over Understanding

We have put our hope in the living God,
1 Timothy 4:10

Not every prayer we utter is answered the way we wish. Sometimes we can easily accept an unanswered prayer, but at other times an unanswered prayer can be a crushing blow. And spiritual darkness can come crashing down upon us when an urgent prayer is not answered. If that is the case, always choose faith over understanding.

Christian author Catherine Marshall tells of a time when she emerged from six months of spiritual darkness following the death of her second granddaughter in 1971, for whom she had prayed that God would heal. In spite of her fervent prayers the infant died, plunging Marshall into a spiritual black hole. After great depression and soul searching this insight came:

"When life hands up situations we cannot understand, we have one of two choices," she wrote. "We can wallow in misery, separated from God. Or we can tell him, 'I need you and your presence in my life more than I need understanding. I choose you, Lord. I trust you to give me understanding and an answer to all my whys—only if and when you choose.'"

◦❦ *Thought for the Day* ❦◦

Without you, my sweet Savior,
I remain in darkness and grief.
Without you, most gentle Lamb,
I remain in worry and fear.
Without you, son of Almighty God,
I remain in confusion and shame.
For without you, I am blind in the dark,
because you are Jesus,
the true Light of the World.
Without you, I am lost and damned,
because you are the God of Gods
and giver of graces.
John of Alverna

Three Healing, Helping Words to Use Often

The Sovereign Lord has given me an instructed tongue,
to know the word that sustains the weary.

Isaiah 50:4

Some of the most important, inspiring, healing, and helping messages we give to one another come in just three words. When spoken or conveyed, those sentences have the power to forge new friendships, deepen old ones, restore broken ones, and heal pained ones. Here are some three-word sentences that should come from our lips frequently:

- *I forgive you.* These words liberate you from feelings of anger, bitterness, and resentment.

- *I miss you.* These words are sure to strengthen and salvage relationships that are cooling.

- *I appreciate you.* These can be spoken and demonstrated. Either way, they will convey that we are not taking another person for granted.

- *Please forgive me.* These words indicate humility on our part and an awareness of a wrong we have committed. They open the way to a restored relationship.

- *I thank you.* People who enjoy good, close friendships are always those who say "I thank you" for the many kindnesses received from others.

- *Count on me.* When you say this, be sure to mean it and then be there when someone needs you, even if it is inconvenient. Your presence during a hard time will be of great and unforgettable comfort.

- *Let me help.* Good people and the best of friends fill needs. When they see a hurt, they do whatever they can to heal it.

- *I understand you.* These words convey complete acceptance and a suspension of judgment. To be in the presence of an understanding, accepting person facilitates emotional healing and better decision making.

- *Go for it.* All of us need cheerleaders in life. This simple phrase conveys confidence and support in another person.

❧ Thought for the Day ❧
Speech is a mirror of the soul;
as a man speaks, so is he.
Publilius Syrus

Upgrade Your Goals

Run in such a way as to get the prize.
1 Corinthians 9:24

A sure way to fire up enthusiasm and zest for life is to take on a major challenge. Defy your current level of living by challenging yourself to do more than you have done and go further than you have gone.

Be inspired by the example of seventy-two-year-old Lynn Edwards who has been training to compete in an Ironman Triathlon World Championship. This ultimate fitness challenge begins with a 2.4-mile swim, followed by a 112-mile bike ride and a 26.2-mile run.

To prepare, this "senior citizen" runs sixty miles, bikes three-hundred miles, and swims four miles a week. Even though the grueling work takes six or seven hours daily, Edwards says the rewards outweigh the sacrifices. "It's hard to describe the feeling, but it's almost spiritual," Edwards says. "If you can do ironman, there's nothing in life you can't do."

Today's text from Saint Paul says, *Run in such a way as to get the prize.* As any racer knows, the only way to win the prize is to train vigorously. To win the prize will mean raising our normal standard and way of doing things.

So, today think about taking on that challenge that you have been considering but have not yet responded to. Today...

- Sign up for a college course to complete your education
- Fill in the form to run the marathon
- Ask for the raise
- Seek out a position with more responsibility and pay
- Make the move
- Apply to medical school, law school, dental school....

❧ Thought for the Day ❧
The adventurous life is not one exempt from fear,
but on the contrary one that is lived in full knowledge
of fears of all kinds, one in which we go forward
in spite of our fears.
Paul Tournier

Energized by Tragedy

I will not keep silent…
I will not remain quiet.
Isaiah 62:1

A deeply traumatic event led Ida Sophia Scudder (1870–1959) to establish the world-famous Vellore Medical College and Hospital in Madras State, India, in 1918.

Born in Ranipet, Arcot (India), Scudder was the daughter of a medical missionary from the Reformed Church in America. In 1893 three men came to her in the night asking Scudder to assist their wives in childbirth. Although her father was a medical doctor and missionary, he was not allowed to approach the women because he was a man. All three women died that night, leaving Scudder horrified at what had transpired.

Rather than curse the darkness of social taboos that created such a tragedy, Scudder decided to light a candle. Determined to make a difference in the lives of Indian women, Scudder applied and was accepted for studies at the Women's Medical College in Philadelphia and Cornell University Medical College.

Dr. Scudder returned to India in 1900 and opened the women's hospital at Vellore. Soon a branch and roadside clinics were added. Because Indian women doctors were urgently needed, Dr. Scudder was determined that the nation of India would have its own women's medical school. She lobbied for five years before being allowed to open a medical college for women in 1918. Supporters in the United States took great interest in her work and engaged in fund-raising for her medical projects. The Vellore Medical College emerged as one of the outstanding interdenominational Christian institutions in Asia.

The lesson from her life is this: When a tragedy strikes our community, let us not be paralyzed by the crisis; let us not curse the darkness that it creates. Rather, let us examine it and allow it to energize and motivate us to avert similar future tragedies. Like the prophet Isaiah, we must not remain silent, nor must we remain quiet.

❧ Thought for the Day ❧
The rung of a ladder was never meant to rest upon,
but only to hold a man's foot long enough to enable
him to put the other somewhat higher.
Thomas Henry Huxley

Lending a Helping Hand to a Single Parent

Defend the cause of the fatherless,
plead the case of the widow.

Isaiah 1:7

Among the most heroic people in our society today are single parents. Parenting always requires tremendous energy and patience, commitment and time. Those commodities are often in short supply even in two-parent homes. The general dynamics of most single-parent families is more stress, less money, possible resentment, and heightened worries about the welfare of their children. Since we all know single parents, let us be sensitive to their needs. Here are some ways to lend a hand:

- Always avoid negative descriptions such as "broken homes," "split family," and the like. Educate and sensitize others concerning such negative labels. Single-parent families are families!

- Encourage your church to provide scholarships so that a single parent can attend a seminar or retreat without additional expenses. Consider making a donation for this cause yourself.

- Genuinely show your interest in a single parent. This creates openness so that a single parent will feel free to call you if a problem emerges.

- Purchase books for your church library or pamphlets for your church literature rack that deal with single-parent issues.

- Offer to provide childcare for a single parent. I guarantee this will be greatly appreciated and will be accepted gladly.

- Near Mother's Day or Father's Day offer to baby-sit the children. Then take them shopping so they can purchase gifts for their single-parent father or mother. Single parents often miss out on these special holidays because their children are too young to shop for gifts.

Pray regularly for a single parent you know. Parenting is challenging enough for two-parent homes but even more so for single parents. Ask for God's blessings of peace, love, hope, joy, peace, and prosperity to flow into the lives of a single-parent family.

❧ Prayer for the Day ❧
Loving and eternal God,
Sensitize me to the needs of single-parent families.
Empower me to respond with loving kindness.
VMP

Blessing Others Through Our Kind Acts

As God's chosen people...clothe yourself
with compassion, kindness....
Colossians 3:12

Pulling her jacket tightly around her, Carol trudged out into the cold, snowy afternoon to look for her fourteen-year-old son, Chris. He had gone out sledding and was an hour late for dinner. As she made her way to the hill where neighborhood children were sledding, Carol reflected on her son's turbulent teen years. *Homework didn't get done, his room was a disaster, and now he thinks he can come and go whenever he wants,* she thought angrily to herself.

Passing her neighbor's house she also thought of their five-year-old son, Mark, who lost his leg in an accident earlier that year. She wondered how Mark was getting along and how the family was adjusting. Although she felt she should call them, she hesitated because she did not know what to say or do.

When she arrived at the hill, Carol found Chris and began to scold him for being late. After listening respectfully and patiently to his mother's stern words, Chris asked if he could explain his tardiness.

"Mom, I was helping Mark sled this afternoon," he began. "It's hard for him to sled. Coming down is fine, but he has to crawl uphill pulling his sled behind him. He gets tired very fast. So today I pulled him up to the top—maybe twenty times. It was great to hear him laughing so much." Chris went on to explain that he tried to leave several times, but Mark pleaded with him to continue sledding.

"When I learned of my son's kindness to Mark, I immediately regretted my harsh scolding of him. As I think of Chris helping Mark, I feel a great deal of pride that he is such a loving, compassionate teenager."

This heartwarming story can serve as a reminder that God expects us to bless others through our acts of compassion, kindness, and love. Although it may be inconvenient or time-consuming, we must not allow ourselves to neglect this important spiritual activity.

❧ *Thought for the Day* ❧
Kindness is the golden chain by which society
is bound together.
Goethe

Encourage Those Who First Encouraged You

I am amply supplied, now that I have received...
the gifts you sent. They are a fragrant offering.
Philippians 4:18

When Saint Paul was imprisoned for the faith, people whom he had previously ministered to sent him gifts of encouragement. Obviously delighted, Paul wrote back: "I am amply supplied, now that I have received from Epaphroditus the gifts you sent. They are a fragrant offering."

That example is a good reminder for the rest of us. We must not forget about the people who shared a word of hope with us or those who provided us with our first opportunity to grow and develop, personally or professionally.

A quick review of our past will reveal that our lives are filled with encouraging people...

- a pastor
- a teacher
- a colleague
- a relative
- a school mate
- a college professor
- a spouse
- a parent
- a neighbor
- a religious
- a Christian educator
- a Sunday school teacher

Remember not only their kindness, but remember them. A time may come when they are in need of a lift. If an opportunity arises to return the encouragement, do it as quickly and as lavishly as possible.

⚜ *Thought for the Day* ⚜
We are here to add what we can to life,
not to get what we can from it.
Sir William Osler

The Power of a "Thank You"

Be thankful.
Colossians 3:15

There are many people whose service and assistance are often taken for granted. Because of that, they may experience times of doubt, discouragement, and despondency about their work and lives. Get creative with your expressions of gratitude. They will provide important support and cheer.

Remember that saying "thank you" is a form of encouragement. And encouragement is oxygen for the spirit. A few simple, sincere words of praise and thanks can quickly animate the most disheartened person.

One December, seventeen-year-old Candi Brown's car overturned. The roof collapsed, crushing her skull. The crews of Engine Company 8 and Med 15 in Grayson, Georgia, rushed to her assistance. At the hospital, doctors told her parents to prepare for the worst.

Because of the efficient skill of the on-site fire fighters and emergency medical technicians, Candi survived. A year later, she and her family served a holiday dinner to the Gwinnett County fire fighters and medical personnel.

During dinner, Candi rose painfully and said, "Thank you for helping God save my life and giving me a second chance. I love you!"

After hearing those heartwarming words fire lieutenant Bobby McKinzie said, "It's rare that we receive this kind of thanks. We were glad to have a part in her life. Today she's definitely touched ours."

Today's text is a simple reminder—*Be thankful*. The writer does not elaborate, possibly because we are to use our own creativity in expressing gratitude to God and to all those around who help, inspire, cheer, comfort, and aid us in so many ways.

❧ Thought for the Day ❧
I can no other answer make but thanks and ever thanks.
William Shakespeare

Trusting God One Day at a Time

He who fears the Lord has a secure fortress.
Proverbs 14:26

"It seemed as though life couldn't get much better. I was a college student—enjoying that experience—and I was fully in love," says Mary Ellen. "I eagerly anticipated marrying Harold after we both graduated."

A year before graduating, Harold began experiencing headaches. New glasses were prescribed but the headaches persisted. A few tests clearly revealed that Harold had a tumor on his brain. "I became bitter and confused," Mary Ellen recalls. "I was angry with God and kept saying 'What good was it for Harold to be such an active, committed Christian?'"

Her parents and Harold's parents prayed for his healing. "The operation was a complete success," the doctor triumphantly announced. Mary Ellen was ecstatic and her anger and bitterness dropped. Harold became stronger day by day and week by week. He and Mary Ellen became formally engaged. "Life couldn't get much better than this," she often said to friends.

Then the headaches returned. Another tumor was discovered on Harold's brain. His mother took Mary Ellen out for lunch on a beautiful spring day and told her, "Harold is going to die." Her low voice was filled with pain and fear. Mary Ellen ran out of the restaurant into a nearby park where she stopped by a huge old maple tree. Weeping, she beat her hands against its trunk until blood appeared. Then she collapsed to the ground exhausted. Harold's mother took Mary Ellen to the hospital emergency room where a kind doctor listened to her pain. He reminded Mary Ellen that she could be of tremendous help and encouragement to Harold in the last weeks of his life. "I can't do it!" Mary Ellen exclaimed. Then the doctor said, "In the Book of Proverbs it is written: *He who fears the Lord has a secure fortress.* That means God will help you."

Harold lived for six more weeks, even less than his family and friends had hoped for. They were difficult days for Mary Ellen. "I found myself still questioning what happened, but I also discovered that by putting myself in God's hands, I could face what I had to face. Today, I'm over sixty years of age. I've had a good life, but through Harold's sickness and death I learned that you can't get through something without a strong hand to help you—the strong hand of God!"

⁓ Affirmation for the Day ⁓
I live within the circle of God's majestic love.
Today I trust God to guide and provide for me,
to reach for the safe, strong hand of God.
VMP

All I Need to Know About Life
I Learned From My Bible

He [God] reveals deep and hidden things; he knows what lies in darkness, and light dwells with him.

Daniel 2:22

Consider these realities on the spiritual theme "All I need to know about life I learned from my Bible":

- Miracles happen.
- Somebody loves me, constantly and consistently.
- I am not alone.
- Love transforms people.
- The majority is not always right.
- Wonderful things happen in dark places.
- You can always go home again.
- Things may look better in three days.
- Death is a transition.
- All things do work together for good.
- A sigh can become a song.
- Tomorrow doesn't have to be the same as yesterday.
- There is a light behind every shadow.
- We get what we give.
- We find what we expect.
- One person can make a difference.
- Everywhere on earth peace is in search of makers.

⫷ *Prayer for the Day* ⫸
Gracious and holy God,
I thank you for my spiritual heritage and education.
I thank you for sending wise, spiritual teachers into my life.
Let me live wisely and pass on to others my accumulated wisdom.
VMP

Exercising Our Privilege of Serving Others

The greatest among you will be your servant.
Matthew 23:11

Each one of us has talents, experiences, insights, and wisdom that can help another person. In today's text Jesus reminds us that there are many who need our sacrifice of time, energy, resources, money, ideas, and prayers. We must remember to share those with others. Think about these truths:

• *There is always someone to teach.* Let us consider being a mentor to a colleague, neighbor, friend, or spouse. Or, let us consider guiding a youth by being a sports coach or school tutor.

• *There is always someone to visit.* Ask yourself: Is someone I know sick? Is someone I know hospitalized? Is someone I know being separated or divorced? Is someone I know suddenly unemployed? Is someone I know in trouble with the law? Is someone I know experiencing great financial problems? If the answer to any such question is yes, then there is someone who needs your visit.

• *There is always someone to help.* Because life is not always smooth sailing, there are always those around us who can use some help. Our assistance can be simply a word of encouragement, a sympathetic listening ear, or helpful advice sensitively offered.

• *There is always someone to love.* Doing this simply requires that we choose to act with kindness and charity. Today, let us begin to reorganize our thinking and our acting in ways that are consistent with our choice to be loving.

❧ Thought for the Day ❧

To love is to give one's time. We never give the impression
that we care when we are in a hurry. To exercise a spiritual
ministry means to take time. If we want to save our time
for more important matters than a soul, we are but tradesmen.

Paul Tournier

When in Doubt, Choose Kindness

A kind man benefits himself,
but a cruel man brings himself harm.

Proverbs 11:17

Two stories about Abraham Lincoln can help us live more wisely...

During the Civil War, Lincoln routinely received letters from soldiers incarcerated for various offenses. One letter came without the usual accompanying letters of recommendation.

"What? Has this man no friends?" the president asked his aides.

"Apparently not, sir," replied one aide.

Pausing briefly, Lincoln responded, "Then I shall be his friend," and he signed the pardon.

When Lincoln learned that General Robert E. Lee had surrendered, thus ending the nation's Civil War, he made an unusual request. On the same day he learned of Lee's surrender, Lincoln walked outside the White House and instructed the U.S. Marine Corps band to play "Dixie."

The wisdom in these Lincoln stories is this: Kind acts always turn darkness into light.

When we treat our enemies with kindness, the darkness turns into light as a foe becomes a friend.

When we extend kindness to those who have opposed us, the darkness turns into light as wounds are healed and disunity gradually gives way to unity.

Where you experience conflict with someone and there is doubt about a course of action, always choose kindness. One kind act can accomplish far more than brute strength or relentless aggression can ever achieve.

∼ Affirmation for the Day ∼
God is kind; I will be kind.
God is merciful; I will be merciful.
God is loving; I will be loving.
VMP

Faith Gives Us Victory

Every child of God is able to defeat the world.
1 John 5:4, *Today's English Version*

Tenth-grade student Eugene Orowitz did not know that his sopho-more year in high school would entirely change his life. Until that year he was extremely shy and completely lacking in confidence. He did not excel in either academics or sports. However, one day as he was watch-ing some senior students throw the javelin on the field their coach asked Eugene if he would like to try. To the amazement of those present, when Eugene tried the javelin soared all the way into the grandstand, where it came to rest. Highly impressed, the coach told the youth he could keep the javelin and invited him to participate in the track-and-field sport. From that moment on, Eugene spent most of his spare time javelin-throwing. Before he left high school, Eugene had thrown the javelin 211 yards, establishing a national record that year among high-school stu-dents. His skill earned him a college track scholarship in California. Eugene seriously considered preparing for the Olympics, but a torn shoul-der muscle ended his javelin-throwing career.

However, he never forgot the feeling he experienced the first time he held a javelin: "I had this terrific sense of excitement and confidence and power. It was amazing. And then, years later the same feeling came to me in another area altogether. My javelin-throwing career was over; I was just getting by with odd jobs when a friend who had a part in a play asked me to rehearse his lines with him. We started reading the script together, and all of a sudden the same sense of excitement and confi-dence and rightness came to me. I knew I wanted to get into dramatics. I knew I wanted to be an actor. I knew I was supposed to be an actor." So, Eugene Orowitz enrolled in acting school, changed his name to Michael Landon, and became famous for his many television roles.

What transpired in young Landon's life was a sudden infusion of con-fidence. And confidence is the vital factor in life, making the difference between success and failure, happiness and disappointment, fulfillment and frustration. According to the Bible, confidence should be a natural by-product of faith: *Every child of God is able to defeat the world.*

⤜ *Thought for the Day* ⤛
God wants us to be victors, not victims;
to grow, not grovel;
to soar, not sink,
to overcome, not to be overwhelmed.
William Arthur Ward

Utilizing the "As-If" Principle

It will be done just as you believed it would.
Jesus in Matthew 8:13

Basically, the "as-if" principle says that to attain the quality you want, start acting "as if" you already had it. One who used the "as-if" principle routinely was Lincoln Kirstein, the legendary director and founder of the New York City Ballet. He credits a former teacher with introducing him to the concept. "He gave me a method which can be lightly called 'as if.' You behave 'as if' something were true. Then you make it happen. We thought of a ballet school, a company, Lincoln Center, long before they happened. By behaving as if it would happen, we wasted no time."

Furthermore, by behaving "as if" we give ourselves the opportunity to grow comfortably and confidently into that role. Consider using the "as-if" principle in these ways:

When feeling intimidated…
    act as if you are completely without fear;
When feeling weak…
    act as if you are strong;
When feeling frightened…
    act as if you are courageous;
When feeling confused…
    act as if you are thinking clearly;
When feeling anxious…
    act as if you are in deep peace;
When feeling discouraged…
    act as if you are extremely confident;
When feeling despair…
    act as if you are full of faith.

✀ Affirmation for the Day ✀
God is now helping me.
God is now guiding me.
I am calm and confident.
I am creative and decisive.
VMP

Living Responsibly

Sow for yourselves righteousness...
Hoseah 10:12

Industrial psychologists and business consultants note the strong link between a sense of responsibility and the confidence that creates success. Gerald Kushel, Ed.D, president of the Institute for Effective Thinking says:

> Over the years, I have observed thousands of managers—and find that the most important quality shared by all peak performers is a sense of responsibility that drives them to excel, regardless of external forces. By contrast, when bad managers fail to achieve their maximum capabilities, they transfer the blame elsewhere—a difficult boss...an unsupportive spouse...uncooperative workers, etcetera.

Kushel cites the example of Harry Truman, who entered politics after his men's clothing store failed. He could easily have walked away from his bankrupt business. Instead, he took responsibility and repaid every dollar he owed. That same characteristic appeared when Truman was a U.S. Senator. He made it his responsibility to learn all about complex legislation pending before his committee. To do that, he arrived at the office early every morning—so early that he became the first senator ever issued his own key to the Senate office building.

We need to monitor ourselves, asking if we are living responsibly...

- Do I accept responsibility for my actions or do I blame others?
- Do I face issues with integrity or do I try to pass off the responsibility to another?
- Do I rise to a challenge or do I turn away?
- Do I deal with difficult matters or do I immediately seek out a rescuer?

⟞ Thought for the Day ⟝
A good name keeps its brightness even
in dark days.
Latin proverb

Accepting Challenges With Faith

*But Moses said to God, "Who am I, that I
should go to Pharaoh and bring the Israelites
out of Egypt."*

Exodus 3:11

The lesson from Moses' reluctance to lead the people of Israel out of slavery and into freedom is this: Rather than give in to your fears, accept a challenge; rather than allow your personal limitations to hold you back, step out in faith. Do this even though the matter at hand may be intimidating and the responsibility comes without much support from others. Doing so provides you with an invaluable opportunity of rising to the occasion, meeting the challenge directly, and triumphing over it.

Mary Lou Forbes was one of the first women to win a Pulitzer prize in journalism for her coverage of the 1950s civil rights movement. During that time Forbes nearly missed out on an important promotion because her boss feared men in the newsroom would not take orders from a woman.

In spite of his hesitation, Forbes saw an opportunity and went to work convincing him to give her a chance. "I told him the men would listen to me because they knew I was a good reporter," she explains. "Still his reluctance has stayed with me to this day. It has been a key to whatever success has come my way. When people categorize you according to preconceived notions, take it as a dare. Tell yourself you can do anything they can do, and you can do it better."

✎ *Prayer for the Day* ✎
O God,
You have carefully created me
and filled me with gifts and talents.
Help me use them lovingly and courageously
to face the challenges of daily life.
VMP

Blessing Others With Encouragement

Encourage and strengthen him...
Deuteronomy 3:28

One of the highest human responsibilities is also the easiest: It is that of encouraging others. Sadly, though, the world is filled with discouragers. Just think how frequently you have come across someone who...

has poured cold water on your enthusiasm,
has laughed at your goals,
has ridiculed your hopes,
has broken your dreams,
has dimmed your vision,
has drained your energy,
has negated your aspiration.

Have a good look at the people around you. Are they positive, supportive, and encouraging of you? Or are they mainly negative thinkers—people who erode your self-confidence by questioning your ability, experience, and aspirations. "Avoid nay sayers and negative types" is the blunt advice given by Rush Limbaugh, host of *The Rush Limbaugh Show,* the nation's highest-rated national radio talk show. "It's easy to find people to talk you out of something. I floundered in radio for twelve years, and all that time everybody told me I should get out of it and that radio wasn't a fair business—because they had failed at it."

Eventually, his negative friends reduced his confidence and so discouraged Limbaugh that he left the radio industry in 1979. He spent five miserable years in a sales job for which he was unsuited. "Finally, in 1983, I returned to radio—my real love—and began my show locally in Kansas City, Missouri. If I had followed the nay sayers' advice I'd still be stuck in that sales job—still unchallenged, frustrated, and feeling empty."

The Bible reminds us we have a duty to encourage people in their lives. Many times a simple word of praise, thanks, or appreciation is enough to keep a person on track. Today's scripture is quite accurate—to encourage is to strengthen a person.

❧ Prayer for the Day ❧
Loving God,
Let me be the one whose life blesses others.
Let me be the one whose words inspire others;
Let me be the one whose actions help others.
VMP

Pass It On

Praise be to the God...of all comfort,
who comforts us in all our troubles, so that
we can comfort those in any trouble with the
comfort we ourselves have received from God.

2 Corinthians 1:3–4

We should use our talents, skills, and experiences to leave the world a better place than we found it. One way to do this is to "pass it on."

For example, if you have received a kindness from someone, the best way to "repay" is to pass it on to another person. A good example comes from a California woman:

Forty years ago, I was a poor student working my way through UC Berkeley. I didn't have enough money to pay my laboratory fees for the courses I needed to take. A counselor for young adults at a community church loaned me the money I needed to stay in school. I kept track of the amount, and when I got a job, I tried to repay her. The woman said simply, 'I didn't miss it. Just pass it on.' That has been my motto ever since. Passing it on is the best way to repay a kindness.

❧ *Prayer for the Day* ❧
Eternal God,
I thank you for your love and kindness in my life.
I thank you for the love and kindness in my life
which has come from others.
Let me pass on love and kindness to those I come in
contact with day by day.
VMP

What Are We Leaving Behind?

What good will it be for a man if he
gains the whole world, yet forfeits
his soul?

Matthew 16:26

Lawyers and financial planners advise everyone to write a will, which legally establishes who will benefit from assets when we die. Along with leaving behind our material wealth, we should consider writing and sharing an ethical or spiritual will in which we leave behind some very important life lessons.

Consider this "will" written by Rabbi Moses Yehosua Zelig Hakohen, a religious leader in Latvia during the 1800s. Here is some of the spiritual wealth he bequeathed to his children and grandchildren:

- Ask forgiveness from every person and be forgiving of everyone, both in speech and deed.

- Prepare yourself in the morning to serve the Creator and pray with utmost devotion.

- Train yourself in the habit of balance, expecting equal amounts of criticism and praise, sadness and joy, pain and pleasure.

- Avoid listening to any obscene speech.

- Trust in God that he will certainly do everything for your benefit.

Another example of a spiritual will left behind are the words below written by John Wesley, founder of the Methodist movement. His philosophy of life is still a good one for us today.

～ Thought for the Day ～
Do all the good you can,
By all the means you can,
In all the ways you can,
In all the places you can,
At all the times you can,
To all the people you can,
As long as ever you can.

John Wesley

Make Your World a Better Place—Part I

Of all that you give me I will give you a tenth.
Genesis 28:22

All of us should live and act in ways that bless, inspire, and uplift others. We should use our talents, skills, and experiences to leave the world a better place than we found it. We should give back to life just as we receive from life. Here are some ways you can make the world a better place:

- *Leave footprints behind.* As we walk through life we leave behind all sorts of footprints. Some are quite visible—diplomas earned, degrees received, jobs held, awards won, status attained, and so on. Work at leaving behind the less visible but more enduring footprints, such as help given, kindness extended, forgiveness offered, love shared.

- *Drive "friendly."* Make it a habit to let other cars into your traffic lane. Be patient with people crossing busy intersections. Give a cyclist or jogger a break. Help a stranded motorist.

- *Be compassionate.* Compassion means we are moved by the struggles, sufferings, and fears of others. Whenever you see someone struggling with life, respond in some way. Even a small act can make a large difference.

- *Take good care of your partner.* Your partner is like flowers in a garden. If you nurture the garden, it will grow beautifully. If you ignore it, the garden will wither up. To help a garden blossom and flower we must know the garden's nature. How much water does it need? How much sunshine? When should nutrients be added to enhance growth?

- *Smile more often.* Day by day, try greeting everyone you meet with a smile—family, friends, colleagues, strangers.

- *Practice charity.* Designate a percentage of your income for charitable and religious causes. When reviewing how much to give be guided by the biblical example of Jacob who gave away ten percent, or a tithe, of all he had. In the Book of Genesis, we read his promise to God: "Of all that you give me I will give you a tenth."

❧ Thought for the Day ❧
We live in deeds, not years.
Phillip James Bailey

Make Your World a Better Place—Part II

Do to others what you would have them do to you.
Jesus, in Matthew 7:12

Here are yet more ways to make the world a better place:

- *Forgive someone.* It's impossible to get through life without being hurt by people. Rather than harbor a grudge and nurse a resentment, let it go. Forgive those who hurt you. Forgiveness ends quarrels, eases pain, restores peace, and promotes spiritual and emotional health.

- *Just be there.* When someone is going through a hard time or experiencing a tragedy just being there can be a tremendous source of hope and encouragement. Comfort a grieving friend. Visit the sick or hospitalized. Hold the hand of someone who is weeping. Make the long drive to a funeral home.

- *Have good manners.* Caring, courtesy, and thoughtfulness seem to be in decline these days. Defy that trend by sending thank-you notes for kindnesses received. Use the words "please" and "thanks" frequently in your speech.

- *Live by the golden rule.* One of the most effective ways of living in harmony with others and promoting peace is to live by the golden rule—*Do to others what you would have them do to you.*

- *Return curtness with kindness.* The world is well supplied with rude people. Whenever you experience rudeness from another person resist the temptation to respond in a similar way. Rather, return curtness with kindness. You will feel better and, possibly, have a positive impact upon the other person.

- *Triumph over tragedy.* Be larger than what comes tumbling over you. Rise to the challenge and overcome. When you triumph over tragedy you not only make your own life better but indirectly improve the lives of others. Your example will inspire them to face their tragedies with greater courage and hope.

- *Make your love felt.* Do not only speak your love but show your love. Shower not only family and close friends with your love but let the showering splash on others—neighbors, colleagues, even strangers.

❧ Thought for the Day ❧
He most lives who thinks most,
feels the noblest, acts the best.
Phillip James Bailey

A Lesson in Love and Courage

Be devoted to one another.
Romans 12:10

One afternoon, Jane toured an art museum while waiting for her husband to finish a business meeting. At the art gallery she encountered a young couple who talked nonstop between themselves. Jane noticed that the woman seemed to be doing almost all of the talking. Jane admired the husband's patience for putting up with her constant parade of words. Distracted by their noise, Jane moved to another part of the museum.

Over the next few hours, Jane encountered the couple as she moved through the various rooms of art. Each time she heard the gush of words and moved away quickly, quite irritated by all the talk. Later, as she was standing at the counter of the museum gift shop making a purchase, the couple approached the exit. Before they left, the husband reached into his pocket and pulled out a white object. He extended it into a long cane and then tapped his way into the coat room to get his wife's jacket.

"He's a brave man," the clerk at the counter told Jane. "Most of us would give up if we were blinded at such a young age. During his adjustment the man made a vow that his life wouldn't change. So, as before, he and his wife come in whenever there is a new exhibit," the clerk explained.

"But what does he get out of the art if he can't see?" Jane asked.

"He sees a lot," the clerk said. "Probably more than you and I. His wife describes each painting so he can see it in his head and mind."

Jane was secretly ashamed of her impatience with the couple. However, upon meeting her husband later that evening she said, "Today I learned something about patience, courage, and love. I saw the patience of a young wife describing paintings to a person without sight and the courage of a husband who would not allow blindness to alter his life."

❧ *Thought for the Day* ❧
Love is like the moon;
when it does not increase it decreases.
Joseph de Segur

Living Peacefully in Spite of Troubles

Peace I leave you; my peace I give you....
Do not let your hearts be troubled
and do not be afraid.

John 14:27

During one hot, dry summer in southern California, a brush fire swept through Topanga Canyon, a suburb of Los Angeles, and destroyed 200 homes. Through newspaper reports Norman Vincent Peale, famed New York City minister and author, realized that one of the homes belonged to a friend of his. Dr. Peale called offering sympathy: "I'm sorry to hear that your house burned down."

Expecting that his friend would be traumatized about the fire and his losses, Dr. Peale was astonished when his friend sounded at peace about the tragedy. "Yes, the house did burn down; but my wife and children are safe, and we're all just as healthy as we were before," he said. "All that we lost were some material things—and they can be replaced." After thanking Dr. Peale for his call of concern, the man concluded saying, "Call me when I have some real trouble."

Obviously, Dr. Peale's friend knew how to remain serene and tranquil in spite of losing his house and belongings. However, most people would not exhibit such calm composure when facing a similar loss. In fact, many experience life as a series of frenzied, feverish, and frantic events—phones ring, the traffic is heavy, an employer is unreasonable, a customer is rude, a personal or professional crisis arises. All such events seem to squeeze out a sense of personal peace in daily life. Jesus acknowledged that life could become upsetting: "In this world you will have trouble" (John 16:33). Yet life can and should be much more than trials, troubles, and the crowding of activities. It is possible to experience personal peace in spite of life's demands. Jesus also said, *Peace I leave you; my peace I give you....Do not let your hearts be troubled and do not be afraid* (John 14:27).

❧ Thought for the Day ❧
The world is too much with us.
William Wordsworth

Using the Serenity Prayer

Godliness with contentment is great gain.
1 Timothy 6:6

In 1928 Reinhold Niebuhr became a professor at New York's Union Theological Seminary. Although he would write many books on ethics and theology, he is best remembered for his serenity prayer:

God, grant me the serenity
to accept the things I cannot change,
courage to change the things I can,
and the wisdom to know the difference.

This is a prayer worth memorizing and imprinting upon the mind. It has the power to break tension and reduce anxiety. Recite it daily. Offer it as your prayer whenever you experience inner turmoil.

Consider the example of Judy, thirty-seven, the owner of a growing but struggling business. Judy has the serenity prayer written on a sheet of paper which she has taped on her bathroom mirror. "Having the prayer taped on the mirror is a healing symbol for me. As I wash my face, I also 'wash' away all my anxieties and worries," she says.

⇜ Thought for the Day ⇝
God does not come and go.
Everywhere and always God is there
in fullness.
Wholly with, always for us.
Richard Bryne

Take Time Off From the World

I would flee far away and stay in the desert.
Psalm 55:7

The pure pleasure of simple quiet eludes most people. Modern life just doesn't leave much room for quiet. Airplanes roar overhead. Cars and trucks honk in gridlock. Elevators play music. The television is on during evening meals. The telephone rings and rings and rings. Couples raising children can often go weeks without sharing a peaceful, quiet moment together.

Yet a quiet time, a regular retreat from the noise and busy-ness, a space from the concerns and routines of everyday life, is necessary for spiritual growth, emotional stability, and human happiness. Temporary flight from the hectic pace of daily life is something we all need.

Think of ways that you can block out time that will add quiet to your life. Here are some ways others have done this:

- A forty-five minute walk each evening after dinner and when the sun has set.
- Spending an hour in a botanical garden.
- Hiking along a mountain trail one Saturday morning.
- Walking on a dirt road, enjoying the surroundings.
- Sitting by a pond, lake, or river in quiet meditation and reflection.

∽ *Thought for the Day* ∽
Each person deserves a day away in which
no problems are confronted,
no solutions searched for.
Each of us needs to withdraw from the cares
which will not withdraw from us.
Maya Angelou

Treating Everyone With Dignity

Rich and poor have this in common:
The Lord is the Maker of them all.

Proverbs 22:2

One Sunday morning in 1865, a black man entered a fashionable Episcopalian church in Richmond, Virginia. When Communion was served, he walked down the aisle and knelt at the altar. A rustle of resentment swept the congregation. "How dare he!" was the mood. Episcopalians used the common cup.

Then a distinguished layman stood up, stepped forward to the altar and knelt beside the black man. It was Robert E. Lee, the former Confederate General. He spoke these powerful words to the congregation: "All men are brothers in Christ. Have we not all one Father?" Instructed and humbled, the congregation followed his lead.

That story has three important lessons. The first one is quite obvious: All of us—black, white, brown—are children of God and, therefore, deserve to treated with respect and kindness.

The second lesson is this: We must have the courage to stand up whenever someone who is "different" from the majority is treated unkindly and with disrespect. We must have the courage of our convictions to stand up for them and stand against those who will abuse another person.

And the third lesson is one of perception: We must train our eye and mind to appreciate the diversity of people, races, personalities, and cultures among us. The human family can be compared to a garden of roses in which there are different colored roses growing. We must see that diversity with joy and rejoice to be among them.

⋙ Prayer for the Day ⋘

Loving and eternal God,
I know that you love all people.
Heighten my appreciation for the diversity
of your creation and let me rejoice in our
common humanity.
Wherever there is injustice and unkindness
let me be the one who speaks out against it.

VMP

Thinking and Thanking

Elisha said to him, "Tell her, 'You have gone to
all this trouble for us. Now what can be done for you?
Can we speak on your behalf to the king
or the commander of the army?'"

2 Kings 4:13

Recently, a man's thoughts revolved around people he especially appreciated. Spontaneously, he called each of them. One had been a professor in college; another was a person who had given him a great deal of encouragement; another was one with whom he enjoyed jogging; and another was a supermarket produce clerk who was always friendly and helpful while he was shopping.

"The response to my calls was amazing and gratifying. It seemed that the calls I made were the first time someone had expressed appreciation to them in this way," the man said.

Motivated by the responses, the man continued his practice of expressing appreciation to various individuals who came his way. On one occasion he extended his practice by writing a letter. The letter-writing was inspired while the man was shopping at a large department store in New York City. When the closing bell rang, most employees made quick exits—all except one. That clerk had been on his way out but when he saw the man still browsing in the store, the clerk laid his overcoat on a chair and helpfully answered all questions the man had about the item he was interested in. The man asked the clerk if he was the floor manager. "No, I'm just a salesclerk on the fifth floor," was the reply.

Upon returning home, the man wrote the store manager telling him of the incident. "In the letter I said, 'This man treated me as if this were his own personal store.'" Two weeks later the man received a letter from he store clerk. He thanked him for writing the manager of the store and added: "I have been promoted to the position of manager of my floor."

Let us take time to think and thank. Let us remember people to whom we are especially grateful and let us tell them how much we appreciate them by a telephone call or a letter.

❧ Thought for the Day ❧
A grateful mind is both a great and happy mind.
William Secker

Correcting Spiritual Nearsightedness

*You...worry your way through life and what
do you have to show for it?*
Ecclesiastes 2:22 (*Today's English Version*)

"Worry is spiritual nearsightedness, a fumbling way of looking at little things, and of magnifying their value," declared Anna Robertson Brown, a nineteenth-century writer.

Interestingly, the word "worry" comes from an old Anglo-Saxon verb *wyrgan,* meaning to choke or strangle. Worry is an "emotional weed." Left unchallenged, it spreads quickly, strangling and choking the inner life. Worry diminishes an individual by making opponents stronger and problems larger than they really are. Worry drains energy, reduces confidence, heightens fear, and impedes positive thought and action. The ancient biblical writer declares, *You...worry your way through life and what do you have to show for it?* Drop worry by beginning to live one day at a time.

A good example is television host Kathie Lee Gifford. Several months ago she learned that a disturbed man threatened to harm her. Even from his jail cell where he is serving two life terms for another crime, he continued to write Gifford threatening letters. "From the start I decided I was not going to worry and let this spoil my life," she says. "I have to hand certain things over to God. It's the living out of my faith that makes me a believer. God doesn't just get rid of hardship or suffering; he heals in the midst of it."

✸ Thought for the Day ✸
Anxiety is the rust of life, destroying its brightness
and weakening its power. A childlike and abiding
trust in Providence is its best preventive and remedy.
Tryon Edwards

Getting Off to a Good Start

Very early in the morning, while it was still dark,
Jesus got up, left the house and went off to a solitary
place, where he prayed.

Mark 1:35

Begin each day with prayer…

Many people find that morning prayer establishes the right foundation for everything that follows throughout the day.

Morning prayer becomes a spiritual anchor that helps us maintain balance and stability, no matter what events emerge. Of course, starting each day with a period of prayer will mean rising a little earlier—Jesus rose while it was still dark in order to spend time in prayer—but even twenty minutes spent in prayer can make a great difference.

During that prayer time begin by expressing gratitude to God for your measure of health and wealth.

Next, commit the entire day to God with all of its opportunities and obstacles, dreams and disappointments. Affirm that you will use the next twenty-four hours wisely. If you're convinced you're too busy to add prayer time consider this wisdom from Saint Francis de Sales: "Every Christian needs a half-hour of prayer each day, except when he is busy, then he needs an hour."

⤞ Thought for the Day ⤝
He who runs from God in the morning
will scarcely find Him the rest of the day.
John Bunyan

Keep an Open House in Your Heart

I ask that we love one another.
2 John 1:5

Maintain an open house in your heart for other people, especially those who are less fortunate and more distressed; those whose resources are decreasing while their burdens are mounting. Create space in your life for them by responding with kindness, compassion, and practical help. Do whatever you can to fuel hope in their lives. Consider these two creative examples:

The first one is that of former Senator and U.S. presidential candidate Robert Dole and his wife, Elizabeth. The couple celebrate their birthdays each year, a week apart, by hosting a party for a roomful of underprivileged teenagers. Although the Doles have very hectic, packed schedules, they make time for such acts of kindness. The Doles consider these kinds of charitable activities extremely important because they directly help others and, indirectly, result in nation-building. The human heart always glows with satisfaction and peace whenever we reach out and help another person.

The other example is that of Lucy, thirty-three, a suburban Chicago mother of two preschoolers, who volunteered to do grocery shopping for an elderly couple who live on her street. "It only takes me an hour a week and I feel so good about doing it," she says. At other times Lucy drives the elderly couple for medical appointments. "By doing this I've made two terrific friends. While my driving and errand-running does help them out, I feel I've benefited much more. I can't begin to describe how much joy this has brought into my life."

❧ *Prayer for the Day* ❧
Eternal and gracious God,
I vow to maintain an open house in my
heart. Let me see and respond to needs
graciously, generously, and gently.
VMP

Avoiding Self-Pity

A deluded heart misleads him.
Isaiah 44:20

Life provides us with ample opportunities to engage in self-pity. We can feel sorry for ourselves because we...

- Don't make more money
- Aren't married
- Are married
- Have children
- Don't have children
- Want a larger house
- Don't drive a newer car
- Don't have more success, etc, etc, etc.

Do not be seduced by the temptation to feel sorry for yourself. Self-pity is fine for a brief moment, but then it must be curbed with a more realistic vision taking over. Allowing self-pity to run a free reign in our lives allows it to become a spreading poison in our system. Before long, self-pity will result in massive bitterness, cynicism, and paranoia. Self-pity is an emotional and spiritual bondage.

If you are tempted to feel sorry for yourself, try eliminating self-pity by adopting a technique that worked for the late actress Joan Blondell. She used a common kitchen timer to pull herself out of a self-pity session. "I set the time for six-and-one-half minutes to be lonely, and twenty-two minutes to feel sorry for myself. And then when the bell rings, I take a shower, a walk, a swim, or I cook something—and think about something else," she explained.

~≈ Prayer for the Day ≈~
Loving and kind God,
Rather than become absorbed in myself, in my pain,
and in my deficiencies, let me become absorbed
in your love and abundance.
VMP

What Are We Looking for in Others?

Why do you look at the speck of sawdust in your brother's eye?

Matthew 7:3

Martha's sixth-grade son handed her his report card with a flourish of excitement. "All A's!" he declared proudly. As he watched Martha look at the report card, the boy was rocking back and forth on his heels with a self-satisfied smile on his face.

Quickly scanning the paper, Martha saw that her son had indeed achieved straight A's. She was not surprised, as he had always been an outstanding student. However, her eyes zeroed in on a letter N, which indicated "Needs Improvement" in conduct. Martha responded, "Well, you did get good grades," she began somewhat reluctantly, "but look at this N in conduct. I know you can do better than that! You need to try harder."

The boy's enthusiasm and smile evaporated. He took the report card back and slowly walked away, his shoulders drooping. Martha turned back to her work, confident that she had parented him well and encouraged him to reach his potential. The next day Martha reflected upon what had transpired between herself and her son and it hit her. "I had stolen his self-confidence and the pride he felt in a worthy accomplishment. Instead of looking at all the great grades he made, I had been looking for his faults."

Martha was guilty of failing to praise him for what he had done right. She focused on his one fault and discounted all the other achievements. Martha was guilty of seeing the "speck" in her son's personality, precisely what Jesus commanded us not to do. Fortunately, Martha felt ashamed of what she had done and apologized to her son. She asked forgiveness, and the sixth-grader hugged her with the complete forgiveness that children give so easily.

Let us reflect on Jesus' command and examine our conscience:

- When I look at others, do I focus on the bad and overlook the good?

- When I look at others, do I look for the speck in the other person or do I see all the wonderful things that person has done?

- Do I choose to praise a person or am I critical of who they are, what they do, and how they live?

～๕ Thought for the Day ๖~

The camel never sees its own hump;
but its neighbor's hump is ever before its eyes.

Arabian proverb

Comforting Those Who Mourn

Weep with those who weep.
Romans 12:15
(New Revised Standard)

Today's advise from Saint Paul means…

- Don't try to explain.
- Don't try to rationalize.
- Don't try to philosophize.
- Don't try to theologize.
- Don't try to justify.
- Don't try to resolve.
- Don't try to solve.
- Don't try to gloss over….

- Just be there!
- Just be there for those who weep.
- Just be there in their grief and pain.
- Just be there with your own tears.
- Just be there to listen and affirm the hurt.
- Just be there with your shoulder on which they can cry.
- Just be there and let them know you are standing by.
- Just be there!

∼ *Thought for the Day* ∼
How shall we comfort those who weep?
By weeping with them.
Father Yelchaninov

A Lesson in Forgiveness

Forgive us our debts, as we also
have forgiven our debtors.
Matthew 6:12

Edwin Markham, the famous American poet, came to his retirement years only to discover that the man to whom he had entrusted his life savings had squandered all his money. Markham was furious with the financial planner and began to brood over the injustice and the loss. Day after day he became more and more bitter.

One day Markham was sitting at his desk. His spirit was deeply disturbed. He found himself aimlessly drawing circles. Finally, he said to himself, "I must forgive him and I will forgive him." As he looked at the circles he had been drawing on the page, Markham's creative spirit once again emerged as he wrote his most famous lines of poetry:

He drew a circle to shut me out,
Heretic, rebel, a thing to flout;
But love and I had the wit to win,
We drew a circle to take him in.

The lesson: Forgiveness does more good for us than for the one who is forgiven. Forgiveness is a source of healing for our frayed emotions, disturbed mind, and angry feelings. When we genuinely forgive, we abandon the impulse to get even, to retaliate in some way. The result is peace of mind, clarity of purpose in life, and freedom from bitterness.

❧ Thought for the Day ❧
He who has not forgiven an enemy has never
yet tasted one of the most sublime enjoyments of life.
John Caspar Lavater

Using Our Mistakes

...our hearts condemn us.
> 1 John 3:20

An artist who was locally known for her vibrant watercolor paintings and creative collages was giving a lecture. When the time came for questions from the audience a man asked the artist how she achieved the fine detail in her collage pieces. "Was each detail created especially for the piece she was working on?" he asked.

The artist laughed and responded, "Making a collage is easy, really. Each section is a cut-up piece of a larger watercolor painting that didn't work out for some reason. In other words, I use my mistakes."

That last phrase—"I use my mistakes"—is worthy of further consideration.

Everyday life would flow much better if we remember that we can use our mistakes to our advantage.

When we take our mistakes and put them to good use, they disappear. However, if we fret about them, the mistakes take on a larger life. They grow and fester until they inflict a deeper and more permanent wound.

The reality is that all of us will make mistakes, some small, some large. Too quickly do we condemn ourselves. Let us be artists at life and find ways of using our mistakes to create something better.

⤜ Affirmation for the Day ⤝
I approve of myself.
I gain wisdom from my mistakes.
God is leading me to a higher good.
VMP

Making a Christmas Pledge

When you make a vow to God
...fulfill your vow.
Ecclesiastes 5:4

As December begins, consider making this Christmas pledge...
Believing in the beauty and simplicity of Christmas, I commit myself to the following eight goals:

1. To remember those individuals who truly need my gifts.
2. To express my love toward family and friends in more direct ways than simple gift-giving.
3. To fan the light as I sense it in others and help it grow, glow, and spread.
4. To examine my holiday activities and traditions in the light of the true spirit of Christmas.
5. To initiate one act of peacemaking within my circle of family, friends, neighbors, and colleagues.
6. To be hospitable and keep an open house in my heart for all things—human and nonhuman.
7. To rededicate myself to the spiritual growth of my family and closest friends.
8. To cease all Christmas preparations by midnight on December 23.

As you commit yourself to this Christmas pledge, ask God to help you be faithful to your vow.

❧ Affirmation for the Day ❧
Today and every day I live in peace and harmony.
Today and every day I act from love.
Today and every day I live with gratitude and joy.
VMP

DECEMBER

Remembering That Christmas Is a Miracle

...the star they had seen in the east went ahead of them
until it stopped over the place where the child was.

Matthew 2:9

The season celebrating Christ's birth continues to be one filled with miracles...

At Christmas stately green trees are transformed into twinkling, glittering, gorgeously ornamented creations of imaginations from the young and the old.

At Christmas animosity is transformed into understanding.

At Christmas anxiety and frustration are transformed into acceptance and peace.

At Christmas modern day "Scrooges" are transformed into benevolent gift-givers.

At Christmas estrangement is transformed into reunion.

At Christmas enemies are transformed into friends. Do you know the World War I story that took place on Christmas Eve on the battlefield?

Enemies were in their trenches. Suddenly in the clear cold air the distinctive notes of "Silent Night" could be heard being played by a homesick bugler.

Soon the English and American soldiers began to sing the words—*Silent Night, Holy Night...*

Then, incredibly, from the German side voices joined in singing *Stille Nacht, Heilige Nacht...*

An informal peace pervaded the trenches. Troops from both sides stood up, left their trenches and exchanged Christmas greetings with the "enemy." Enemies separated by the trenches of war were transformed, briefly, into comrades celebrating Christmas.

As we move through the month, let us remember, first and foremost, that Christmas continues to be a miracle. Let us look for miracles all around us this December.

⤖ Thought for the Day ⤖

Jesus Christ, the condescension of divinity,
the exaltation of humanity.

Phillips Brooks

When God Sends Hot Chocolate

*Be strong and courageous. Do not be afraid
or terrified...for the Lord your God goes
with you; he will never leave you nor forsake you.*
                                        Deuteronomy 31:6

"No hot chocolate on Christmas Eve?" Christine, a teenager, asked her mother. "Next year," promised the mother as she quickly looked away.

In that family hot chocolate was a Christmas Eve tradition. But this year they could not afford even that simple item. Jack, the father and main breadwinner, was laid off six months earlier. Because unemployment in their area was high, he decided to begin his own business. Working out of the house basement, he struggled to make the business grow but was unsuccessful. The family finances were further strained when the transmission on their car failed.

To make ends meet, their oldest daughter contributed her earnings from her first full-time job. Neither of the two girls ever complained about doing without. Still, as the year drew to a close, the family financial picture looked extremely bleak.

During the church service on Christmas Eve, the mother found her spirits sagging rather than being lifted by the message of hope delivered by the minister. Her anxiety over family finances blocked out the joyous music and scriptures of hope that evening.

When the service was over, people greeted and embraced one another. As the mother and her daughters bundled up in coats, scarves, and gloves preparing to return home, one of the youth workers called the daughters over saying: "Wait a minute. I have something for you." Then she pulled a ribboned jar from her bag saying, "Merry Christmas." The gift was a hot-chocolate mix.

Interestingly, the youth worker did not know about the family tradition of hot chocolate on Christmas Eve. Nor did she know that this simple gift became a powerful reminder to the family that God had not forgotten them and their plight. Let us think about that incident, connecting it to the text for this day: *He will never leave you nor forsake you.*

❧ *Prayer for the Day* ❧
Loving God,
I praise you for your faithfulness
and unconditional love.
Help me live day by day
aware of your loving concern.
VMP

Giving the Gift of Love at Christmas

So when you give to the needy...
Matthew 6:2

Sometimes the most memorable gifts are not those that come in boxes and are colorfully wrapped. The gifts most remembered are gifts of love. Here are ten suggestions for giving love at Christmas:

1. Address Christmas cards for someone with a vision handicap or someone with a muscular disorder.

2. Offer to baby-sit one evening for a couple with small children. That will give them time alone or time to do some last-minute shopping.

3. Invite someone from overseas who is living in this country to spend Christmas with you and your family. You will benefit by learning more about another culture and your guest will not spend this major holiday alone.

4. Write a special Christmas letter of appreciation to a priest, minister, or college professor who has made a difference in your life.

5. Adopt a lonely senior adult. Take that person out for dinner or bring a special basket filled with treats. Ask the senior to share a special Christmas memory with you.

6. Organize a collection box of food staples for a needy family. Deliver it personally.

7. Offer to run errands for someone who is housebound, perhaps an elderly person or someone ill or injured.

8. Offer to take older relatives, grandparents, or neighbors shopping. Many older people are without transportation.

9. Invite some neighborhood children into your home on some cold, overcast day, play board games or rent a movie. Remember back to your childhood when you were bored because there was no one to play with.

10. Buy an extra Christmas tree and give it to a family whose finances are tight and who might hesitate to make such a purchase.

✜ *Affirmation for the Day* ✜
I honor the birth of Christ by giving the gift of my time,
the gift of my talents, the gift of my love.
VMP

Applying the Law of Compensation

Those who hope in the Lord will renew their strength.
Isaiah 40:31

December is an ideal time of year to review the natural "gifts" that have been given to all of us from our creator. It is interesting to note the most successful among us have as many or even more weaknesses than the general population. The difference is this: Rather than dwelling on their weaknesses and handicaps, they compensate by building on the natural strengths and gifts that they possess.

In a famous study by Victor and Mildred Goertzel, entitled *Cradles of Eminence,* the home backgrounds of three hundred highly successful people were investigated. Many of these three hundred individuals were men and women whose names are well known: Franklin D. Roosevelt, Helen Keller, Winston Churchill, Albert Schweitzer, Gandhi, Albert Einstein, and Sigmund Freud. The Goertzels' intensive investigation into their early home lives yielded these surprising findings:

- Three-fourths of the children were troubled either by poverty, by a broken home, or by rejecting overpossessive or dominating parents.

- Seventy-four of eighty-five writers of fiction or drama and sixteen of the twenty poets came from homes where, as children, they saw tense and painful psychological drama played out by their parents.

- Physical disabilities, such as blindness, deafness, or crippled limbs, characterized over one-fourth of the sample.

Those results raise this question: How did these people manage to go on and achieve outstanding accomplishments? Most likely, they applied the law of compensation. They chose to focus on their strength and not their weakness, their talent and not their handicap.

In this season of gift giving, let us take the time to review the diverse gifts we have been naturally endowed with by our kind Creator. And, let us resolve to tap our hidden potential for our benefit, for the good of others, and for the glory of our Creator. No matter what has happened to us in the past, the promise of God is that we can renew our strength.

≈ *Affirmation for the Day* ≈

God is good and has blessed me with many talents.
I am completely willing to learn more about myself.
It is safe for me to act on my strengths.

VMP

December 6

Feeling Good When the Weather Is Bad

See! The winter is past.
Song of Songs 2:11

"Winter is a disease," declared French poet and playwright Alfred De Mussett. Many people can identify with that statement. Various factors make winter a gloomy and even depressing season. From November through March it's dark longer while the weather is colder, cloudier, and wetter. It is a time of year when people experience diminishing energy and increasing lethargy. In the winter it seems as though there is more sickness in the form of colds and the flu. During winter, both the emotional and spiritual life can suffer.

Yet winter can be a creative, productive, and informative time. Here are some ways to beat the winter blues and feel good when the weather is bad:

- *Read for encouragement.* A very effective way to reduce and even eliminate winter blues is to arm yourself with self-help and inspirational books. Finding these will mean a pleasant trip to a bookstore or library.

- *Begin an exercise program.* Shorter days and longer nights present an ideal opportunity to work out at a gym or health club after work. Not only will your body improve but so will your mood. Research reveals that exercise beats back the blues.

- *Reconnect with a friend.* Call someone whom you have not been with or spoken to for some time. Enjoy a meal together.

- *Bake a dessert.* Double your recipe and give half as a surprise to someone in your neighborhood or place of work.

- *Arrange to go on a retreat.* Keep your eyes and ears open for a weekend retreat either in December or January. The intellectual and spiritual formation will linger long after this winter is gone.

- *Remain patient.* Try recalling that seasons come and go. It will not be long before winter is over—*See! The winter is past.*

⚜ Thought for the Day ⚜
Each moment of the year has its own beauty...
a picture which was never seen before and
which shall never be seen again.
Ralph Waldo Emerson

Extending and Expanding Christmas Joy

Yet I will rejoice in the Lord, I will be joyful in God my Savior.
Habakkuk 3:18

The joy of Christmas can be greatly extended and expanded when we give of ourselves to those who need us. This year try some of the following:

- Be the first to wish everyone you meet "Merry Christmas."

- Bake or buy delicious coffeecakes. Give them to neighbors on Christmas Eve.

- Give your place in line to someone who looks as though she or he has had a long, tiring day. Or, give up your seat on a subway or bus to someone carrying a lot of packages.

- Be especially courteous to harried sales personnel.

- Give an anonymous gift of money to someone laid off.

- Give someone with failing eyesight a subscription to a large-print magazine.

- Compliment at least one person each day for the rest of the month. Your compliment may be their most remembered gift this year.

- Give tickets to a Christmas performance to someone who could use a break but couldn't otherwise afford to go.

- Offer to watch your neighbor's house, feed their pet, water their plants, and so on, while they are out of town for the holidays.

- Donate leftover food from a party to a homeless shelter.

- Buy an extra bag of nonperishable groceries when you shop and donate it to a food pantry or to an impoverished family.

- Buy a special Christmas card, mail it to someone who greatly influenced or helped you. Be sure to express your appreciation for their help and influence on you.

∼≪ *Thought for the Day* ≫∼
The princes among us are those who
forget themselves and serve mankind.
Woodrow Wilson

Warrior Angels

Then the Lord opened the servant's eyes, and he looked and saw the hills full of horses and chariots of fire all around Elisha.

2 Kings 6:17

Angels are connected to the Christmas stories of Jesus' birth. They appear on many Christmas cards. Here is a true story for those who may be skeptical about the presence of angels in today's world. It concerns a small woman who weighs eighty-five pounds, is slightly over five feet tall, and who walks with a noticeable limp because of rheumatoid arthritis.

Once a week she visits a bank to deposit the offering from her Sunday school class. As she left the bank one day she heard a woman screaming in the parking lot. There a ski-masked man, weighing about two hundred fifty pounds and more than six feet tall, was beating the woman as he tried to steal her moneybag. The two were struggling when he finally struck her with a powerful blow, knocking her to the ground.

The smaller, frail woman had an urgent inner feeling that she needed to take action. Obeying her inner voice she limped toward the mugger, pointed her gnarled finger at him and repeated, "No! In the name of Jesus, no!" As she advanced, the woman became aware of a strong presence with her and knew she was not facing the mugger alone. The man in the ski mask continued his assault, pausing only to glance contemptuously at the tiny woman. But as he looked over her head, his eyes filled with terror. He began to back up as if in shock. Abruptly, he turned and ran for his life.

While others did not know what made the mugger flee, the woman had no doubt what the man saw. She was aware that standing behind her was an angel, a warrior angel whom she described as at least nine feet tall. The striking figure intimidated and terrified the mugger.

That modern incident has a parallel in today's ancient text concerning the prophet Elisha. When he and his servant were surrounded by soldiers of an enemy ruler, the servant became hysterical. Quietly but firmly, the prophet prayed for his servant. When the servant opened his eyes and looked into the hills, he saw an army of warrior angels there to protect him and Elisha—*Then the Lord opened the servant's eyes, and he looked and saw the hills full of horses and chariots of fire all around Elisha.*

The ancient story and the modern one give us something more to consider when we think about the role of angels in daily life.

⊰ Thought for the Day ⊱
When angels come, the devils leave.

Arabian proverb

Teaming Up With God to Make a Difference

You have…increased their joy.
Isaiah 9:3

The ninth chapter of Isaiah is the prophet's anticipation of what will happen when God appears among people in the form of the "messiah." People's joy will be increased. During this time of the year, let us be especially open to the needs of others. Let us resolve to team up with God in order to make a difference so that someone's joy will be increased. Consider the experience of Elaine, an Indiana resident who delivered gifts to a family in need.

When she arrived, the children's mother invited her in. Elaine quickly learned the woman was a single mother with five young children. Their tiny apartment was sparsely furnished. Although Christmas was less than ten days away, there wasn't a single decoration in the apartment—no brightly decorated tree, no sequined stockings, no manger scene, not even a candy cane.

Although Elaine left one gift behind for each child, she was stung by the starkness of the apartment. The more she thought about it, the more it disturbed her. Knowing that the local discount chain store had been generously involved in community projects, Elaine approached the manager. She told him about the family in need and asked if his store would help her pass along some Christmas joy. Immediately the manager authorized a small benevolent budget. He assigned two store employees to help Elaine select a tree, ornaments, tree lights, tree stand, skirt, topper, and even an extension cord.

When other store employees learned about the project, they donated money to purchase additional gifts for the mother and her five children. Soon, a store shopping cart was filled with brightly gift-wrapped presents. Before leaving the store to make her delivery, another employee stopped Elaine and gave her an envelope. It contained $200 and was "to help the mother with expenses in January," the employee explained.

Although no one person can relieve all the suffering in a community, one person can make a large difference to one family. As we team up with the Divine, the joy of another family can be increased.

⊰ Thought for the Day ⊱
The assured Christian is more motion than notion,
more work than word, more life than lip,
more hand than tongue.
Thomas Benton Brooks

Tapping Into the Faith of Another Person

We look for light, but all is darkness.
Isaiah 59:9

Sometimes our own faith reserves drop dangerously low—"We look for light, but all is darkness." This can happen due to spiritual neglect or because of some harsh life circumstance. When that happens, it is important to seek out other persons who are full of faith and tap into their strength in order to replenish our own. A good example is Laura D. Bridgman, born in 1830. Sadly, an attack of scarlet fever left her blind and deaf. At that time such individuals were classified with the insane and often thrown into badly run state asylums to live out lonely lives in darkness and silence. They were not only ignored but often mistreated.

Providentially, Laura was spared such a horrible future because Dr. Samuel Gridley Howe, a prominent educator, took a special interest in her situation. Dr. Howe persuaded Laura's family to let her attend his school, the Perkins Institution, a unique school for the blind in Boston. He personally took on the immensely difficult task of teaching her to communicate. An eager and bright student, she soon learned to rapidly spell out words with her fingers. This breakthrough created a sensation throughout the United States and Europe, with many dignitaries traveling to the Perkins Institution to visit with Laura.

As she grew older, many of her friends, relatives, and teachers died. Her faith was severely tested and turned into a dark night of the soul when her beloved sister, Mary, died suddenly. Laura was distraught and wrote in her journal: "I did not feel myself in the care of God or the Savior for weeks." She found it impossible to pray. After several months she traveled to New Hampshire where she "spoke" with her mother and others about her soul crisis. Gradually, she began to feel renewed by the richness of their faith. Their belief animated and energized her faith. "I heard Jesus speak down from his throne into my heart....He illumined my heart with glory and light and grace," she later wrote.

Let us remember her experience and learn to tap into the faith of others when our faith is dim and weak.

❦ *Prayer for the Day* ❦
Loving God,
I thank you for
surrounding me with people who
are full of faith, hope, and love.
When I am weak, let them be my strength.
VMP

Pray When You Can

Pray continually.
1 Thessalonians 5:17

Scholars of spirituality note that ways of praying have been varied and appropriate for different times and cultures. The monastic model of praying at specific times and working at others, for example, is not a natural fit for most of us. Today's culture almost seems to promote addictive, frantic, surface activity. Because we are so busy with life's daily demands, it is difficult to carve out time for prayer.

One way of increasing daily prayer is by praying when you can and sometimes while on the move. Here are some examples:

- *Pray while commuting.* If you drive to work, turn off the radio and work your way through a prayer program. If you use public transportation, forgo reading the newspaper or magazine and use the time for quiet prayer, devotional reading, and meditation.

- *Pray while standing in lines.* It's amazing how much time is spent standing in line: banks, grocery stores, the checkouts. Use that time for prayer.

- *Let emotions lead you to pray.* If you are dealing with an obnoxious and difficult person, remind yourself of Jesus' words "Love your enemies." Pray for that person and for the ability to deal with him or her wisely and gently.

- *Step into a church during the week.* Thankfully, many churches still keep their doors open during the week. Take the opportunity to break up your day with brief periods of prayer and meditation. This can be done during lunchtime or while out shopping.

- *Pray while getting ready for the day.* When you rise and begin a morning routine—brushing teeth, showering, applying make-up—think through your day, the people you will meet, the decisions that need to be made, and pray about those matters. Ask God to bless you and all whom you will come in contact with.

- *Create more time by fasting.* Today's text combines prayer with fasting. Once in a while, skip a meal and use that time for prayer. It can lead to better physical and emotional health.

❧ *Thought for the Day* ❧

A Christian is more music when he prays.
John Donne

Giving the Gift of Hope

We have this hope as an anchor for the soul.
Hebrews 6:9

"The most thoughtful gift I've ever received cost very little. It was given by a stranger who touched my life for only a few moments, but changed my thinking, strengthened my faith in God, and inspired my entire attitude about life," says a woman named Sara.

At the time, she was at the Mayo Clinic in Minnesota awaiting the results of a battery of neurological tests. Doctors were searching for the mysterious cause of her periodic blurred vision and profound fatigue. With Sara in the waiting room was another patient, also awaiting the results of her tests. As strangers sometimes do when they face a similar crisis, Sara and the older woman shared fears and problems. The older woman talked about grandchildren, and Sara spoke lovingly of her two grade-school children and worried husband.

After several hours, the older woman was summoned into a private office. She emerged relieved and smiling, telling Sara her only problem was a slight elevation in blood pressure. "I hope your test results are as promising as mine," she told Sara and added, "If they aren't please try to find comfort in this little message." She extended her hand and pressed a small laminated copy of Reinhold Niebuhr's Serenity Prayer into Sara's palm. "God grant me the serenity to accept the things I cannot change, courage to change the things I can, and the wisdom to know the difference."

Almost immediately Sara was called to the neurology department where the physician told her she had multiple sclerosis. The doctor told Sara there were three distinct types of MS, but she had the "best" kind. It would not likely cripple her nor result in her death, he explained.

"I don't enjoy having the 'best' kind of MS, but I find immeasurable contentment in the message a caring stranger gave me," she says. "When hopeless depression threatens, I read those simple, fulfilling words and am reminded a Higher Power offers hope and refuge to all. Receiving that message was the most thoughtful gift I've ever received."

Today's text speaks of the blessings that come to those who trust in God. Consider how you can give this precious gift of hope to someone.

❧ Affirmation for the Day ❧
I rejoice in God's love and mercy for all people.
I am God's messenger of hope.
It brings me joy to plant seeds of hope.
VMP

Some Ways God Responds to Our Prayers

I have heard the prayer and the plea you have put before me.

1 Kings 9:3

I prayed for help.
   God gave me friends and said, "Turn to them."
I prayed for the poor.
   God said, "Live simply that others may simply live."
I prayed for peace.
   God said, "It starts with you. Love your neighbor."
I prayed for strength.
   God showed me I was stronger than I thought.
I prayed for deeper faith.
   God said, "Faith unaccompanied by action is dead. Get busy helping others."
I prayed for the sick.
   God said, "Visit them. Listen to them. Your presence will be a source of healing."
I prayed for help with temptation.
   God gave me a conscience and said, "Follow it."
I prayed for guidance.
   God said, "Trust me and live one day at a time."
I prayed for healing.
   God said, "My grace is all you need."
I prayed for tranquillity.
   God said, "Stop rushing. Be still. Be quiet. Listen."
I prayed for a lighter burden.
   God gave me a stronger back.

❧ *Thought for the Day* ❧

Keep praying, but be thankful that God's answers are wiser than your prayers!

William Culbertson

Choose to Beat Self-Defeat

Be strong in the Lord.
Ephesians 6:10

During World War II, Fred Spencer was a soldier stationed in a small garrison on the island of Singapore, just off the tip of the Malay Peninsula. The British believed that Singapore was impenetrable to invasion from the north because of the dense jungles protecting it. Any attack would have to come from the sea. However, the Japanese quickly advanced down the peninsula demanding an unconditional surrender. The British had only a few days' food, less than a day's water, and very little ammunition, so they quickly surrendered. Singapore fell without a fight.

Spencer escaped and spent nine months in the jungle before he was able to rejoin his unit. Previously while he was in the garrison, living on the edge of the jungle, the only information he had about the jungle were statements he heard from others, and they were conflicting reports. On the one hand, he was told the jungle was filled with snakes and insects, brutal wild animals, and poisonous fruit. It was assumed anyone lost in the jungle would die quickly. On the other hand, Spencer heard the jungle was a lush, tropical paradise with plenty of fresh water and edible fruit, a place where anyone could live with relative ease and comfort.

After his war experience, Fred Spencer wrote a best-selling book titled *The Jungle Is Neutral*. It was based on his nine-month experience hiding. The jungle neither attempted to destroy him nor support him. He learned that his survival depended on the amount of effort he put forth to survive. It was up to him to make of his environment whatever he chose. By choosing wisely, he survived and triumphed over adverse circumstances. Fred Spencer chose to beat self-defeat, rallying internal resources to work for his own best interests.

Spencer's experience offers this parallel to life in general. It is not accurate to declare that life is a "jungle"—a dangerous place filled with many pitfalls and hazards. Life itself is neither out to destroy nor to support us. It is neutral and returns joys and rewards directly in proportion to the effort put forward. Unfortunately, when some people experience personal crises or professional setbacks, they engage in self-defeating behaviors. Today's biblical text is a reminder not to grow impatient and despairing. Whenever there is a personal or professional crisis, steps can be taken that will either improve or erode the circumstances.

❧ *Thought for the Day* ❧
Where there is no hope there can be no endeavor.
Samuel Johnson

Try God Wholeheartedly

You yourselves have seen what I did to Egypt,
and how I carried you on eagles' wings.

Exodus 19:4

Here are some fabulous facts…

- Whatever your problem, it can be solved.
- Whatever your crisis, it can be managed.
- Whatever your sorrow, it can be transformed.
- Whatever your anxiety, it can be relieved.
- Whatever your sin, it can be forgiven.
- Whatever your wound, it can be healed.
- Whatever your dilemma, it can be mastered.
- Whatever your pain, it can be eased.
- Whatever your failure, it can be reversed.
- Whatever your challenge, it can be overcome.
- Whatever your suffering, it can be remolded.
- Whatever your burden, it can be lightened.
- Whatever your addiction, it can be broken.
- Whatever your setback, it can be overturned.
- Whatever your weakness, it can be changed.

—if you…
TRY GOD WHOLEHEARTEDLY.

❧ *Thought for the Day* ❧
All beginnings require that you unlock new doors.
Rebbe Nachman of Breslov

Sometimes Faith Is More Than Getting a Miracle

Let him who walks in the dark, who has no light,
trust in the name of the Lord and rely on his God.
Isaiah 50:10

While on vacation in England, Geoff and Wanda were completing a day of touring when it began to rain. As Geoff carefully guided their rental car through a busy intersection, an oncoming car barreled over the hilltop and hit them broadside. Their eighteen-month-old daughter was killed instantly and their four-year-old son went into a deep coma from brain hemorrhaging. As word reached their family and friends in the United States, people began to pray for their son's recovery. "We were absolutely convinced that our faith—bolstered by the prayers of hundreds of believers around the world who were told of the accident—would produce a miracle." But their son died three days later.

The couple's ensuing grief was intense and fierce. There were many moments of anger and rage, despair and disillusionment, over the senseless tragedy. Gradually, the couple learned that sometimes faith is more than getting a miracle. "I am convinced now that faith is hanging on until the end, that its purpose is not to get supernatural intervention. Rather, it is to get up each morning and trust God for strength, comfort, and courage to accomplish his work for the day," Geoff now says.

The couple grew in faith and learned these spiritual lessons:

1. God empowers them with the kind of faith that survives when the miracle doesn't come.

2. In times of great crisis they came to trust that, out beyond the fog and pain, God still reigned and did not abandoned them.

3. God can be trusted with the outcomes of life's confusions.

4. Even when God doesn't choose to take away the suffering or remove the evil, God does send strength, peace, and hope.

❧ Prayer for the Day ❧
Loving God,
Strengthen me in those times of fog and confusion;
those times when nothing works according to plan;
those times when life becomes tragic and senseless.
Strengthen me in those times, O God.
VMP

Feel the Fear and Do It Anyway

*Trust in the Lord with all your heart and lean not
on your own understanding.*

Proverbs 3:5

Movie mega-star Sylvester Stallone did not allow fear to stop him in his goal of becoming a top Hollywood actor. For more than five years, Stallone earned very little as an actor and writer. "I had been rejected by every casting agent in New York City. I lost out on what seems like five thousand auditions. I still can't laugh about it now. It was a cruel experience," he says.

His twenty-ninth birthday was an especially desperate time. His wife was pregnant, the landlord was about to evict them, and together the couple had total life savings of $106. Desperate, Stallone decided he had to "write the kind of screenplay that I personally enjoyed seeing—heroism, great love, dignity and courage, people rising above their stations, taking life by the throat and not letting go until they succeeded."

So, in three and a half days, Stallone wrote the first draft of *Rocky*. Then he tried to sell it, with himself in the title role. Amazingly, United Artists offered him $75 thousand for the screenplay, but said they wanted a star for the lead. Despite his financial situation, Stallone turned them down. "I wrote it and I have to do it," he explained. The studio kept increasing its offer, and Stallone kept turning them down.

Finally, at $350 thousand, he said he wouldn't sell the screenplay "for a million dollars" if he wasn't the star. Stallone told studio executives he would "rather bury the script in the backyard and let caterpillars play Rocky" than see another actor in the role. The studio gave in. Although he was in excellent physical condition, Stallone had to get into even better shape to play a championship prize fighter. For the next five months, Stallone worked out long hours in a gym with fighters who "hit me so hard, sometimes I couldn't even remember my phone number."

Then, after twenty-eight days of shooting, the movie was completed and entertainment history was made. The key to Stallone's success was not only his talent but his ability to keep moving ahead, even though he felt fear.

Today's biblical text reminds us to feel the fear and do it anyway because people of faith are to *trust in the Lord*.

✎ Thought for the Day ✎

I have accepted fear as a part of life—especially
the fear of change. I have gone ahead despite
the pounding in the heart that says: turn back.

Erica Jong

The Importance of Receiving Help

"So guard yourself in your spirit."
Malachi 2:15

Struggling with a multiple sclerosis flare-up, Bobbie was finding it impossible to get her clothing in place after using a rest room at work. *I hated the problems I was experiencing—not being able to walk or stand long enough to get dressed or rise without help,* she thought. As she struggled Bobbie again weighed the value of her current working life against that of disability retirement.

She had a wonderful family and a successful twenty-five-year career. But now her MS problems were overwhelming her. The questions that haunted her included these: Could her family cope with her disability? How much longer would her employer be understanding before forcing her into a disability retirement? Should she give up now? Overcome with frustration and the current humiliating circumstances, Bobbie cried out loud with great anguish. Just then a coworker came into the rest room. She was a young woman, a "born-again" Christian. Upon hearing the cry, she asked Bobbie if she could help.

"Go away!" Bobbie sobbed. "I'm too much of a burden. People get tired of helping someone like me."

But the woman walked over and began to assist, saying gently, "Never turn down or hesitate to ask for help. Remember, your need is someone else's opportunity to give. And we all need to give. Right now, it's just as important for me to give as for you to receive."

That woman's wisdom has echoed in Bobbie's mind many times over the ensuing twelve years. "And in that time, help both sought and offered has allowed me to lead a full life," Bobbie says.

Eventually, Bobbie did take early retirement. Today she needs help much more often, but that young woman's profound understanding continues to remind her that kindness willingly received is a kindness given in its own right. Let us apply the words of the prophet—*guard yourself in your spirit*—being certain we are not too proud and too arrogant to receive assistance that is sincerely and generously offered.

~≈ Prayer for the Day ≈~
Loving God,
Keep me from the kind of pride which does not allow me
to receive acts of kindness from others.
Remind me that just as I reach out to people in need,
others do the same for me when I am needy.
VMP

Setting the Right Tone for Each Day

The Lord turns my darkness into light.
2 Samuel 22:29

We must cooperate with God in turning *darkness into light*. Too many of us spend days of darkness rather than bright, glorious days of light. Here are eight tips for having a better day every day:

1. Begin and end the day with five minutes of silence, followed by a time of prayer.
2. Listen to your inner guide.
3. Put yourself in charge each day before you get out of bed.
4. Affirm that you will speak softly and lovingly, especially to your family.
5. Take all nonessentials off your agenda and schedule the amount of time really needed for important tasks and errands. This will keep you from feeling pressured and frenzied.
6. Commit yourself to avoiding negative people.
7. Do one thing each day that moves you closer to your goals.
8. Exercise sometime during the day. This can be an early morning jog, a brisk walk at lunch, or a workout after work at home or at the gym.

Following these eight steps is a way of giving yourself loving kindness daily. It will also empower you to maintain inner balance and see the world more lovingly.

⚜ Thought for the Day ⚜
A day is a miniature eternity.
Ralph Waldo Emerson

Making Christmas More Fulfilling

With their mouths they express devotion,
but their hearts are greedy.

Ezekiel 33:31

This time of year is so hectic, busy, and commercial that the very pace of life in December can extinguish the reason for the season. Be sure to fill your life with "spiritual pauses" in order to make the Christmas season more fulfilling. Here are some suggestions:

- *Make time for extra prayers daily.* In addition to regular times of prayer and meditation, add more prayer moments during the day. For example, cut back on watching television by just a few minutes. Replace that time with a quick reading from the Bible or other devotional book. Conclude with a brief prayer. Or, set your alarm for fifteen minutes earlier to pray for world peace.

- *Make a new friend.* Reach out to someone who is currently just an acquaintance and try to establish a friendship. Invite that person for dinner or coffee. Give him or her a small gift at Christmas.

- *Compliment someone for making the world better.* If someone you know is making a difference in the community, call and thank them. Or, write a letter of praise and appreciation. Either gesture will surely please that individual.

- *Write a generous check to a charitable organization.* There are many worthwhile groups working hard and, usually on shoestring budgets, to make the world a kinder, gentler place for the less fortunate. December is a good time to write out a generous check because their needs are usually greater this month.

- *Conduct an examination of conscience.* Reflect on today's biblical text from Ezekiel. Ask if your words match your deeds. If so, thank God. If not, ask for God's help in making the necessary changes.

❧ Thought for the Day ❧

It is always a feast where love is,
and where love is, God is.

Dorothy Day

God's Powerful Angels

With the tip of the staff that was in his hand, the angel of the Lord touched the meat and the unleavened bread. Fire flared from the rock, consuming the meat and the bread. And the angel of the Lord disappeared.

Judges 6:21

A few years ago, Judith Rowsey and her nine-year-old daughter were driving through Oklahoma City. The winds were very strong. In the opposite lane, Judith saw a flatbed truck loaded with four-foot by eight-foot plywood boards driving toward her.

Suddenly, a strong gust of wind blew three of the plywood sheets off the truck. The boards flew straight for the windshield of Judith's car. She remembers hearing her daughter scream and instinctively shield her face. Judith had only enough time to utter this one word prayer: "Father!"

Incredibly, Judith saw an angel appear at the front of her car. She says he looked like a clean-cut, boy-next-door football player, only larger and extremely muscular. He looked into Judith's eyes and smiled. Then, with little effort, the angel deflected the plywood boards one after another.

"Did you see that?" Judith asked. "Did you see the angel?"

"No I didn't!" answered her daughter, who was still shaking with fear.

Judith Rowsey says that was the most thrilling moment of her life. "Those plywood boards were coming toward us, I prayed, and God sent his angel. God preserved our lives!"

The Bible often refers to angels. Usually they are powerful and protective figures. Let us reflect on angels and thank God for providing these divine emissaries to help us.

⤖ *Prayer for the Day* ⤖
Dear God,
You are so kind, loving and compassionate.
I thank you for all the ways in which you
show me your love,
provide me your protection,
send me your light,
and deliver me from harm.
VMP

Lightening the Load of Life

Carry each other's burdens.
Ephesians 6:2

Everyone has some time in his or her life when problems seem overwhelming. Such pressures erupted in the life of Gloria, a young single parent with a physically challenged child. Gloria had just found a job when her two-year-old's pediatrician strongly recommended surgery. Gloria went ahead with the procedure, even though the health insurance connected with her new job did not cover the entire medical costs.

While sitting in the surgical waiting area, Gloria broke down into uncontrollable tears. "I could not hold back the tears. I cried because this little boy had to have an operation. I cried because I didn't have the money. I cried because I felt so alone through all of this," she says.

Gloria was surprised by the pediatrician, who suddenly walked into the room. "Everything went well," the doctor said, gently taking her hand. "Everything will be all right. Please don't worry."

After bringing her son home, Gloria waited nervously for the hospital and surgical bills to arrive. When they didn't she called the hospital billing department. However, they told her the bill had been paid in full. She then called the pediatric surgeon's office and was told, "You don't owe anything. The doctor hopes your little boy is doing well." Today Gloria says, "Although it's been several years since that happened, just thinking about the kindness of that surgeon and hospital administrators warms my heart."

That story is a good example of Saint Paul's words from his letter to Galatian Christians: *Carry each other's burdens.*

﹥ᔐ *Prayer for the Day* ᔐ﹤

Loving God,
Continue to sensitize me toward
the needs of others.
Use me to help lighten the load of
another who is struggling from
the harsh demands of life.
VMP

Unexpected Christmas Joy

Supply him liberally.
Deuteronomy 15:14

No matter how commercial and materialistic this season becomes, the true meaning of Christmas continues to break through in the expressions of sympathy, understanding, compassion, and love. As this heartwarming story shows.

The story is set in Vermont and involves a family of four. Steve, the father, came down with an illness. Rather than recovering from it, the illness worsened and doctors could neither explain nor treat it. Finally, physicians told Frances, his wife, that she should alert their children that their father was dying. It was a low, depressing point for the family as Frances struggled with ways to explain their predicament to Samuel (age five) and Katherine (age three). In order to be closer to extended family, Steve and Frances moved to Brattleboro, Vermont. Unexpectedly and miraculously, Steve began to improve.

Consequently, they began to prepare for what they hoped would be a normal Christmas. Even though money was tight due to Steve's job loss and high medical expenses, the parents were determined their children would have gifts at Christmas. After buying some gifts at a local discount store, Frances returned to her car with the purchases. Sitting in the car she realized that one item had been forgotten. Carefully locking the driver's-side door, she left the car. Upon returning she saw the passenger-side door open. Someone had stolen their Christmas packages.

Upset and furious, Frances drafted a letter to the editor of the local newspaper explaining what had happened. It was addressed to "whomever stole my Christmas packages." She concluded by listing her name and street address in case the thieves might be moved to return the packages. The letter was in the paper the following day. Soon gifts of all kinds began mysteriously appearing on the doorsteps. There were dozens of gifts, as well as $500 in cash. Steve and Frances were moved to tears by the outpouring of sympathy and kindness from strangers in a new community. The response was unexpected, but welcome. The parents replaced the gifts that had been stolen and gave all other gifts plus leftover money away to other needy families in the town.

As this Christmas season comes to an end, let us think of ways we can be the source of unexpected Christmas joy to others all year long.

❧ *Thought for the Day* ❧
Kindness effects more than severity.
Aesop

Learning to Deepen Our Compassion

Spend yourselves in behalf of the hungry.
Isaiah 58:10

Mary, an office manager in a large midwestern city, tells of stepping off the subway and making her way to the office. Just outside the entrance to her building was a homeless man she had seen many times before. He looked about thirty, had his cap pulled over his ears, and was huddled in the cold under a tattered blanket. "I quickly looked away, and by the time I walked into my office, I had put the man out of my mind," she says.

At the end of her workday, as Mary was leaving her office she noticed a woman wearing an expensive red linen and silk suit. "The woman was classy and I wondered where she bought such an elegant outfit and how much it cost her," Mary recalls thinking to herself. As they both stepped outside the building, Mary saw the homeless man again but was stunned to hear the woman in the red suit greet the man saying, "Hi, Steve. Need any money for the weekend?" Then she took out some bills and pressed them into his hand.

"I hadn't even wanted to look at the man, but this woman had called him by name, talked to him, touched him, and wished him a nice weekend," Mary vividly remembers. "What she demonstrated was something I needed: a deeper understanding of compassion. Clearly that woman had a lot more going for her than great clothes."

It is commendable that Mary was observant enough to learn an important spiritual lesson via the homeless man and the woman in the red suit. Perhaps we can take a cue from her experience as well. Life provides us with ample opportunities to deepen our compassion for others.

Rather than look the other way, we should stretch our hearts and souls to respond with kindness and generosity. It may not always be possible for us to assist with material things but at the very least we can offer a smile and a silent prayer of blessing to those in need of kindness.

~ Thought for the Day ~
It has hands to help others. It has feet to hasten to
the poor and the needy. It has eyes to see misery
and want. It has ears to hear the sighs and sorrows
of women and men. That is what love looks like.
Saint Augustine of Hippo

Christmas in August and All Year Round

*This is what the Lord says: "Maintain justice
and do what is right."*

Isaiah 56:1

One year Martha and her husband asked themselves, "How can we make Christmas last year round?" they came upon the plan to keep the Christmas spirit alive all year by giving gifts to special individuals each month. They call their project the "Spirit of Christmas Mission."

In January, they chose babies as recipients of their first gift-giving project, in keeping with the celebration of Jesus' birth. After reading about a local group that helped unwed teenage mothers and their babies, Martha called to find out what they needed. "Everything" was the reply. So she and her husband went on a shopping spree, loading their cart with disposable diapers, formula, juices, baby food, bottles, blankets, socks, cloth diapers, and infant outfits. "As we delivered our gifts to the center where babies filled the nursery cribs, we thought of the baby Jesus wrapped in swaddling clothes, his crib in a manger."

In February, Martha's daughter shared her concern over a neighbor, a single mother who was struggling financially. "She gets food stamps," the daughter explained, "but can't use them to buy any paper products or soap—only food." Martha and her husband "showered" the young woman and her six-year-old son with paper goods, soap, laundry detergent, and toothpaste.

In April, Martha and her husband responded to a challenge from their pastor who asked the church to remember the homeless. She and her husband cleaned out closets and chests donating all extra, blankets, sweaters, and jackets to a homeless shelter.

During June, Martha was intrigued by a news story on a shelter helping battered women. She wondered to herself, *What would a woman need if she had to leave home suddenly and seek shelter?* That month she purchased a variety of personal-care items—toothbrushes, combs, mirrors, tissues, toothpaste, shampoo, hand lotion—and mailed them to the shelter.

Other months Martha and her husband donated clothing and toys to a home for troubled children and served meals to a terminally ill young man and his family.

ᕗ Thought for the Day ᕙ

Christmas is not a time nor a season, but a state of mind.
To cherish peace and goodwill, to be plenteous in mercy,
is to have the real spirit of Christmas.

Calvin Coolidge

An Important Lesson From African Americans

*I know, my God, that you test the heart
and are pleased with integrity.*
1 Chronicles 29:17

Beginning today and continuing for seven days, African Americans celebrate Kwanzaa. Although defined as a nonreligious holiday conceived in the late 1960s, its seven principles can greatly aid our spiritual growth. As one year draws to a close and a new year begins, everyone— black and white, male and female—can benefit by reviewing the seven principles that make up the basic framework of the Kwanzaa celebration. Today let us *test the heart* by examining them.

1. *Unity.* How can I better live in unity with all those around me? What attitudes do I need to change to establish clearer and strong unity within and without?

2. *Self-determination.* Am I mature enough to accept responsibility for my life or am I in the habit of blaming others? Do I have the convictions to establish personal goals and move steadily toward them?

3. *Collective work and responsibility.* Do I understand that my success in work is both a blessing and a responsibility; that the more I earn, the more I should share?

4. *Cooperative economics.* Am I guided by a harsh, rigid, self-centered capitalism in which only the strong thrive or can I have a work ethic that is permeated with compassion, especially toward those whose resources—emotional, physical, mental, spiritual—are limited?

5. *Purpose.* Do I try to discover a purpose for my life and work? Am I faithful to that understanding on a daily basis?

6. *Creativity.* Knowing that God has endowed me with talent and creativity, do I tap into it, using God's gifts for myself and for others?

7. *Faith.* Am I faithful in all the events of life, large and small? Do I ask God for help, guidance, and direction, or do I go it alone?

❧ Prayer for the Day ❧
Eternal and loving God,
Help me to use my life honestly and well this day and every day,
so that others will be blessed, so that God will be glorified,
and so that I will experience satisfaction and fulfillment.

VMP

An ABC Prayer for Wholeness

To you, O Lord, I call.
            Joel 1:19

Loving God, in your mercy grant me these gifts:

Attitude, that I might view people and life positively.
Balance, for stability in life's stormy times.
Courage, to back up my convictions.
Devotion, that I would be in communion with you daily.
Eyes, to see the needs all around me.
Faithfulness, to tasks and responsibilities which are mine.
Generosity, to share from my material and spiritual wealth.
Humor, that I can see the lighter, brighter side of life.
Inspiration, that I might be a source of encouragement to others.
Joy, that my life can bring cheer into saddened lives.
Kindness, toward all living creatures, large and small.
Loyalty, that others can count on me.
Mercy, to offer and receive forgiveness.
Nearness, to you, your love, your grace.
Obedience, that I might faithfully do your will.
Peace, even in the crises of life.
Quietness, to hear your still, small voice.
Receptivity, that I will always be open to your guidance.
Simplicity, that I will not be overly concerned with material possessions.
Trust, in you to lead me through the darkest days.
Unity, that I might experience harmony between the divine and the human.
Valor, to be courageous where there is injustice.
Willingness, to change my habits, my mind, and my spirit when necessary.
X-ray eyes, to discern the meaning of events.
Yieldability, a spirit that is open, pliable, responsive to your call.
Zest, to live with joy and passion.

⇝ Prayer for the Day ⇜
Lord,
Oil the hinges of our hearts' doors
that they may swing gently and easily to welcome
your coming.
A New Guinea Christian Prayer

Calling a Spiritual 911 Number

He who dwells in the shelter of the Most High
will rest in the shadow of the Almighty.

Psalm 91:1

A man was stressed out because of work pressures. His company was downsizing, and he felt it was only a matter of time before his position might be eliminated. Concurrently, he had a job offer from another company, but it was a much lower paying position. If he said no to the job offer and remained with his present company, he could end up unemployed in a few months. On the other hand, if he took the new job, he was not sure his family could make ends meet on the lower salary.

One of his closest friends called to offer encouragement, both emotional and spiritual. He concluded their conversation by advising him to "use the spiritual 911 number." He explained it was a "code" for Psalm 91:1.

"As soon as I got home that evening, I turned to that psalm in my Bible. It lifted my spirits enormously," the man recalled. The psalm begins with this reminder that all of us live within God's close circle of care and love: *He who dwells in the shelter of the Most High will rest in the shadow of the Almighty.*

It goes on to remind us of God's faithful, daily support—including protection: "Surely he will save you from the fowler's snare... no harm will befall you, no disaster will come near your tent" (verses 2 and 10).

The psalm also clearly states that God assigns angels to watch over us, guiding us safely through difficult—even dangerous—times: "For he will command his angels concerning you to guard you in all your ways" (verse 11).

The next time you face tough choices or difficult times, remember to "call" the spiritual 911 number. Read the text slowly. Review the words carefully.

❧ *Thought for the Day* ❧

Over and over again, God gives us far more that we have
any right to ask. We call this "grace," which goes to much
farther than "law" requires God to go. And God's mercy
goes so much farther than mere human justice goes.

Glen Clark

Some Good Resolutions for the New Year

There is a time for everything, and a season
for every activity under heaven.

Ecclesiastes 3:1

The end of December is a good time to begin thinking about setting goals for a new year. Here are some suggestions:

1. *In this new year I will think positively.* Dwelling on negatives leads to an unbalanced view of life. It violates the biblical mandate to be a thankful, grateful person. In this new year, remember to view difficult times as opportunities for growth and change.

2. *In this new year I will delight in life.* Most of us need to find the healthy balance between labor and leisure, to experience more joy. Let us look for more opportunities to play, laugh, and delight in daily living.

3. *In this new year I will remember that fitness counts.* I will begin, maintain, and increase a regular exercise program. God has given me a healthy body, and I will do all I can to keep this body in good shape. Today I will be thinking about an exercise program that is right for me.

4. *In this new year I will "chill out."* Too many of us live hectic, frenzied lives. We need to find ways of living more simply, naturally, and in ways that are not constantly depleting our physical and emotional strength. I will find ways to spend quiet time in meditation, spiritual reading, prayer, and reflection.

5. *In this new year I will move toward wholeness.* Along with trying to establish emotional balance, I will try to have a balanced diet. I will seriously find ways to decrease the amount of processed foods, fast foods, junk foods, fats, and sugars that I consume. I will work at replacing them with healthy servings of vegetables, fruits, and grains.

6. *In this new year I will try to make a difference.* I will remember that as a responsible citizen I must work to enhance the quality of life not just for myself, but for my community. I will help out as a coach, school volunteer, or by joining with a group dedicated to helping others.

❧ Prayer for the Day ❧
Loving God,
I thank you for the talents and experiences I have.
Guide me to improve on those and to use them
in ways that help others bring greater fulfillment
to my life, and please you.
VMP

A Radical New Year's Resolution

The Lord Jesus himself said: "It is more blessed
to give than to receive."
Acts of the Apostles 20:35

As another year draws to a close, many of us think about making New Year's resolutions. These are usually commitments to actions that will improve the quality of our own lives or the lives of those around us. One woman took a highly creative and radical approach to her New Year's resolution. Her resolution began to evolve during a candlelight prayer service in late December. There, Martha prayed and strongly felt, *This year I want to reach out to others.*

However, she was not sure how to implement her resolution until she was browsing through the newspaper. There she noticed rows and rows of ads for 900 numbers. "People are so lonely and just want someone to talk with," she said to her husband. After further prayer and conversation with her spouse, Martha paid for a classified ad which read: "You're lonely and discouraged. Maybe you just need someone to talk to—someone to listen who's also been through tough times. Don't call a 900 number; call…" With the placement of the ad, Martha prayed, "God, help me share love and hope with others. Help me find just the right words."

Soon calls came. One was a university student from China who was lonely and homesick. Martha listened kindly and offered words of encouragement. Another call came from a teenage girl who was depressed. Her boyfriend of two years was killed while riding his motorcycle. She was grieving his loss. Again, Martha listened kindly and said she would pray for her.

Throughout the entire year, whenever the calls ebbed Martha placed another ad. As the year came to an end, Martha had the satisfaction of knowing that her creative and radical New Year's resolution was a source of hope for many people during the preceding twelve months. Perhaps her example can nudge us into considering other creative resolutions that help people.

～ *Prayer for the Day* ～
Loving God,
Guide my thoughts as I reflect upon
the year past and the year ahead.
Lead me to a creative resolution for
the new year, one which is good for
people and brings you honor.
VMP

Choosing Wisely

I have set before you life and death,
blessings and curses. Now choose life.
Deuteronomy 30:19

A woman identifying herself simply as "a country girl in Indiana," wrote to an advice columnist to relate the story of her life, which was initially characterized with poor choices. As a teen she became involved with "Tony." He was a man of questionable character and integrity. Her family and friends urged "country girl" to terminate the relationship. She disregarded their counsel, choosing to believe "Tony" would change once they were together and had a child.

The woman lied to her parents, saying she was pregnant so they would have to allow her to marry "Tony." "The next three years were hell," she recalls. They moved twenty-seven times. "Tony" had—and lost—thirty-two different jobs. He was in jail periodically for some "minor" offense. On one occasion "country girl" lived in a car and on the beaches in Mexico with their six-week-old baby.

Her husband was also violent with her. She received three stab wounds, several loose teeth, and her eyes were blackened frequently. Under his influence she began to drink, do drugs, shoplift, panhandle, and engage in prostitution. "Country girl" had to give up custody of her daughter before her first birthday. It would take her thirteen years to end the relationship and stop drinking and doing drugs. Thanks to AA and intensive therapy, she is now happily married to a stable, healthy person.

As one year ends and a new one begins, an excellent resolution would be to make wise choices every day. Our lives are a series of selections. Set before us are decisions about "life and death, blessing and curses."

It is up to us to make good, healthy, wise, sound decisions about our lives. It is up to us to choose relationships, projects to do, activities to participate in, friendships to cultivate. Let us resolve to choose wisely. And when a decision is exceedingly complicated and confusing let us not hesitate to seek out the guidance of God through prayer.

≈ *Prayer for the Day* ≈
Eternal and loving God,
You have made me free to be who I want to be.
You have made me free to grow or not grow,
to feel joy or experience pain.
As a new year emerges, give me the wisdom,
insight, and maturity to choose all things wisely.
VMP

About the Author

Victor M. Parachin studied at the University of Toronto School of Theology, where he received a Master of Divinity degree. He worked as a reporter, feature writer, and editor at *The Catholic Register* (Toronto). Currently, he is a freelance writer and author. His previous works include: *The Lord Is My Shepherd: A Psalm for the Grieving; Our Father: A Prayer for the Grieving; Scripture Passages to Inner Healing;* and *Daily Strength: One Year of Experiencing the Psalms.* Parachin is married and has three children.